DATE DUE

CHILDREN
OF
POVERTY

STUDIES ON THE EFFECTS OF SINGLE PARENTHOOD, THE FEMINIZATION OF POVERTY, AND HOMELESSNESS

edited by

STUART BRUCHEY
UNIVERSITY OF MAINE

A GARLAND SERIES

THE MIDDLEGROUND

THE AMERICAN PUBLIC
AND THE ABORTION DEBATE

BHAVANI SITARAMAN

GARLAND PUBLISHING, INC.
NEW YORK & LONDON / 1994

Library of Congress Cataloging-in-Publication Data

Sitaraman, Bhavani, 1960–
    The Middleground : the American public and the abortion debate /
Bhavani Sitaraman.
        p.   cm. — (Children of poverty)
    Includes bibliographical references.
    ISBN 0–8153–1572–4 (alk. paper)
    1. Abortion—United States—Moral and ethical aspects.   2. Abor-
tion—Massachusetts—Greenfield—Public opinion.   I. Title. II. Series.
HQ767.15.S58   1994
363.4'6—dc20   93–49087
                                                                              CIP

Printed on acid-free, 250-year-life paper
Manufactured in the United States of America

Contents

Preface

The idea for this study emerged in 1986 when I was a graduate student in Sociology at the University of Massachusetts at Amherst. I had read Kristin Luker's book on pro-choice and pro-life activists and was intrigued by its implications for understanding the general public's stance on abortion. The deep and persistent polarization of the abortion issue among activists appeared to be in sharp contrast to the relatively stable, moderate position assumed by many Americans. Luker's work showed that abortion is only "the tip of the iceberg," and beneath it lay a host of concerns related to changing structures of work, family, and gender roles in American society.

During this same period I was introduced to the Factorial Survey Method in a seminar taught by Peter H. Rossi. The method was ideal in exploring the abortion belief structure through the use of computer generated vignettes that combined a broad range of dimensions that shaped an abortion situation. Thus my combined interests in the methodical technique and the topic of abortion resulted is this study.

Few studies of public opinion on abortion had been designed with the breadth and range of questions to explore the belief structure surrounding attitudes toward abortion. Furthermore, the shifts in the abortion debate since legalization in 1973 have added new dimensions to the issue that have not been captured satisfactorily in existing national data sources. This led to the decision to gather primary data. In this study, I place public opinion on abortion within the context of attitudes and beliefs in the domains of sexuality, reproduction, human life issues, and gender roles. Abortion attitudes in particular are explored in greater detail using the factorial survey design.

The study design resulted in two survey instruments, a conventional survey and a factorial survey. The sample for the study consisted of 420 respondents from Greenfield, a moderate sized town in Massachusetts. With limited funding, I personally completed two-thirds of the total 291 telephone interviews.

I am grateful to many hearts and minds for making it possible to bring this work to completion. I am particularly indebted to my mentor, Alice Rossi, who took a personal and professional interest in me early in the course of my graduate training. Alice Rossi had been an active member in the efforts to legalize abortion in 1960s. She had also designed the original items on abortion attitudes that became part of the battery of questions that appeared annually in the General Social Surveys. When I first communicated my interest in this research project, she encouraged me with great enthusiasm. As the chair of my dissertation committee, she never settled for less than the best, providing critical, detailed, and prompt feedback to every draft. Both by example and through active involvement, Alice Rossi has shaped my professional development.

I also extend the deepest appreciation to Peter Rossi, Andy Anderson, and George Levinger. Peter Rossi provided both financial support that was critical to the implementation of this study, and crucial advice in the design and analysis of the factorial survey. Andy Anderson has taught me much of what I know about statistical analysis. He always stressed the importance of letting the substantive issues dictate the statistical analysis.

The most important people behind the scenes of this project have been close friends. I am grateful to Cathy Hammond for sacrificing many evenings to help with a substantial portion of the telephone interviews. The 'Dissertation Brigade' provided a friendly setting in which to explore shared anxieties and fears about the solitary experience of writing. My heartfelt thanks to its enthusiastic members, Jay Demerath, Jeff Will, Georgia Willis, In Soo Son, Debbie Sellers, and Sally Gallagher. Special thanks to Dee Weber for her friendship, computing advice, and personal commitment to bring this project to completion. I am also grateful for the support and friendship extended by Tim Black and Rhys Williams, who engaged me in many intellectually stimulating debates on a wide range of issues. Lastly, I extend my warmest appreciation to my mother. She was patient and understanding when study abroad made it impossible for us to see each other for several years.

1

Historical and Conceptual Context

In January 1989 the Supreme Court agreed to hear a Missouri appeal that proposed greater restrictions on legal abortions, leading observers of abortion politics to speculate that a possible reversal of the existing abortion law may be in the offing. A few weeks later, the President of the United States announced his support for overturning the 16-year-old Roe v. Wade decision that made abortions legal. This announcement was timed close to the annual march in Washington by Right-to-Lifers, which is another reminder of the intense political conflict abortion represents in contemporary American life. In the 1980s national elections came to symbolize the fears and hopes of both supporters and opponents of legal abortion. While the battle over abortion continues in the headlines of the morning paper and the evening television news, the majority of Americans show ambivalent support for abortions. Jean Elshtain expressed the sentiments of many Americans when she wrote, "I am in fact part of a larger majority that opposes both abortion on demand, and an absolute restriction on abortion...Americans who are irrepressibly pragmatic, yet stubbornly ethical and moral in their concerns" (1984:48).

The ambivalence toward abortion is in part a response to the conflicting options that confront men and women in modern society. Abortion represents both choice and coercion, and pits individual rights against obligations to family and community. At the societal level, the conflict over abortion can be viewed as one among many responses to long-term secular trends in values and life circumstances. The moral controversy has surfaced at a time when Americans are experiencing significant changes in their sexual and reproductive behavior, and in the organization of family life which has traditionally been the social context of intimate relationships among adults, and between parents and children. Today, a teenager who decides to terminate an unintended pregnancy hopes to postpone childbearing to an appropriate time in the future, when she will be prepared both financially and emotionally to assume the responsibilities of parenthood. Similarly, the necessity of full-time employment, financial burdens, and the desires to have fewer children prompt an adult married woman to resolve a pregnancy in an abortion. Such cases constitute the majority of abortion decisions in contemporary society, and illustrate the incompatibility of unplanned parenthood and competing social roles for many couples. Furthermore, neither legal access to abortion, nor its widespread incidence can easily resolve the moral challenge it poses to deeply ingrained norms that dictate a respect for the preservation of human life. Even if an abortion is only a remote possibility in an individual's life, the prevalence of legal abortions has brought to the surface moral questions that Americans have to contend with as parents, spouses, partners and children.

This study is concerned with the ways in which people organize their attitudes toward abortion. The focus of our study is on moral approval of abortions rather than support for the legality of abortions, or its impact on the political behavior of the public. We explore two conceptually distinct aspects of abortion morality: characteristics of abortion situations that impinge upon moral acceptance of abortion, and social and ideological attributes that individuals bring to bear upon their judgments of abortion decisions. We investigate a variety of positions individuals take on abortion, and try to place these views in the context of a coherent belief structure. We recognize that moral responses to abortion are subject to many influences that arise from an individual's past history, current life circumstances, as well as an overall value orientation toward sexual and reproductive matters. Both structural factors such an as an individual's social group characteristics, and ideological factors like beliefs and attitudes toward a variety of issues related to abortion can have independent, as well as interdependent effects on abortion morality. We begin with a historical sketch of abortion politics that provides the long-term context to situate the moral issues that dominate the current abortion debate. We then discuss social science research on attitudes of abortion activists and the general public, which provides a focused context for the substantive and methodological approach of this study.

Abortion in Historical Context

The history of abortion in the U.S. is the story of the evolution of a moral debate. The actors in this debate have included physicians, lawyers, social workers, women's rights activists, and theologians. At various points in the history of abortion, concerned groups with seemingly opposed interests have joined forces in their attempts to either restrict or facilitate access to legal abortions. The ebb and flow of abortion politics has also corresponded to shifts in fertility values and behavior, and changes in the sphere of economy and family. Despite some similarities in the social trends that stimulate public concern over abortions at different historical periods, the issues central to the abortion problem have varied as a function of political groups that claimed custody over the issue.

In the 19th century, the emergent group of educated physicians defined abortion in medical and technical terms. Later in the century, campaigns for restrictive abortion laws took on a eugenics tone, stimulated by concern over the falling birth rate among native white women compared to the very high birth rates of immigrants. Fears related to population growth in the U.S. and developing countries in the aftermath of the Second World War, combined with health concerns related to illegal abortions, set the stage for the reform of 19th century abortions laws in the 1950s and early 1960s. By the end of the 1960s, feminist involvement in the abortion debate led to the treatment of abortion as a problem of "women's reproductive rights," and now in the 1980s, the issues posed before the American public are the irreconcilable moral questions concerning the sanctity of human life, and conflicting reproductive rights of pregnant women, spouses and parents.

The First Wave of Restrictive Abortion Laws

A typical advertisement for abortion services in the 1845 Boston Daily Times featured the following message from Madame Restell, a pioneer in commercial abortion services in the 19th century (Mohr 1978: 48).

Madame Restell's experience and knowledge in the treatment of female irregularity, is such as to require a few days to effect a perfect cure. Ladies desiring proper medical attendance will be accommodated during such time with private and respectable board.

In the early part of the 19th century abortion was not publicly discussed: Early abortions were legal and usually performed under the guise of menstrual regulation. Acceptable abortions were performed prior to quickening (when a woman first feels fetal movement in the womb). Midwives and pregnant women themselves induced abortions, and American women's knowledge of these services came from a variety of home medical literature. A fetus during this early stage was not considered a human being, and abortions were viewed as a point on the continuum including contraception. A historian writing on this subject concludes that "even as late as 1872 (indeed until 1884) embryotomy had never been condemned by any Roman Catholic authority. Nor had therapeutic abortions on medical indications ever been condemned by any such authority before 1895" (Means 1970:21). The absence of any legal regulation of abortions was also due to a lower incidence of abortions among married women compared to single women. Historians speculate that the abortion rate closely approximated the illegitimacy rate (Mohr 1978, Potts 1985). Hence, two factors that kept abortion out of public discussions were lack of adequate knowledge in diagnosing pregnancies prior to quickening, and low visibility that surrounded abortions among unmarried women. These two factors changed in the latter half of the 19th century, and set the stage for restrictive abortion laws in the United States.

In the 1830s and 1840s the U.S. entered the demographic transition, paralleled by a declining birth rate and a sharp increase in abortions among married women. Between 1850 and 1900, the United States population was also transformed from being predominantly agrarian to largely urban and industrial. The birth rate dropped from an estimated 7.04 children per woman in 1800 to 3.56 children per woman by 1900 (Mohr 1978). Contemporary demographers associate a sharp rise in induced abortions and contraceptive usage, during early phases of transition from high to low fertility in developed countries, with a multi-phasic response on the part of families to limit fertility (Davis 1949). By the middle of the century, American women were aborting roughly one in five pregnancies, and abortion clients tended to be largely white, married, and native-born (Mohr 1978). Increased visibility of abortions that accompanied a shift in the characteristics of women having abortions was observed in the greater volume of commercial advertisements for abortion services.

On the scientific front, the invention of the microscope, development of cell theory from observations of plant life, and studies of animal reproductive behavior, provided a new perspective in embryology that questioned the old doctrine of quickening. The nascent class of professional physicians drew from this new body of scientific knowledge in the 19th century, and began to view pregnancy as a continuous process from conception to birth (Luker 1984). Consequently, the criterion of quickening as a borderline between permissible and criminal abortions became problematic. The debunking of the quickening doctrine as unscientific created a moral dilemma for theologians, while providing educated physicians with a claim to "technical expertise."

Abortion provided 19th century physicians with a cause to advance their professional status, as well as to cut out competition for female clients from midwives and quacks, who had until then enjoyed a monopoly over reproductive medicine. Education in the best institutions, claims to scientific knowledge of reproductive processes, and the official backing of the American Medical Association, provided a firm base from which physicians could urge the passage of restrictive abortion laws. Once pregnancy was viewed as a continuous process from conception to birth, a distinction between therapeutic and criminal abortions became difficult to sustain. The claim to 'technical' knowledge prevented opposition from women and other professionals, and physicians assumed 'moral stature' as guardians of human life (Luker 1984). It should be noted however that physicians were less interested in outlawing all abortions than in gaining custody over abortion decisions.

Later in the 19th century a new demographic concern emerged, a fear of 'race suicide' that provided additional support for the anti-abortion crusade. The perception that abortion was practiced by native, Protestant women encouraged virulent anti-Catholic and nativist rhetoric in efforts to persuade American legislators to pass laws that would restrict legal abortions to life-threatening circumstances.

The relationship between 19th century feminists and abortion, although ironic from a contemporary standpoint, provides a clue to the social context of abortions. In the late 19th century, marriage and motherhood became full time occupations for most middle and upper class women in America (Rossi 1973). Industrialization first attracted native single women, and later a greater proportion of immigrant women into the factories, while creating a spatial and ideological separation of the world of work and the world of family life (Chafe 1972). The 'cult of true womanhood' stressed moral qualities of piety, purity, domesticity and submissiveness that corresponded to the roles middle class women assumed in their lives: daughter, wife, and mother (Welter 1966). In this context, 19th century feminists engaged in social causes that extended their moral superiority and responsibility from the home to the public arena. They campaigned for a right to vote and a right to education rather than a right to control their sexual and reproductive behavior.

An increasingly negative view of sexuality in the 19th century (Rossi 1973), coupled with moral responsibility that came with the cult of domesticity, meant that abortion degraded the moral status of women. It symbolized the unfortunate circumstances women were forced into as a result of uncontrolled male sexuality. A similar response seems to have resurfaced among feminists-for-life in the 20th century, when they view abortion as the outcome of coercive sexuality and male irresponsibility, rather than the expression of women's choice in reproductive decisions.

With moral questions largely untouched, 19th century laws criminalized abortions, except for cases where it was necessary to save the life of the mother. These legal changes did not reduce the number of abortions performed, because abortion to save the life of the mother came to be broadly applied to the mental, physical and social condition of the woman. As Luker points out:

> Given the competition for clients, an ideology that physicians were protectors of women and some ambiguity about the indications for abortion, one can easily imagine situations where physicians would be willing to give their women patients the abortions they wanted under the rubric of saving their lives (1984:37).

Twentieth Century Challenge to Abortion Laws

Following a period of public silence, abortion emerged once again as a political issue in the 1950s based on the health risks of illegal abortions, and a fear of population explosion in many developing countries. The first impetus for abortion reform came from concerns among physicians and public health professionals about the morbidity and maternal mortality associated with illegal abortions. An additional problem for physicians was the legal risks in performing abortions, as the line between therapeutic and criminal abortions continued to blur. The cure for several diseases that could affect pregnancy outcome rendered unnecessary the performance of abortions to save the life of the pregnant woman.

The decline in fertility that began in the latter part of the 19th century continued throughout the 20th century, with a sharp fall during the Depression and a temporary rise in the post-war period. The Baby Boom of the latter period is now considered an anomaly, in light of the long-term trend toward declining fertility in the United States. The demand for abortions exceeded those that could be legally obtained, and estimates of abortions vary from one in four live births to one in five births (Luker 1984). The Kinsey study reported that almost 90 percent of pre-marital pregnancies had ended in abortions, and the abortion rate peaked among women of child-bearing years during the Depression (in Luker 1984). The continued use of abortions by women, especially married women to limit births, meant that the law had to change to accommodate the fertility behavior of American women.

While the Baby Boom in the U.S. signalled a crisis in population growth at home, a decline in mortality had not resulted in a subsequent decline in fertility in many developing countries. The neo-Malthusian sentiment of the times was that population growth was the root cause of poverty. In the backdrop of the global population crisis, and the War on Poverty program of the Johnson Administration, the U.S. government took an active role in extending family planning services to indigent women. The Catholic church's opposition to government involvement in family planning represented two concerns (Rosoff 1988): First, support for contraceptive services could eventually encourage sterilization and abortion; and second, government involvement violated civil liberties of minority groups who would be obvious targets of fertility control efforts. Hence, the dissent from the Church during this early period, and pressures from the anti-abortion front in later years would keep official definition of family planning limited to specific contraceptive services; and the eligibility criteria for poor, unmarried, and minor women would become increasingly problematic.

During the first phase of reform, mostly male professionals in medicine, law, and public health urged the reform of existing abortion laws to include a broader definition of therapeutic abortions: factors such as the social and psychological well-being of the pregnant woman were justifiable considerations in a decision to terminate a pregnancy. Early reformers followed the path of Scandinavian countries in proposing the establishment of hospital boards that would oversee requests for abortions from women for a wide variety of reasons (Rossi and Sitaraman 1988).

By the mid sixties, a new group of activists entered the debate, redefining the role of physicians in the abortion issue, once and for all. Feminist involvement in the abortion issue changed the language of the debate from the reform of existing laws to repeal of all abortion laws. The National Organization for Women (NOW) took up the abortion issue in 1967, and the National Association for Repeal of Abortion Laws (NARAL) was also formed around the same time. The abortion issue cost NOW the allegiance of many Catholic members, who departed to form the Women's Equity Action League (WEAL) with an exclusive focus on economic rights for women (Rossi and Sitaraman 1988).

The feminist view of reproductive rights had two key elements. One idea implicit in the concept of reproductive rights was that of 'bodily integrity' - a woman's need to control her body and procreative capacities (Petchesky 1984). Second, given the social organization of gender roles, it was women's life circumstances that were most affected by a pregnancy. Hence biological and social components of women's reproductive activities provided the basis for a claim to abortion as a woman's rights issue. While the biological facts of pregnancy and childbirth gave women a unique vantage point from which they could argue for their abortion rights, the social context of reproduction today has challenged the idea of women's sole rights in making abortion decisions.

The feminist call for the repeal of all abortion laws also challenged physicians' control over abortion decisions. Feminists argued that physicians should act as professional counsellors on abortion decisions made by women for what ever reasons individual women themselves judged as valid. For example, radical members of the Society for Humane Abortions (SHA) not only referred women to illegal abortionists as an act of civil disobedience, but also kept a close check on the practice of such abortionists, by asking female clients to report back to them on the terms and conditions under which abortions were performed (Luker 1984). Religious groups such as the Episcopalian Church, the United Church of Christ, the Methodist Church, the United Presbyterian Church among others took a public stand in favor of abortion rights. Clergyman from these denominations contributed by referring women to clinics (in New York City) that provided abortion services.

While secular and religious activists joined forces, structural changes in the area of work and family provided the framework within which abortion took on a new meaning. Dramatic changes in the traditional roles of men and women appeared as more women, especially those with children under the age of six, entered the paid labor force. The pattern of women's increased participation in paid employment indicated both change and continuity in the history of women's work. Women had participated in equal share with men in the farm economy of the Colonial period. Given the long-history of women's contribution to the household economy, the role of the full-time homemaker (at least for middle and upper class women) was peculiar to the changes that Industrial Revolution brought about (McLaughlin et al 1988). These changes not only created a spatial separation of women's productive and reproductive activities, but created a new meaning of work, narrowly conceptualized as paid employment outside the home. In 1890 two percent of married women were employed outside the home. The proportion of women in the labor force increased by one percent during the depression years, and 40 percent of the married women in the labor force were from the middle-class (Chafe 1972). The Second World War had a tremendous impact on women's paid employment; the proportion of women in the labor force increased from 27.4 percent in 1940 to 35 percent in 1944 (U.S. Bureau of Census 1975), with 75 percent of the new entrees composed of housewives (Ryan 1983). Post-war attempts to resurrect women's traditional responsibilities as mothers and wives, and to reclaim jobs for men returning from the war were only partially successful. In 1950 51.2 percent of the women in the labor force were married, a quarter of the women working had children under the age of 18, and 12 % had children under the age of 6 (U.S. Bureau of Census 1975).

The trend in women's employment has been one of increased and continued participation, often leading to a simultaneous assumption of multiple roles of wife, mother, student, and worker. Increase in women's educational opportunities and delayed marriages also indicated shifts in traditional roles of women. Between 1960 and 1987, the proportion of ever married women in the age range of 20 to 24 declined from 73 percent to 39 percent (Westoff 1988). Delayed marriages, commitment to education and paid employment went along with a greater incidence of pre-marital sex and pregnancies. In 1950, 14 percent of all births to women under 20 were out of wedlock; by 1986, this proportion had increased to 61 percent (Westoff 1988). Marriage did not always precede childbearing and for many, children did not appear in family plans immediately after marriage.

The traditional ideology of the family did not fit the structural realities of American life, and this discrepancy began to be expressed in the abortion debate. The campaign for rights was loud and clear in the sixties from a variety of sources. The Civil Rights Movement, the campaigns for gay-liberation, the counter-culture, and the women's movement made the time ripe for the consideration of abortion as a woman's private right. The efforts of the abortion activists culminated in 1973, with the Supreme Court ruling in Roe v. Wade that legalized abortion on demand during the first trimester of pregnancy was permissible.

The Court viewed abortion as a private matter between a woman and her physician. The Court also made its moral position clear by defining fetal life as beginning at viability (after six months in the pregnancy, when fetal life can be sustained outside the womb), thus denying the full status of personhood to fetuses younger than six months. After the first trimester, states have the right to impose restrictions on abortions, unless the health of the mother is in danger. And after viability, states may regulate abortions in the interests of fetal life, unless it is deemed medically necessary (Butler and Walbert 1986).

Developments Since Roe v. Wade

The Supreme Court ruling evoked a sense of victory among the pro-choice supporters, while taking the pro-life activists by surprise. The early pro-life organizers had been male Catholic professionals with low levels of exposure to abortion (Luker 1984). This ruling by the highest court in the country attacked deeply held beliefs regarding the sanctity of life advocated by the Catholic Church. It is important to clarify the position of lay Catholics on the abortion issue. As with contraceptive issues, some differences of opinion divided the Catholic hierarchy from the Catholic laity. There were already signs of an end of Catholic-Protestant differences in fertility behavior and attitudes (Westoff and Jones 1979, McCready and Greeley 1972). The first public opinion survey on the topic of abortion was used to downplay the Catholic Church's opposition to abortion in the sixties, by showing minimal differences in attitudes of lay Catholics and Protestants (Rossi and Sitaraman 1988).

In the early seventies the pro-life movement owed much of its organizational activities to the Catholic Church. Even before 1973, the Church had begun to organize right-to-life committees. The National Council of Catholic Bishops formulated a "Pastoral Plan for Pro-life Activity" which sought to establish a network of parish level committees that would (a) effect the passage of a pro-life amendment b) elect pro-life sympathizers to local and party organizations, (c) monitor officials on their abortion stand, and (d) work for qualified candidates who would vote for a constitutional amendment and other pro-life issues (Petchesky 1984). In the late 1970s, and in the 1980s Fundamentalist Protestant groups and individuals joined forces with the Catholic Church and conservative politicians. Given this coalition of religious and political interests, some see the anti-abortion campaign of the 1980s as the symbol of the resurgence of right-wing conservatism in the country. Writers point to the marriage of interests between what has been called the "New Right" and the "New Christian Right" (Guth 1983, Kater 1982, Petchesky 1984). The New Christian Right members include televangelists, clergymen, committees, organized structures such as the Religious Roundtable, Christian Voice, and the Moral Majority (Guth 1983). The Christian Voice emerged in 1979 as a merger of anti-gay, anti-pornography and pro-family groups on the West coast, while the Moral Majority, founded by Jerry Falwell, has more of a Southern flavor. The unique characteristics of these groups has been the use of communications media, direct mail, television, press and 'pulpit politics' to focus public attention on individual 'Christian' or moral issues. However, the political and ideological roots of the organized pro-life movement is distinct from the 'New Right.'

The New Right represents a network of activities, organizations, and constituencies that have all targeted themselves against ERA, Salt II, affirmative action, federal social programs, and government regulation of business (Himmelstein 1983). The themes that characterize the New Right are (1) economic libertarianism, (2) social traditionalism, and (3) militant anti-communism. The New Right is thus 'new' in its inclusion of social issues in the political agenda. While the religious anti-abortion elements are using the New Right to lobby in Washington, the political Right has found a way to mobilize a broad based electorate to the pro-life movement. The alliance is not so clear-cult, since many pro-lifers are also pacifists, support welfare programs, and oppose the conservative policies of the political right. The myriad interest groups involved in the anti-abortion movement are further illustrated by a feminist pro-life caucus that opposes other issues, and Catholic church affiliated groups that have challenged the Reagan Administration's position on nuclear arms (Petchesky 1984). Clearly, the abortion debate in the eighties presents no united front on the part of abortion opponents, for there are moral absolutists on the pro-life side and political pragmatists on the side of the political right. In the past two years, ideological divisions within the evangelical movement have become evident, and media exposure of scandals of evangelical celebrities has dampened their charisma.

Although attempts to pass a Human Life Amendment that would outlaw abortions have failed, pro-lifers have been partially successful in limiting de facto access to abortion in some instances (Blake 1981). The passing of the Hyde Amendment in 1976 restricted the use of Medicaid funds for abortion. The same year, the Court ruled that states could not impose a blanket spousal consent requirement for all abortions, although such consent after viability is still open to debate. In 1980 the court upheld a congressional ban on the use of federal Medicaid funds for abortion, except in situations where the mother's health was in danger. In 1983, the Supreme Court struck down an Ohio ordinance that required a 24-hour waiting period prior to the performance of an abortion. The same year, the court upheld a Missouri law requiring the presence of two physicians for the performance of late abortions, and parental or judicial consent for minors seeking abortions. The track record of the Supreme Court since the landmark decision in 1973, has been to uphold the spirit of the Roe v. Wade decision legalizing abortions. A potential threat to this steadfast support for legal abortions emerged in the Court's decision to hear appeals in the Missouri and Pennsylvania cases.

The Missouri appeal challenged the existing abortion law in fundamental ways: it barred the use of public funds to counsel women on abortions; it prohibited the use of pubic hospitals to perform abortions, except in life-threatening instances; it required that doctors assess fetal viability before performing abortions beyond 19 weeks of pregnancy (Newsweek 1989). Past defeats in securing support for these same restrictions dampened the optimism of right-to-life activists, who expected the Court to allow more restrictions at the state-level, while essentially reaffirming the woman's right to abortion (Newsweek 1989). The Supreme Court ruled on Webster v. Reproductive Health Services upholding two new restrictions on legal abortions. First, women who seek abortions beyond 20 weeks of gestation would be required to undergo medical tests to assess fetal viability. Second, public facilities and employees would be prohibited from performing or assisting with abortions that are not necessary to save the life of the mother. While, the court abstained from overturning its earlier ruling n Roe v. Wade, it clearly relegated greater powers to individual states to decide their own abortion laws in the future. Three years later another serious challenge to Roe emerged with Planned Parenthood of Southeastern Pennsylvania v. Casey.

On June 29th, 1992 the Supreme Court once again affirmed the 1973 Roe v. Wade decision by a 5-4 vote as it also upheld restrictions on abortion in a Pennsylvania law. Despite fears that conservative appointments to the court under Reagan may lead to a shift in the court's view of Roe v. Wade, the moderate positions of Justices Sandra O'Connor and Anthony Kennedy have deferred any immediate challenges to the Roe decision. A new focus on "undue burden" has emerged as the criteria for judging state restrictions on abortion. Undue burden is defined as a "substantial obstacle in the path of a woman seeking an abortion before the fetus attains viability." (New York Times, 1992). This same criteria allowed the court to uphold some of the restrictions including a 24-hour waiting period, counselling of alternatives to abortion, and parental or judicial consent for minors seeking abortions. On the other hand, the court struck down a provision that required married women to inform their husbands of the abortion decision as unconstitutional.

The politics of abortion continues to be played out in all branches of the government. Abortion politics had a spill-over effect on the government's funding of family planning agencies at home and abroad, and scientific research on contraceptive technologies (Rosoff 1988). Funding for family planning services has not increased in the past 15 years, and in the Reagan era, a strong ideological opposition to abortions led to attempts to defund national and international organizations that engage in abortion related activities. Both the International Planned Parenthood Federation and the United Nations Fund for Population Activities suffered funding cuts as a consequence of their refusal to withdraw from abortion-related activities.

Soon after assuming office, President Clinton rescinded the 'gag order' prohibiting federally funded clinics from counselling about abortion, and removed the ban on using fetal tissue for scientific research. These efforts have reversed the conservative presidential policies of the past twelve years.

Additional political and legal challenges to abortion arise from the moral implications of recent developments in reproductive medicine. Fetal blood transfusions, fetal monitoring techniques such as amniocentesis, ultrasonography, fetoscopy, and semi-delivery for surgical purposes have turned "the anonymous fetus into a patient" (Francoer 1985:2). Medical advances will further complicate the definition of viability as ever-younger fetuses can be sustained outside the womb. Pre-natal diagnosis and care create an ambivalent situation for parents who will be torn between emotional investment in the pregnancy and the possibility of having to abort a defective fetus (Rothman 1988). Scientific gains in contraception, neo-natal care, and infertility raise new ethical issues, for which neither the public nor the legal system seems to be well prepared.

The Structural-Ideational Context

The linking of abortion to the politics of family, sexuality, and human life issues is indicative of long-term shifts in life circumstances and value orientation in many aspects of social life. Structural changes in the organization of work and family life underscore the current and continued salience of abortion in family plans. Long-term trends in values and beliefs provide the ideational context for the discussion abortion attitudes.

Contemporary trends in marriage and childbearing show the persistence of normative pressures to parent, as well as immense diversity in the timing and sequence of transition to parenthood (Rindfuss, Morgan and Swicegood 1988). Close to 90 percent of Americans will marry some time in their lives, and increased childlessness reflects patterns of delayed childbearing, rather than a commitment to childlessness. Rindfuss, Morgan and Swicegood (1988) demonstrate that the timing and sequence of transition to parenthood from the 1920s to the 1980s have been characterized by swift responses to economic conditions that either facilitate or obstruct early family formation and childbearing. Hence, delayed marriages and childbearing, along with high levels of childlessness that dominated the Depression Era were indications of a collective response to high levels of unemployment and loss of family income. Similarly, high inflation and moderate levels of unemployment in the 1970s and 1980s have resulted in delayed entry into parenthood, and levels of childlessness that may surpass those observed during the Depression. The collective response of individuals of all reproductive age groups in tailoring their fertility behavior to economic conditions is also consistent with cultural norms regarding parenthood which require all individuals to marry and raise children *once they can afford them*. Hence, normative pressures to parent can remain strong, while individuals adapt to economic circumstances by changing the timing of parenthood and the size of their families.

Increase in women's labor force participation since the 1960s has also contributed to contemporary patterns of childbearing. The majority of women who enter the work force are likely to stay employed for longer periods of time because they are faced with the necessity of contributing to an adequate standard of living for their families. In 1980, wives aged 25 to 34 were 70 percent as likely to be employed as single women (McLaughlin et al 1988). Furthermore, the rates of labor force participation for mothers and childless married women had also become identical by 1980. The expansion of the service and professional sectors has mandated higher levels of education for both men and women. In the 1980s, two out of five women obtained at least some college education, pushing trends toward a convergence of men's and women's levels of educational attainment (McLaughlin et al 1988). A commitment to higher education is an additional factor that has contributed to the changing patterns of family formation. Even among teenage mothers, whose early entry into parenthood is in sharp contrast to current patterns, the salience of education and future employment is likely to result in reentry into school following childbirth (Rindfuss, Morgan and Swicegood 1988). And among teenagers who are highly committed to education, an unwanted pregnancy is more likely to result in an abortion.

The number of abortions performed each year is close to 1.5 million (Tietze 1983,1986), and a recent sample survey of American women who had abortions reveals that majority of these women terminated a pregnancy for a number of social and economic reasons (Torres and Forrest 1988). Most common reasons cited for an abortion were financial burdens, bad timing, and competing work-family responsibilities. A German Survey also reported that more than half the women gave financial problems as a reason for their abortions (Sachdev 1988). While such reports indicate adaptations by individual families to economic circumstances and conflicting social roles, a corresponding change in attitudes toward abortion has not necessarily followed. Our discussion of public attitudes in the next section will show only partial public support for abortions based on social and economic circumstances. The link between attitudes and behavior at the individual and societal levels is too complex to be reduced to simple causal statements. There is some evidence that structural changes discussed above have also been accompanied by parallel long-term shifts in value orientation in many Western developed nations.

In a recent essay (Rossi and Sitaraman 1988) we attempt to place abortion in the context of secular ideational trends observed in many European countries, which also apply to the United States. The senior author of this essay first observed links between the secularization thesis tested by Lesthaege and Surkyn (1988) and the American abortion debate. Lesthaege and Surkyn (1988) use trend data from the European Value Studies that span the years between 1970 and 1986. In their conceptual framework, secularization represents a trend toward the declining influence of religious institutions in many private aspects of life. Such a secular trend has also been accompanied by a highly individualized value orientation in social, political, and economic domains of life. Among the European respondents, a positive approval of sexual permissiveness, unmarried motherhood, educational qualities of independence and imagination, support for easier divorce, an emphasis on greater worker control, and a tendency to engage in public protest are indicators of a value orientation that stresses individual discretion as opposed to institutional control. By contrast, an emphasis on public morality and greater religiosity are highly correlated with greater acceptance of institutional control on matters of personal morality. From a long-term point of view, their analysis shows that a secular trend becomes evident in each younger cohort of respondents expressing a greater tendency to uphold individualized values (Rossi and Sitaraman 1988). Within this framework abortion attitudes become part of two domains that represent values in the area of marriage and family, and religion and morality.

In the American context there are several indicators of such changes in value orientation that can be inferred from attitude trends even over a short period of time. The convergence of Catholics and Protestants in fertility behavior and attitudes is one instance of the decline of the Church's control over sexual and reproductive behavior of lay Catholics. Only 1 in 4 young respondents in a 1984 Gallup poll reported a high degree of confidence in organized religion, and 82% of Catholics and 74 percent of Protestants believe that a person can be a good Christian without having to attend church (D'Antonio 1985). Attitudes are also changing to accommodate contemporary patterns of work and family life. Fifty-eight percent of respondents in a 1985 Gallup Poll found pre-marital sex morally acceptable, compared to only 24 percent in 1969 (McLaughlin et al 1988). Compared to thirty years ago, more Americans now approve of mothers with young children working outside the home. Tolerant attitudes toward pre-marital sex and women's employment should not be taken to indicate a decline in the salience of marriage and family life. Thornton and Freedman (1982) report that 90 percent of adolescents report they will marry, a figure that has changed little between 1960 and 1980. The majority of Americans are also likely to include children in their life plans.

Greater acceptance of pre-marital sex and women's employment, along with the continued salience of marriage and children probably imply a simultaneous recognition of traditional normative pressures and changing patterns of work and family life. During a long process of fundamental changes in values and life circumstances that span many decades, a telescopic vision of public behavior or attitudes at any one point in history cannot yield clear-cut patterns of change. Furthermore, changes in many of the value domains discussed may take place at a different pace. Attitudes toward women's employment can change more quickly, especially with a greater acceptance of themes in feminist ideology that provide legitimacy for combining familial and non-familial roles. On the other hand, human life values which also underlie attitudes toward abortion are not easily responsive to change. To test the empirical validity of changes in values discussed in this section would require longitudinal data that covers a wide variety of topics such as those found in the European Value Studies. This study, like many others, is limited to an inspection of the structural and ideological correlates of abortion attitudes found among a sample of the public polled at one point in time. The long-term trends sketched here provide some insight into interpreting variation in the abortion attitude structure found in our sample.

Research on Abortion Attitudes

Social science research on abortion was stimulated by the controversy surrounding abortion in the mid sixties. The same period saw an increased interest in charting trends in attitudes and behavior in many aspects of marriage and family life. The counter-culture, the feminist movement, and the 'sexual revolution' of the sixties made visible dramatic shifts in family life that led to a monitoring of attitudes toward divorce, children, pre-marital and extra-marital sex, and gender roles among other issues. Research on abortion attitudes has shown two major emphases. The earliest and most common are studies that trace changes over time in public opinion on abortion (Arney and Trescher 1976; Westoff, Ryder and Moore 1969). The second, more recent, type of study has attempted to identify the social and ideological correlates of abortion attitudes among political activists (Granberg 1987, Ginsberg 1989, Luker 1984, Markson 1985), and extends such research to an analysis of public attitudes toward abortion. (Granberg and Granberg 1981, Scott and Schuman 1988).

Abortion Activists

Studies of abortion activists attempt to portray contrasting belief-structures that encompass moral views toward abortion. Researchers have highlighted various aspects of abortion ideology by placing it in the framework of contemporary family politics (Luker 1984), by tracing its origins to the politics of the counter-culture (Markson 1985), by treating it as an anti-feminist backlash of recent decades (Petchesky 1984), and by relating abortion views to contrasting value orientations toward many aspects of modern political and social life (Granberg 1987).

Luker (1984) concludes from her study of California pro-life and pro-choice activists that abortion is at the 'tip of the iceberg' of a host of concerns related to sexuality, motherhood, gender roles and family. She portrays the abortion conflict as a conflict about gender roles and identities between two types of women. The ideological responses of abortion activists arise from trajectories that their lives have followed. A typical pro-life activist is a Catholic woman, who married early in life, has three or more children, attends church regularly, and has been a full-time housewife and mother for most of her life. By contrast, the pro-choice activist comes from a higher income background, has fewer children, is strongly committed to a professional job, is not affiliated with any religion, and rarely attends church. The lifestyle choices made by these women form the basis of contrasting value orientations in matters of sexuality, marriage and motherhood. Different value orientations in turn reaffirm the lifestyles chosen by pro-choice and pro-life activists.

The pro-life view of the world is composed of a conservative morality in sexual matters, including an opposition to pre-marital sex, extra-marital sex, and homosexuality. Pro-life activists also show support for the 'separate but equal' organization of gender roles and responsibilities within the traditional nuclear family. In contrast, pro-choice women support a permissive sexual morality, uphold a firm belief in planning their reproductive lives around other social roles, and have a more relativistic view of human life in general.

Granberg's analysis (1987) extends the contrasts between the two groups to include a wide variety of values. Using the Rokeach Terminal Values measure, Granberg found that the Missouri pro-life members ranked salvation high on their list, whereas pro-choice members ranked it the lowest on their list of most important values.

The importance of family security, national security, and inner harmony among pro-life activists is also contrasted with an emphasis on an exciting life, pleasure, equality, and a sense of accomplishment among pro-choice activists. Granberg's analysis extends the abortion views of activists beyond the family-gender framework to embrace a broader set of value domains.

Attitudes of the American Public

Social scientists have drawn upon the profiles of abortion activists to test the strength of support for abortion among the American public. The focus on public attitudes toward abortion has also been at the heart of monitoring responses to legal and political challenges to abortion laws. Conflicting reports on levels of public support for abortion are quite common, and figures vary as a function of samples and questionnaire items. Media polls on abortion have proliferated in response to political developments, and measure public attitudes with varied emphases ranging from moral approval of abortions, support for legality of abortions, political salience of the abortion issue relative to other issues, and support for specific state level referenda that affect legal access to abortions.

According to a 1989 Gallup poll, 58 percent of respondents did not want the Court to overturn the Roe v. Wade decision (N.Y. Times January 10, 1989). Similarly, according to a New York Times/CBS poll conducted in January 1989, 61 percent of respondents said a woman should be allowed to have an abortion if she wants one and her doctor agrees to it. More specific questions have captured greater ambivalence among the public: In the same N.Y Times/CBS poll, 46 percent agree that abortions should be legal as they are now, 41 percent support legal access only under conditions of rape, incest, or life threatening circumstances, and 9 percent said abortions should never be permitted. Also people are more likely to support abortions, if the questions focus on a woman's right rather than fetal life. Researchers for a 1980 media poll experiment found that 29 percent of respondents favored a constitutional amendment prohibiting abortions; the figure rose to 50 percent when respondents were asked if they would favor a constitutional amendment protecting the life of the unborn child (N.Y. Times January 10, 1989).

Studies of the political salience of abortion note that abortion ranks lowest in importance compared to economic and national security issues in the public's view. A 1987 NARAL poll showed that only 8 percent of the respondents cited abortion as an issue that concerned them the most. The remaining respondents cited AIDS (15%), education (25%),and the federal budget deficit(47%) (Donovan 1988). An open-ended question included in a survey conducted in 1985 by the Survey Research Center in Michigan asked respondents to name the most important problem facing the country. None of the respondents mentioned abortion--Unemployment, economic problems, and the threat of nuclear war were cited as issues of prime concern (Scott and Schuman 1988). In 1980s similar surveys demonstrate the lack of impact of abortion politics on voting behavior -- A strong pro-choice stance on the part of incumbents does not threaten their reelection in federal elections (Donovan 1988). Support for abortions is not divided along party lines either. The NARAL poll reported only a slightly smaller proportion of Republican voters who opposed the constitutional amendment banning abortions (48 percent compared to 64 percent of Democrats).

While the political salience of the abortion issue measured in terms of candidate support or voting behavior may be quite low for the general public, moral salience of the abortion issue is harder to demonstrate. In fact, measures of moral approval of abortion over the past two decades show remarkably stable support for abortions that is contingent upon a variety of circumstances. We use repeat items found in the General Social Surveys to chart the trend in public attitudes toward abortion from 1965 to 1988.

Table 1.1 shows the proportion of respondents in each year that approve of a woman's right to an abortion under six different circumstances. The trend observed is a sharp increase in approval for the various health and social concerns between 1965 and 1972, and a remarkably stable level of approval from 1973 to the present. During this same period, Catholics' attitudes toward abortion converged with attitudes found among Protestants, a trend that was especially marked among young Catholics under 30 years of age (McCready and Greeley 1972). A slight drop in approval of abortion observed in 1978 and 1982 has been attributed by some to intensified efforts on the part of the right-to-life movement, just prior to the period of decline. Such a hypothesis has not been tested, and the

Table 1.1
Percent Approving of Abortion for Six Different Reasons:1965-1988

Reasons Year:	65[a]	72	73	74	75	76	77	78	80	82	83	84	85	87	88
Rape[b]	56	75	81	83	80	81	81	81	80	81	80	77	78	78	77
Maternal health	71	83	91	90	88	89	89	89	88	89	87	88	87	86	86
Fetal defect	55	75	83	83	80	82	83	80	80	81	76	78	76	77	76
Financial problems	21	46	52	52	51	51	52	46	50	50	42	45	43	44	41
Unmarried woman	18	41	48	48	46	48	48	40	46	42	38	43	40	41	38
No more children	15	38	46	45	44	45	45	39	45	46	38	41	39	40	39

[a] The data used in this table for 1965 are from Rossi(1966), and the data for the years 1972 to 1985 are from the NORC Cummulative codebooks(1988)

[b] "YES" responses as a percent of "yes," "no," and "dont know" responses.

shifts in approval are minor compared to a relatively stable pattern of approval that has emerged over the past several years. The trend data indicate that the public has generally moved toward a position of consensus regarding abortion for health reasons, while over half of the American public still opposes abortion in the discretionary situations. Of these latter circumstances, poverty elicited the most favorable response and family size limitation the least, while among the hard reasons, maternal health received overwhelming approval (Ebaugh and Haney 1985). The level and pattern of support for abortions was in place before the Supreme Court decision in 1973 that legalized abortions. In fact in 1975, less than 50 percent of Americans even knew about the Supreme Court decision (Blake 1977).

Abortion approval varies to some extent by socio-demographic characteristics of the public, but most variation is limited to complex interactions between religion and church attendance. Catholics are less approving of abortions than Protestants, but attitude differences are also marked between secular Catholics and those who attend church regularly; the latter seem to be closer to fundamentalist Protestants who are more likely to oppose abortions for a variety of reasons. Moderate differences in abortion attitudes also emerge as a function of education, race, age, and gender (Ebaugh and Haney 1978). Blacks show less support for abortions than whites, but they are also more likely to support abortions that are based on economic reasons (Hall and Ferree 1986). Age differences associated with abortion attitudes are not linear, and trend data show more conservative views among both very young and very old age groups (Ebaugh and Haney 1978, Blake 1984).

The second type of attitude research in recent years has attempted to uncover the broader ideological structure underlying abortion attitudes (Barnatt and Harris 1982, Benin 1985, Blake 1971, Blake and del Pinal 1981, Deitch 1983, Ebaugh and Haney 1980, Finlay 1981, Granberg 1978, Granberg and Granberg 1978, 1980, Singh and Leahy 1978, Scott and Schuman 1988). These analyses take into account the recent polarization of the abortion debate itself and seek to find evidence of support for either the pro-choice or pro-life platform among the general public. The question posed is whether the public in general shares the ideological structure of attitudes articulated by the activists. Strong correlations have been found between attitudes toward pre-marital sex, euthanasia, suicide and abortion attitudes, while weak correlations have been found between sex-role ideology and abortion attitudes. Blake's (1981) analysis focused on the middle majority of the public who support abortions on some conditions but not others. She concludes that fence-sitters on abortion are closer to the pro-life position than the pro-choice position, since many of them hold conservative views on suicide, euthanasia and politics. Scott and Schuman (1988) focus their analysis on extreme groups of the public who support or oppose abortions under all circumstances. Their analysis suggests that opponents of abortion among the general public are more likely to consider the issue of importance than supporters; black opponents are less likely to consider the issue important than white opponents of abortion; and pro-choice women are more likely to consider abortion as an important issue than pro-choice men.

The Present Study

The present study draws upon previous research on activists and the public, but departs in its methodological and substantive focus. In Chapter 2, we discuss the methodological limitations of existing data on abortion attitudes and provide a rationale for the procedures used to collect data for this study. We also discuss in detail the measurement of abortion attitudes and attitudes in other domains investigated in this study. The factorial survey design is used to measure attitudes toward abortion. This design allows the use of highly specific abortion situations that approximate a range of real life abortion decisions. By varying life course characteristics of pregnant women, their personal resources, and life circumstances that prompt an abortion decision we are able to investigate in greater detail public approval of abortions along a variety of situational dimensions.

In recent decades several issues have been linked to sexual and reproductive politics, for which data do not exist in standard attitude polls. We specifically designed questions that would tap attitudes in the area of teenage parenting under different conditions of parental and partner approval, attitudes toward different methods of artificial reproduction, and gender role attitudes that focus on salience of family and employment roles. A number of socio-demographic variables were also measured that allow us to relate abortion attitudes to social group characteristics of respondents. Of special significance is data on respondent's exposure to abortion experiences of self, partners, relatives and friends, which can be linked to their abortion attitudes. Chapter 3 of this study is the first of three analysis chapters. In it, we examine the relative impact of characteristics of abortion situations and respondents on abortion attitudes. The data for this analysis comes primarily from hypothetical abortion vignettes used to measure attitudes. Since we explore a variety of dimensions that characterize abortion decisions, we are able to isolate the key characteristics of abortion situations that trigger the most variation in approval levels. This analysis not only extends previous measurement of abortion attitudes, but also provides empirical justification for the approach used in more conventional surveys. A second major issue addressed in this chapter concerns the reciprocal influences of characteristics shared by vignette women and respondents who judged abortion vignettes. We match respondents and vignettes on three shared characteristics: age, marital status, and parity.

In Chapter 4, the focus on the abortion belief structure is extended to encompass a broader structure of beliefs and values of which abortion attitudes are a part. The analyses of attitudes and beliefs in each of the four belief domains - abortion, sex and reproduction, gender roles, and human life - deal with both the dimensionality and commonalities that characterize these four belief domains. In addition we integrate two different approaches to the measurement of abortion attitudes that reveal a very similar structure of attitudes toward abortion.

The last of the empirical chapters (Chapter 5) extends the analysis in Chapter 6 to sub-groups of the sample. We examine variations in the belief structure among groups of respondents defined by age, religion, gender and personal exposure to abortions. The concluding chapter summarizes key findings from the study, and discusses the implications of these findings for the current abortion debate, and future social science research in this area.

2

Methodology

In this study we explore the structure of abortion attitudes using two research instruments designed to measure variation in abortion attitudes at two levels. First, we wish to examine attitudes in the abortion domain by focusing on the distinguishing characteristics of abortion situations themselves. The factorial survey approach is used to explore the situational dimensions of abortion that trigger the most variation in approval of abortion. On another level, we are concerned with respondents' value orientation as expressed in the relationship between attitudes toward abortion and attitudes in related domains. For this purpose, we employ a customary survey instrument which includes several items that measure attitudes in areas identified in past studies as closely linked to abortion attitudes. Some clarification of the terms *attitudes, values* and *beliefs* as used in this study is in order. There is a substantial body of social psychological literature that attempts to distinguish among these concepts. In this study we will consider only the commonly held distinctions between these concepts. By attitudes we mean preferences for an object or situation. In this study survey items measure attitudes toward specific aspects of abortion by asking respondents to rate the degree of their approval or disapproval of abortion under different conditions. Similarly, we measure attitudes in domains such as sexuality and gender roles with questions that elicit approval or agreement with specific types and instances of sexual behavior and gender role arrangements. The term *belief* refers opinions that imply a deeper level of personal commitment (belief in God, salvation, personhood of the fetus) rather than likes or dislikes toward more discrete issues. And, *values* refer to a higher level of orientation that embraces a range of specific attitudes and beliefs. An example from this study would be values regarding human life which are manifested in specific attitudes toward euthanasia, suicide, abortion and beliefs regarding the personhood of the fetus. The focus of measurement in this study is attitudes, whereas values are largely inferred when we attempt to correlate attitudes across various domains to in an effort to test the data for a coherent belief system.

The preceding chapter discussed historical developments in abortion politics and social science response to such developments through research over the past two decades. Empirical research on abortion activists and the general public amidst the ongoing debate about abortion has led to social science attempts to link public attitudes toward abortion to positions articulated by activists on the abortion issue. Activists tend to adhere to an internally consistent set of arguments for or against abortion, which are embedded in a larger set of beliefs and values that shape their lives. There is much less coherence to the beliefs of a heterogenous public: the salience of the abortion issue varies tremendously among individuals and attitudes toward abortion may not be consciously premised on a particular set of values. In contrast to bi-polar positions taken by activists, we find greater variation in the positions taken by the general public, in the conditions under which abortion is judged acceptable, and in the positions taken on issues related to abortion.

In this chapter we present the rationale for the collection of primary data on abortion attitudes, the design features of the two research instruments used in this effort, and the details of execution of the survey. These methodological issues will be addressed in the following order: first, an overview of methods and techniques used in previous studies of abortion attitudes, with a discussion of the limitations of secondary analysis of such data to answer questions posed by this study. Next, we focus on specific problems encountered in previous measurement and interpretation of abortion attitudes: confounding effects of context and order of items, and interpretive issues regarding the discrepancy between public opinion and public behavior in the abortion area. The factorial survey method is proposed as a partial solution to some of the methodological and conceptual problems raised in conventional survey approaches to the study of abortion attitudes.

A second level of analysis concerns the structure of abortion attitudes defined in a larger context of a value orientation. This analysis seeks to describe relationships between attitudes toward abortion and attitudes in other related domains. We will discuss the measurement of these attitudes in the telephone survey used in this study. Lastly, we sketch the scheme of analysis to be followed in the empirical chapters to follow.

Past Measurement of Abortion Attitudes

Social science methodology reflects the ambience of a culture and its historical roots. The earliest attempts to measure and investigate abortion attitudes date back to the mid sixties amidst the political climate of abortion reform movements in several states in the United States. The continued interest in gauging trends in abortion approval parallels the persistent political debate surrounding abortion in the post-legalization period since 1973. The first systematic measurement of attitudes toward abortion began in 1965, when a national survey commissioned by Lawrence Kohlberg included questions designed by Alice S. Rossi and administered in the NORC[1] survey (Rossi 1966). Since that time, with the institution of the General Social Surveys in 1972, these items have been included almost every year, with trend data on abortion attitudes spanning more than a decade. The original items on abortion approval included six different justifying circumstances ranging from rape to unmarried status. These items began with a lead question asking respondents whether or not they "think it should be possible for a pregnant woman to obtain a legal abortion.." (Rossi 1966:9), and the reasons cited were: (1) "If the woman's own health is seriously endangered by the pregnancy," (2) "If she became pregnant as a result of rape," (3) "if there is a strong chance of serious defect in the baby," (4) "If the family has a very low income and cannot afford any more children," (5) "If she is unmarried and does not want to marry the man," (6) if she is married and does not want any more children." (Rossi 1966:9). These same items were incorporated into other polls such as Gallup and the National Fertility Survey, and now constitute the standard measurement of abortion attitudes used in trend analysis. In addition, polls including media surveys and those sponsored by activist groups on both sides of the abortion debate, have included a variety of questions that tap other aspects of abortion in response to legal and political developments in the 1970s and 1980s. Questions on approval of abortion in the absence of spouse approval were included once, in 1977, in the GSS survey. Media polls timed during the presidential election campaigns attempted to measure the impact of public views toward abortion on candidate preferences and electoral outcomes.

The earliest and most common of social science studies have used the original six items to trace changes over time in public attitudes toward abortion (Arney and Trescher 1976, Westoff, Ryder and Moore 1969). The second, more recent type of study has attempted to uncover the broader ideological structure underlying abortion attitudes (Barnatt and Harris 1982, Benin 1985, Blake and del Pinal 1981, Deitch 1983, Ebaugh and Haney 1980, Finlay 1981, Granberg 1984, Granberg and Granberg 1978, 1980, Singh and Leahy 1978). These take into account the recent polarization of the abortion debate among activists and seek to interpret support for either the pro-choice or pro-life platform among the general public. A third type of analysis concerns the short-term impact of public opinion on national electoral outcomes or abortion policies (Donovan 1988, Granberg 1987, Vinovskis 1980).

The use of national survey data for analysis of abortion attitude structure has several advantages. First, the vast amount of data collected facilitates trend analysis as well as analysis of attitudinal structure, because the data set contains items on several related issues. The most widely used national poll data comes from the cumulative General Social Surveys conducted by NORC. Secondary analyses of these data use items that tap attitudes toward abortion, women's employment, family size aspirations, human life values, and sexual morality. These surveys provide large representative samples which facilitate generalization of findings to the U.S. population. Since there is widespread use of such data sets among social scientists, there is a considerable body of methodological criticism aimed at improving design and measurement of items used in these surveys. Despite these advantages, there is also a downside to the eclectic nature of the content of national polls.

The NORC surveys, the most widely used data set in analyzing abortion opinions, have been geared toward trend analysis with repeat items each year. As a consequence, these measures are not sensitive to the increasing complexity and changing context of the abortion issue. Further time and space constraints limit detailed exploration of specific issues in amalgam surveys covering many attitude domains. The spread of content in these surveys is largely 'reactive' to social-political trends viewed in the short-run and in isolation, with less emphasis on long-term trends in values that date back several decades preceding the first attempts to measure the attitude domains in question. Omnibus surveys of this type are more likely to be guided by pragmatic policy implications of issues viewed from a short-run point of view.

Our interest in analyzing the contemporary structure of abortion attitudes with sensitivity to changes in the abortion issue over time provided the rationale for collecting primary data rather than analyzing existing data sets. Two research instruments were designed to answer questions posed by this study: (1) a closed-ended telephone interview including questions on abortion values, values in related areas, and some socio-demographic characteristics of respondents and (2) a factorial survey instrument, each containing 20 descriptions of hypothetical abortion situations that was mailed to respondents following the telephone interviews. An age-sex stratified sample was drawn from the 1987 street census of Greenfield, Massachusetts. We begin with a discussion of the features of the factorial survey instrument.

The Factorial Survey Approach

The most crucial aspect of an abortion situation that has received singular attention in political-legal debates as well as in survey research has been the reason for which a woman seeks an abortion. The focus on motives stems logically from an historical emphasis on explicit conditions that warranted approval for the performance of a legal abortion. The actual experiences of individuals who have faced an abortion decision challenges such a unidimensional portrayal of the circumstances surrounding abortion. A recent survey conducted by the Alan Guttmacher Institute found very few women had only one reason for having an abortion: the modal response was four reasons (Torres and Forest 1988). The women in this study reported a combination of factors : financial constraints, bad timing, lack of a marriage partner, and conflicting work-family responsibilities at the time of pregnancy were all involved in their abortion decision. The measurement of abortion attitudes in surveys so far has not incorporated such complexity of factors into their design. Real life situations are far more complex and multi-dimensional than a series of discrete survey items can portray. Even women who share one reason for an abortion may differ on other circumstances that contributed to the decision to abort, such as age, marital status, number of previous childbirths and financial standing. For example, many women may say they had an abortion because of 'bad timing;' of these women, some may go on to cite their age or poverty, while others cite family size, or conflicting responsibilities of schooling and careers. If attitudes are to some extent embedded in real life experiences, then judgments regarding the acceptance of an abortion solution will vary with respect to the relative salience of the various situational factors.

The factorial survey method permits us to explore such complexity in abortion situations. It is not possible with conventional survey techniques to present a large variety of descriptions of real life abortion situations to a respondent to judge. Time and resource constraints often do not permit such an endeavor. Even if we were to come up with hundreds of carefully crafted abortion situations that represent the diversity apparent in the real world, a methodological solution is necessary to disentangle the impact of each of the situational factors upon the respondent's overall decision to approve or disapprove of an abortion.

Elements of the Factorial Survey Design

The factorial survey design originally developed by Peter Rossi (Rossi and Nock 1982) combines useful features of the conventional survey technique and experimental design. The underlying premise of the factorial survey approach is that individuals weigh several aspects of an object or situation in arriving at a judgement. Individuals use judgement principles that are socially shared and individually arrived at, depending on the nature of the situation.

Some attitude domains reflect a higher degree of societal consensus than others. Investigation of obligations toward various types of kin shows a high degree of normative consensus on what types of kin rank as important (Rossi and Rossi 1990). Definitions of what constitutes child abuse or sexual harassment are likely to reflect a low level of social consensus, and hence greater intra-individual variation in judgments of such situations. The factorial survey approach permits us to distinguish between social and individual components of attitudes. It is also possible to isolate the variation in attitudes that is due to factors describing an object or situation and the variation due to characteristics of respondents making the judgments.

Factorial surveys, as the name implies, combine the orthogonal design properties from the experimental tradition and the variety and complexity of the survey approach (Rossi and Anderson 1982). The experimental stimuli or the survey item in the factorial survey design is a hypothetical description of an object or situation. The factors or independent variables that go into producing the hypothetical situation are referred to as dimensions. In our study several situational components describe an abortion decision. We will refer to these as the dimensions of abortion situations. Some of the dimensions along which abortion decisions vary are age, marital status, health and financial position of the woman, her reproductive experience, reasons guiding the abortion, and the gestation period. These dimensions represent conceptually distinct components of an abortion situation. Each of these dimensions in turn can include highly specific levels of information (or in the statistical sense values that an independent variable assumes). If age is a conceptually distinct dimension from marital status, a specific age or marital status category (e.g. 18 year old, unmarried woman) is a more specific level of information.

In using the factorial survey method, we begin with a set of substantive dimensions that describe an abortion decision. The next step is to decide upon the specific levels of information that describe each of these substantive dimensions. The vignette design approximates an orthogonal design when computer-generated random combinations of a level from each dimension produces several unique descriptions of abortion situations. The item that is finally evaluated by a respondent is an abortion vignette: a short description of a particular situation produced by a computer-generated random combination of the substantive dimensions in the design. Each respondent receives only a small sample of the thousands of vignettes produced, but the analysis of the situational components uses on each individual vignette as the unit of analysis rather than the individual respondent.

There are several methodological advantages to such a design: thousands of unique abortion situations to analyze; the ability to isolate independent effects of each situational characteristic; the random ordering of vignettes within the total sample removes the problem of confounding order and context effects that is encountered in previous studies. The premise of this method is that the structure of general attitudes or beliefs can be systematically discerned from highly specific situational stimuli. We turn now to a discussion of the dimensions and levels used in constructing the abortion vignettes.

Abortion Vignettes: Dimensions and Levels
In this study the ten substantive dimensions that describe the context of the woman's abortion decision are roughly classified into five different clusters:

1.   *Life Course Position*

     #1 Age
     #2 Marital Status
     #3 Parity

2.   *Personal Circumstance*

     #4 Health Status
     #5 Economic Status

3.   *Circumstance of the Pregnant Woman*

     #6 Overt reasons woman has for seeking an abortion

4.   *Phase of Gestation*

     #7 Number of months pregnant

5.   *Relational Context*

     #8 Quality of couples' relationship
     #9 Parental Approval/disapproval
     #10 Partner's Approval/disapproval

Within each dimension a 'Blank' level was included which would appear in approximately 8 to 12 percent of the vignettes. The 'blank' level is essentially the absence of any information on that particular dimension. In analytical terms, this category can be used as a reference point from which the impact of particular levels of information can be assessed. However, some researchers caution that the use of blank levels in vignette designs can be risky.[2]

Life Course Position

#1. *Age*: Reproductive norms are closely tied to beliefs about the proper timing and context of parenthood. Age then, is not only a biological marker of reproductive capacity from early teens to late forties, but also a social indicator of appropriate timing of entry into parenthood. Biological capacity for reproduction may range from age 14 to 48, while social approval of pregnancies may be restricted to a narrower range from age 18 to 38. Given concern over teenage pregnancies and ambivalent attitudes toward pre-marital sex, abortion values may be modified as a function of the age of the woman in question. We may then predict a disapproval of abortions in the socially defined age range for parenting and an approval of abortions for very young women (14 to 15 years old) and very old women (over 45 years old). A wide range of age levels was included in the design (15, 18, 21, 25, 30, 35, 40, 45 and a blank category that appears as no information on age).

#2. *Marital Status*: Marital status distinguishes between legitimate and illegitimate contexts for parenting. Despite claims to a sexual revolution there is still widespread discomfort with childbearing outside of marriage. The levels within the marital status dimension were limited to a broad classification of 'married' or 'unmarried.' We expect a greater sympathy toward abortion decisions of unmarried women than married women. A blank level was used in this dimension, but 'married' and 'unmarried' were weighted to produce a larger proportion of vignettes that would contain descriptions of actual marital status, with a smaller proportion that would contain no information on this dimension.

#3.*Parity*: Completed family size of the woman is relevant to the perception of the current pregnancy. In Western industrialized societies marked by low fertility, a large family is no longer a cherished ideal. Instead we find a delicate balance between disapproval of voluntary childlessness and families with too many children. Family size norms will have direct implications for approval of abortion as one of the means of fertility control. Women who desire an abortion of a sixth or seventh pregnancy may elicit greater approval than women with no previous births or one to two children. To test for the impact of actual parity of individual women on approval of abortion, the dimension contained descriptions of family size ranging from no children to a maximum of 6 children, with the level describing no previous children weighted to represent over 30 percent of the descriptions. The childless category was weighted in this way since the choice of levels in this dimension (childless women. vs. women with previous births) logically determines the inclusion of the level describing desired childlessness as a reason for an abortion in a dimension that appears below. We wished to have a sufficient number of vignettes that included a description of this reason for analysis, and so we weighted this level in the parity dimension.

Personal Circumstance

   #4.Health Status: Maternal health has been one of the oldest justifications for acceptance of an abortion and elicits overwhelming approval among the public. The inclusion of a dimension on general health status of the woman permits us to check if health status has an effect on abortion approval, independent of whether it is a reason for obtaining an abortion. Three levels describe general health as being "excellent," "average" and "very poor". This general description was preferred to a more detailed depiction of health condition, since there are so many specific conditions of illhealth and few ways to denote good or excellent health.

   #5. Economic Status: The inclusion of information regarding the woman's household income, was premised on the rationale that contemporary family planning ideology is based on a cost-benefit calculus. The emphasis on fewer children who are provided with quality care, results from the high cost of rearing children in today's society. The financial position of the household might be crucial to judging whether the woman can actually provide quality care for a child if the pregnancy were carried to term. Hence, the public may approve of an abortion in the case of a woman with a low household income, and disapprove of an abortion for a woman with a high household income. Five levels of household income ranging from

$1000 a week to $100 a week were included, along with a 'blank' level.

Personal Circumstance of the Pregnant Woman

#6. Reasons for an Abortion: This dimension pertains directly to the abortion decision. Ten different circumstances that surround the abortion decision were included, that cover a range of health related and social personal concerns that underlie an abortion decision. In every case the decision was assumed to be voluntary and one that the woman desired. Conventional situations used in previous surveys have been elaborated in this dimension, with particular emphasis on the discretionary reasons guiding abortion.

In over two decades of heated discussion about abortion, health related exemptions (such as rape, fetal deformity, and maternal health) account for only a small proportion of the abortions actually performed in the U.S. trend data on abortion attitudes show a saturation of approval among the public for the various physical-health reasons for abortion; it is the discretionary reasons that point to divisions among the public in moral approval of abortion. Further, since a large majority of women seek abortions for various personal reasons, it seems pertinent to explore the variation in moral judgments with specific discretionary circumstances that characterize their abortion decisions. The six conditions presented in previous studies as overt reasons for seeking an abortion are: rape by stranger, fetal deformity, harmful pregnancy, desire to limit family size, financial problems, unmarried status. To this list we added four more circumstances; desire to remain childless, father's refusal to marry the woman, incestuous rape (rape by brother), and pregnancy resulting from an extra-marital relationship. A 'blank' level was also included in this dimension, which would allow us to determine the overall approval of abortions when no information regarding the motive for terminating a pregnancy is present. A slightly larger proportion (6 out of 10) levels describe personal-social reasons for abortion and a smaller proportion include health related reasons (4 out of 10).

Phase of Gestation

#7.Number of Months Pregnant: Given all this complex scenario to an abortion situation, respondents might still weight their approval

of abortion by the actual gestation period. Historically, acceptance of abortion has been far greater very early in pregnancy than during the second trimester. Views toward the fetus may vary markedly as a function of gestation stage: from an embryo or 'product of conception' in the first 8 to 10 weeks to an almost or complete human being after the 16th or 20th week of gestation. Even in radical pro-choice circles, there is discomfort concerning unregulated access to late abortions, an ambivalence that is linked to stage of fetal development and concerns for maternal health.

Relational Context

   #8.Quality of Couples' Relationship: The quality of a couple's relationship (defined as 'happy' or 'unhappy') provides an additional dimension for the evaluation of the abortion decision. The couple's relationship defines the emotional context in which the child would be raised, were the pregnancy carried to term. A pregnancy resulting in abortion in the context of an unhappy relationship may evoke greater sympathy than an abortion in the context of a happy relationship.

   #9. Parental Approval/disapproval:

   #10. Partner's Approval/disapproval: Abortion decisions are often arrived at through consultation with close family members and friends. Lovers and parents are likely to play an important role in how a young unmarried woman decides to resolve her pregnancy. The involvement of such close individuals may both facilitate and complicate an abortion decision. Despite the legal and political definition of abortion as a 'woman's right' or 'choice', most women cope with the views of several significant others such as parents and spouses when they face the question of dealing with a pregnancy. These two dimensions provide an opportunity to determine the relative salience of close relatives' views toward an abortion. The views of parents may be more salient to young women's abortion decisions, while partner or spouse's views play an important role in older women's decisions. The emphasis in this dimension is on approval, rather than 'consent' which has an overly legal connotation limited to minor women's situation.

   Table 2.1 provides the distribution of levels within each of these dimensions in the study design. The percentages refer to the proportion of the total sample of vignettes in which each level within a dimension has been included. The levels marked by an asterisk in this table identify situations presented in previous surveys as overt reasons for an abortion. The following is a sample vignette used in this study that illustrates several features of the factorial design.

> *Jean is a 45 year old married woman with two children. Her household income is $300 a week. She and her husband have a very happy relationship. She is in excellent health and is five months pregnant. She does not want to have any more children. She has decided to have an abortion, a decision her husband approves of and her parents disapprove of.*

Circle the number below that best expresses your opinion of this woman's decision to have an abortion.[3]

Strongly Approve	*Approve*	*Not Sure*	*Disapprove*	*Strongly Disapprove*
1	2 3 4	5 6	7 8	9

In the sample vignette the parts delineated in boldface refer to specific levels of information that vary for each vignette produced from the random combination of the dimensions. In this study each respondent was presented with 20 vignettes, each followed by the nine-point rating scale ranging from strongly approve to strongly disapprove. The vignette packet was mailed to 291 respondents who had completed a telephone interview. Of this total, 217 returned completed vignette packets. Since each respondent rated 20 vignettes, the total number of unique ratings of abortion situations is 4340 (217 x 20). The next chapter will present results from the analysis of the vignette data. We turn now to a discussion of other attitudinal domains and respondent characteristics measured in this study.

Table 2.1

Percent Distribution of Vignette Characteristics (N = 4340)

Levels	Proportion of Vignettes
Age	
15 year old	10.7
18 year old	11.8
21 year old	11.1
25 year old	10.8
30 year old	11.3
35 year old	10.3
40 year old	12.0
45 year old	10.1
(Blank)	12.1
Marital Status	
Married woman	45.0
Unmarried woman	43.7
(Blank)	11.2
Number of Children	
(Blank)	11.0
No children	34.1
one child	11.0
two children	11.4
three children	9.6
four children	9.6
five children	6.8
six children	6.8
Weekley Household Income	
$1000	17.4
$800	18.4
$600	19.0
$300	18.4
$100	18.3
(blank)	8.6
Quality of Relationship	
happy	44.0
unhappy	45.0
(Blank)	11.0

(continued on next page)

Table 2.1 (contd)

Health Status

excellent	29.7
average	30.2
very poor	30.0
(Blank)	10.0

Gestation Period

two months	17.6
three months	18.8
four months	17.7
five months	19.0
six months	18.2
(Blank)	8.6

Circumstances Surrounding Pregnancy

Raped by her brother	11.2
*Raped by a stranger	10.2
*Pregnancy may be harmful to her health	11.2
*The fetus has been diagnosed as deformed	11.5
*She thinks raising a child at this time is beyond her financial means	10.9
She had sex with man, other than her husband, and is sure he caused the pregnancy.	10.4
*She does not want to have any more children.	8.0
*She is unmarried and does not want to marry the father.	5.8
She is unmarried and the father does not want to marry her.	5.2
She does not want to have any children at all	3.5
(Blank)	12.2

Parent/Partner Approval

her partner approves of.	11.8
partner disapproves of.	11.3
parents approve of.	10.9
parents disapprove of.	10.7
partner approves of and parents approve of	11.8
partner approves of, parents disapprove of	9.9
partner disapproves of,parents approve of	11.5
partner disapproves of, parents disapprove of	11.2
(Blank)	10.9

Respondent Characteristics

The vignette design elaborated on the situational characteristics of abortion and their potential relevance for approval of abortion. Situational components provide a partial explanation of the moral reasoning behind acceptance or rejection of abortion. The accumulated life experiences and ideological baggage that individuals bring to bear on abortion situations also accounts for a significant proportion of variation in public attitudes. These may be referred to as characteristics of persons evaluating an abortion situation, which include social-demographic attributes; personal reproductive experiences, and attitudes toward a host of issues closely tied to abortion.

The view of abortion morality as embedded in a larger cluster of beliefs and values that constitute an individual's world-view has received increased attention among social scientists who have studied abortion activists. A pro-life view of the world includes a conservative sexual morality, a respect for preservation of human life that finds expression in opposition to suicide and euthanasia, and adherence to a traditional conception of gender roles and family relations (Luker 1984). By contrast, the pro-choice view embraces a respect for choice in decisions to terminate individual life, a liberal sexual morality, and egalitarian gender roles (Luker 1984).

In our attempt to identify the structure of abortion views a number of key attitude domains were identified and measured in a questionnaire administered in a telephone interview. These include: attitudes in the area of sexuality and reproduction; human life preservation themes; attitudes toward gender relations; political participation in the abortion debate; degree of support for the pro-choice and pro-life positions; secular influences measured through educational attainment and religious influences measured through church affiliation and attendance; personal reproductive experiences (actual family size and experience with abortion); and some standard socio-demographic characteristics. The rationale for the choice and measurement of these ideational dimensions is discussed next.

Attitudes Toward Abortion

The telephone interview began with a few items on abortion attitudes that have been used in national surveys. These items measure approval under various circumstances used in these surveys with a few new ones: if the woman was suffering from AIDS, and in the case of voluntary childlessness. Moral approval of abortion was also measured in the context of spouse' views (for married adult women) and partner's and parents' views (for minor unmarried women). An item was also included that asked respondents whether they would consider an abortion for themselves or their women partners under four different circumstances. These items (in addition to the elaborate measurement of abortion situations in the vignettes) allow us to compare our sample with representative samples of the U.S. population found in national surveys. Since the telephone interview took place before the vignette packet was mailed to respondents, the inclusion of these items at the start of the interview alerted respondents to the substantive focus of the study. While comparison of the two methodological approaches (vignette and questionnaire) is limited due to different rating scales used in their design, the correlation of responses based on the two measures will provide an additional check of internal validity.

Human Life Values

Pro-life activists have defined the abortion debate as centering on the protection of human life. The term pro-life rather than 'anti-abortion' refers to a positive concern for human life and an opposition to situations that endanger its preservation. Hence, this concern extends beyond abortion to include opposition to euthanasia, suicide, and in some cases, capital punishment. Questions were included in the interview to tap respondent's attitudes toward suicide and euthanasia, two situations that approximate human life values implicit in abortion views better than views regarding gun-control or capital punishment.

The life-preservation theme is central to the proposal for a Human Life Amendment to the constitution. The opposing views of pro-life and pro-choice activists are found not in greater or lesser regard for human life, but in differing views of what is 'human' in the definition of life, and a range of circumstances that justify termination of fetal life in the interests of a woman's social, psychological or physical well-being. As a consequence, a crucial indicator of acceptance of abortion hinges on what point in a pregnancy is defined as the onset of human life. Hence we included a question on when human life begins: at conception, very early in the pregnancy, later when the fetus is viable, or at full-term birth. Respondents who view human life as beginning at later stages of a pregnancy may be more approving of an abortion at an earlier phase of a pregnancy.

Attitudes in the Domain of Sexuality and Reproduction

In all societies fertility limitation has often been accomplished indirectly through norms governing sexual unions between individuals, marriage, and family formation. From a conservative viewpoint, marriage precedes and legitimizes sexual relationships, which in turn is necessary for human procreation. By contrast, a liberal sexual morality sees sex, marriage, and pregnancy as distinct aspects of an individual's life, and the pursuit of sexual pleasure can take place independent of the institution of marriage or without a pregnancy necessarily resulting in a birth.

A more direct regulation of human fertility has been achieved through values that underlie the use of contraception, induced abortion and infanticide. In the 20th century we have benefitted from the miracles of modern science that facilitate the twin goals of either fertility limitation or fertility enhancement with increasing technological sophistication. While contraceptive and artificial reproductive techniques have opposing objectives, they share in common the separation of long standing causal links between sex and pregnancy. However, the ideology of 'choice' and 'rational planning' implicit in these technologies has developed quite independently from long-standing cultural norms underlying sexual behavior, pregnancy, and its outcomes. In a symbolic sense contraceptive and reproductive technologies are 'artificial' means of control over the creation of human life. Abortion, depending on an individual's sexual morality, either encourages 'deviant' sexual behavior while denying the natural outcome of pregnancy in childbirth, or it provides a back-up to failed contraception and a solution to problematic pregnancies, if the woman is not prepared to accept the birth of a child. To measure values in this domain, we included items that tap attitudes toward pre-marital sex, extra-marital sex, homosexuality, contraceptive use by teenagers, teenage parenting, and various methods of artificial reproduction.

Family and Gender Roles

Many social scientists have viewed the current struggle over abortion as expressing a conflict between traditional and modern-liberal views of family and gender relations. Luker (1984) identifies pro-life activists as largely composed of women who view motherhood as a primary source of prestige and meaning in women's lives. Their own life choices point to the salience of marriage and motherhood over paid employment and careers. In contrast, pro-choice activists are professional women with few children who espouse an egalitarian management of work and family responsibilities between men and women. In this context, abortion to terminate an unwanted pregnancy carries different meanings for the women involved, ranging from an assault on deeply held views regarding motherhood to an acceptance of abortion as the solution to conflicting responsibilities between education, employment, and family.

The long term trend in American society (as in other developed countries) has been toward increased and continued involvement of women in the paid labor force throughout most of their reproductive years. Female employment stimulated by economic necessity, rather than ideology has resulted in demands on males to participate to a greater extent in childcare and housework. The corresponding change in gender role ideologies has been slow to evolve. Reports of women who have abortions indicate conflicting demands of work, school, and family as underlying reasons for abortions (Torres and Forest 1988). Individuals who are sensitive to such conflicts in families and who view changes in gender roles in a positive light are less apt to emphasize women's reproductive roles over other responsibilities. A liberal shift in gender role ideologies will pave the way to increasing acceptance of abortions under a variety of personal and social circumstances.

The domain of gender roles is extremely broad and complicated, and our attempt was to isolate a sample of issues involving gender roles that would be linked to attitudes toward abortion. The questions we designed tap attitudes toward women's employment, egalitarian sharing of childcare and housework, parental responsibility for childcare, salience of work life over family life, and support for increased representation of women in political office.

Political Identity, Participation and Abortion Support

In the 1970s and 1980s abortion became an issue of concern in local, state and national elections. The Republican and Democratic parties have identified themselves symbolically on the two sides of the abortion issue in the campaigns for Presidential elections in 1984 and 1988. However, analysis of public opinion indicates no reciprocal influence between party identification or preference and support for abortion. In this study political identity is measured in terms of a general liberal-conservative dimension rather than party identification. More specifically, questions were included to measure active involvement in abortion politics (attending meetings, engaging in volunteer work, or contributing money to pro-choice or pro-life organizations) and degree of support for the pro-choice and pro-life positions.

Personal Reproductive Experiences

Personal reproductive experiences include experience of previous births as well as abortions. Actual family size that exceeds the desired family size implies decisions to carry an unwanted pregnancy to term. Parents who have made such decisions are less likely to consider any pregnancy as 'unwanted,' or to view an additional child as unwanted in light of their personal experience. In our interviews, few respondents gave a desired family size that was smaller than their actual parity. A desire to remain childless, or to limit family size to one or two children, may pre-dispose individuals to sympathize with abortions to prevent additional children. A powerful test of abortion values is personal exposure to abortion. A personal experience with abortion or knowledge of the abortion experience of close friends and relatives is a real life situation requiring individuals to reconsider or reaffirm previously held values. Positive experiences may strengthen approval of abortion, while decisions wrought with pain and ambivalence may result in negative views toward abortion. Questions on personal experience with abortion will provide a clue to the link between abortion experience and abortion attitudes. The increased incidence of legal abortion among women of all reproductive ages necessarily means increased exposure of the public to abortion experiences of significant others, with important implications for change in attitudes toward abortion. Given the sensitive and private nature of these questions, they were included as part of the vignette packet mailed to respondents rather than in the telephone interview.

The ideational domains discussed above represent some of the more immediate influences on abortion views. The abortion controversy is only one aspect of larger changes in values and beliefs in the society. The political salience of this issue for the general public is only minimal, compared to other economic and political issues facing the country. Hence the correspondence between the various ideational dimensions in explaining abortion views among the general public is likely to be modest.

Sample and Survey Execution

A random sample of over 500 respondents was drawn from the annual street census of Greenfield, Massachusetts. Greenfield is a mid-sized town in Western Massachusetts located close to a major university. The annual street census of the town provides a listing of household members and their ages. The sample was stratified by four age groups (19-25, 26-40, 41-60 and 61 and above) and sex to produce equal numbers in each age-sex category. Furthermore, only respondents who could be reached through the telephone were included in the final sample. The stratification of the sample in such a way necessarily leads to a loss of representativeness, although representativeness can be achieved through appropriate weighting of the sample. A age-sex stratified sample was chosen since we were more interested in investigating the structure of abortion values within sub-groups of the population. Several national surveys have documented trends in general attitudes toward abortion, which have remained fairly stable over the 1973 to 1988 period. Few studies have investigated the structure of attitudes within sub-groups of the population defined by age, gender and religious orientation. Time and resource constraints required a small-size sample. In order to maximize the opportunity for sub-group comparison we sought to obtain at least 50 respondents in each of the eight age-sex categories.

The four age categories, with arbitrary cut-points, present interesting analytical possibilities. Previous studies of abortion have paid little attention to the influence of age. Age is a composite indicator of influences due to history, experiences of cohorts and position in the reproductive phase of life. The ideal sample to disentangle these varied influences would be a panel design with longitudinal data on values in the various domains, including abortion. Previous analysis of the relationship between age and abortion attitudes shows no evidence of a linear relationship. The simple impact of chronological age showing increasing opposition to abortion is hard to interpret. A cohort perspective on attitude change seems more plausible and promising in terms of trends toward greater acceptance of abortion. Based on a cohort perspective, we would predict that respondents who grew up and raised families prior to political debates of the sixties and early seventies would have different views on abortion compared to respondents who grew up in the post-legalization period. For today's elderly men and women the fact of illegality of abortion in their early life may predispose them to more conservative views on abortion. By contrast, young men and women who have grown up in an era of legal abortions may be inclined toward greater approval of abortion. It is likely that cohorts would vary in approval of the life circumstances involved in an abortion decision, as well.

As increasing numbers of Americans become exposed to legal abortions for a variety of reasons, their experience will reflect a greater sensitivity to the issues that have been publicly discussed only in the past two decades. Age differences in attitudes may reflect differential impact of abortion experience and abortion politics as cohorts move through a controversial phase of the abortion debate. Hence it is possible that cohorts may also vary by religious affiliation in their response to abortion. Results from a pilot study conducted on college students indicated that young Catholics are more approving of abortion than young Protestants, and a personal experience of abortion has a positive impact on abortion views for Catholics, but not Protestants.

For these reasons, age will be an important dimension in our analysis. We have hypothesized that abortion attitudes are embedded in a broader context of values that influence attitudes toward sexuality, reproduction, human life values, and gender roles. It is only in the past two decades that links between these attitude domains and abortion opinions has been articulated. Therefore, it is quite likely that we will find among older respondents a structure of attitudes that relates abortion to human life issues, but not to gender role or sexual ideology. By contrast, among younger respondents who have been exposed to the political arguments of recent times, we may find an ideological structure that combines attitudes in the areas of abortion, gender roles, sexuality and reproduction.

The youngest and oldest age groups were oversampled since we anticipated problems in contacting young respondents (who move more often) and getting cooperation from older respondents. Given the sensitive nature of the abortion topic, care was taken to inform respondents in advance about the nature of the study. A personalized letter was mailed that informed respondents they would be contacted

Table 2.2
Demographic Profile of the Sample

Characteristics	Percent
Sex	
Males	47.8
Females	52.2
Religion	
Catholic	43.6
Protestant	42.5
Jewish	1.0
Other	3.5
No Religion	9.1
Dont Know	.3
Marital Status	
Never Married	20.1
Married	64.9
Divorced	7.3
Widowed	7.6
Education	
Less than High School	5.2
High School	29.0
Some College	32.9
College Graduate	21.3
Graduate School	8.7
PHD or Professional Degree	2.8
Median Income Range	$25,000 - $35,000
	N = 291

by phone to participate in a 30-minute interview on their personal views on abortion and other issues. At the end of the telephone interview, respondents were told that they would receive some additional questions in the mail that were part of the study. The packet containing abortion vignettes and three items on personal experience with abortion were mailed to respondents who had completed the telephone interview. Two weeks after the mailing of the packets at least two follow-up calls were made to stress the importance of returning completed vignette packets. The data collection phase spanned six months from September 1987 to February 1988.

Of the 420 respondents who were contacted on the phone and found eligible to participate in the survey, 291 completed the telephone interviews. Of these 291 respondents, 217 returned completed vignette packets. Problems in contacting very young respondents and a higher refusal rate among the oldest age group resulted in less than the expected number in the four age groups. Table 2.2 provides the demographic profile of the respondents in the final sample.

The sample contains almost equal proportions of males and females. There are also close to equal numbers of Catholics and Protestants, which is not surprising for a sample drawn from Massachusetts. The distribution of respondents between the four age groups is slightly disproportionate, with the highest percentage of respondents in the age range of 26 to 40 (31.7%) and the lowest percentage in the 19-25 year range (18.3). Two-thirds of the sample, given the age distribution, consist of married respondents, while one-third are never married, divorced or widowed. The sample is predominantly white (except for one Oriental and one Black respondent), with a median income in the range of $25,000 to $35,000.

Organization of Analysis Chapters

The following three chapters will present empirical findings on the situational and ideational components of abortion attitudes. Chapter 3 focuses on the relative salience of the situational dimensions in predicting abortion approval. The situational components will be further analyzed in terms of two other vignette dimensions; age and gestation period. Some respondent characteristics that match those of the women in the vignettes will be considered jointly in an analysis of the reciprocal influences of respondent and vignette characteristics on abortion approval. Thus

Chapter 3 sets the stage for the analysis of the ideological structure of abortion attitudes in the two chapters to follow.

Chapter 4 focuses on the larger ideational context of abortion attitudes, and we explore the links between moral views toward abortion and attitudes and beliefs in three other belief domains. Chapter 5 extends this analysis to sub-groups of the sample differentiated by age, religion, and gender.

Notes

1. National Opinion Research Council

2. Andy Anderson notes that it is difficult to interpret how individuals evaluate blank levels. From the design point of view a blank level represents lack of information on a particular dimension of the abortion situation. This does not mean that all respondents ignore the absence of information on that particular dimension. Some individuals may attribute certain information based upon information that is provided on other related dimensions in the vignettes (Personal communication).

3. The scale was reversed in subsequent analysis such that all high scores indicate positive approval of abortion.

3

Dimensions of Abortion Situations

Abortion attitudes are subject to a variety of influences: from life circumstances that produce an unwanted pregnancy; from past experiences of adults; and from the broader set of values closely related to abortion attitudes. An individual's attitudes toward abortion are situated within a larger belief system and become modified as a function of personal reproductive experiences: These two issues are explored in the chapters to follow. Attitudes toward abortion are also subject to further variation when individuals evaluate concrete abortion decisions made by others. When we consider all the complex factors that define attitudes toward abortion, various features of a hypothetical abortion situation are likely to have significant though limited impact on an individual's moral approval of abortion. This is the first of two issues we explore in this chapter. The second issue is an assessment of the relative impact of respondent and situational attributes on abortion attitudes, and the interactions between them as they affect abortion attitudes.

The results reported in this chapter are organized in a manner that progressively illustrates the contribution of situational and respondent characteristics to variation in abortion approval. We begin with the analysis of abortion vignettes that shows the combined contribution of all the situational dimensions to abortion attitudes to pinpoint the situational factors that trigger the most variation in approval of abortion. Second, we compare the profile of abortion attitudes found in the vignette analysis with the most recent national survey data, to demonstrate the persistence of general patterns of approval across methods and datasets. We then explore interactions among situational factors in the vignette, which further refine general approval of abortion circumstances.

In the second major section of this chapter, we focus on additional contributions of important respondent characteristics to the structure of abortion attitudes. The respondent characteristics included in this analysis are life course attributes like age, marital status, and parity; personal reproductive experiences (childbirths and abortions); secular influences measured through educational attainment, and religious influences measured through church affiliation and attendance; sex and family income of the respondent. We explore interactions between attributes shared by respondents and vignette women (age, marital status, and parity), as these factors together shape opposition to or support for abortions. In conclusion, we estimate the separate and combined impact of respondent and situational factors.

Marginal Distribution of Approval

Each respondent (from a total of 217 respondents) rated 20 abortion vignettes, yielding a total vignette pool of 4340 ratings. Since the major substantive focus of this chapter is on the characteristics of abortion situations, the unit of analysis is the vignette rating rather than an individual's mean response to 20 vignettes.

Table 3.1 presents the distribution of approval ratings on the 9 point rating scale for all vignettes rated by respondents. A major proportion of the ratings cluster around the approval and disapproval ends of the scale, with only a small proportion of the ratings in the middle range of the scale. This points to a polarization of responses in terms of definite approval or disapproval of abortions. The substantial spread across the rating scale is fortunate in that there is considerable variance for us to explore in analyzing abortion attitudes.

A median rating of 7.0 with a mean rating of 5.6 indicates that over 50 percent of the respondents show positive approval of abortion under a variety of circumstances. This is also indicated by a greater proportion of ratings that show strong approval (23.8%) compared to strong disapproval (15.8%). If we collapse the 9 points on the rating scale to represent three equal parts of approval, ambivalence, and

Table 3.1
Distribution of Vignette Rating Scores

Response	Score	Percent
Strongly Disapprove	1	15.8
	2	3.1
Disapprove	3	12.3
	4	3.1
Not Sure	5	9.2
	6	5.3
Approve	7	20.0
	8	6.8
Strongly Approve	9	23.8
Mean = 5.61 Median = 7.0 Std.dev. 2.87		N = 4315

disapproval, only 17.6 percent of the scores fall within the middle range of ambivalent responses to abortion situations.

Table 3.2 provides a more detailed profile of vignette ratings, with mean ratings of the levels within the nine dimensions. The F statistic tests for significant variation among the mean responses within each of the nine dimensions. Six of the nine abortion dimensions show statistically significant variation in approval levels: the woman's health, economic standing, the phase of gestation, overt reasons for the abortion, and the relational context of abortion decisions. No significant variation in mean ratings are found for the three dimensions that describe the life course attributes of the vignette women: age, marital status, and parity.

The greatest variation in approval of abortions is found within the dimension that describes overt reasons for an abortion. Abortion as a solution for pregnancies resulting from incestual rape evokes the highest approval rating (6.9 on the 9-point scale), and voluntary childlessness evokes the lowest approval rating for a decision to abort(4.4). These two situations challenge reproductive norms in very different ways. Given the strong negative feelings that incestual

Table 3.2
Mean Ratings of Vignette Levels

Dimensions	Mean	SD	Significance
Age			
15	5.6	2.9	(N.S)
18	5.6	2.8	
21	5.4	3.0	
25	5.6	2.8	
30	5.5	2.9	
35	5.7	2.8	
40	5.6	3.0	
45	5.9	2.9	
(Blank)	5.5	2.9	
Marital Status			(N.S.)
Married	5.6	2.9	
Unmarried	5.6	2.9	
(Blank)	5.5	2.9	
Number of Children			(p = .08)
None	5.5	2.9	
One	5.5	3.0	
Two	5.5	2.9	
Three	5.8	2.9	
Four	5.6	3.0	
Five	6.0	2.7	
Six	5.8	2.9	
(Blank)	5.7	2.9	
Weekly Household Income			(p = .001)
$1000	5.3	2.9	
$800	5.6	2.9	
$600	5.5	2.9	
$300	5.8	2.9	
$100	5.9	2.8	
(Blank)	4.8	2.9	
Quality of Relationship			(p = .01)
Happy	5.5	2.9	
Unhappy	5.8	2.8	
(Blank)	5.6	3.0	

Table 3.2 (contd).

	Mean	SD	Sig.
Health Status			(p = .000)
Excellent	5.4	2.9	
Average	5.5	2.9	
Very poor	6.1	2.7	
(Blank)	5.4	3.0	
Number of Months Pregnant			(.000)
Two	6.0	2.9	
Three	5.8	2.9	
Four	5.7	2.8	
Five	5.3	2.9	
Six	5.1	2.9	
(Blank)	5.8	2.8	
Circumstances/Reasons for Abortion			(.000)
Rape by brother	6.9	2.4	
Rape by stranger	6.5	2.7	
Fetal deformity	6.5	2.5	
Harm to mother's health	6.3	2.7	
Woman does not wish to marry	5.2	2.9	
Father does not wish to marry	5.2	2.9	
Extra-marital relationship	5.0	2.9	
Financial constraints	4.7	2.8	
Family size limitation	4.6	2.9	
Woman wants to remain childless	4.4	2.9	
(Blank)	4.9	2.9	
Partner/parents' Views			(.01)
Partner/Parents approve	5.7	2.9	
Partner/parents disapprove	5.5	2.9	
Partner approves/parents disapprove	5.9	2.8	
Partner disapproves/parents approve	5.7	2.8	
(Blank)	5.5	2.9	

N = 4315   Overall Mean   5.6   SD = 2.9

relationships arouse in all societies, a child resulting from such a relationship disrupts the very basis of familial relationships, and hence abortion is considered to be an acceptable option. By contrast, voluntary childlessness implies the woman wants to prevent any current and all future pregnancies; hence an abortion premised on such intentions may be viewed as a direct attack on the value of children and parenting.

Respondents draw sharp distinctions between the physical-health related grounds for abortions and the social-personal circumstances that underlie abortions. Greater approval is shown for abortions to prevent harm to the mother's health or the birth of a deformed child, than for the six social-personal reasons cited for an abortion. In most previous research, the physical-health related circumstances have been labeled as 'hard' reasons. The common characteristic that underlies all the 'hard' reasons for abortions (rape, physical harm from pregnancy, or a deformed fetus) is that they represent circumstances over which a woman has very little control and hence she cannot be held personally responsible. By comparison, the 'soft' reasons represent a range of situations (pre-marital or extra-marital sex, desire to limit family size or remain childless, and financial problems) in which an individual woman may be perceived as having personal responsibility for failure to contracept, for engaging in deviant sexual behavior, or for disregarding the value of parenting. As a result, individuals may believe that a married woman can avoid an abortion by adding an additional child to the family, or an unmarried or poor woman can give the child up for adoption. Some ranking is evident among these five social reasons for an abortion: Abortions to limit parity, remain childless, or those based on personal financial problems, show lower mean approval than abortions to prevent an illegitimate birth in the context of a pre-marital or extra-marital relationship.

As expected, abortions in the first four months of a pregnancy evoke greater approval than those in the fifth or sixth month of a pregnancy. Both health and economic status are conducive to approval of abortions, but only under extreme conditions of poverty and very poor health status. Respondents also vary their approval with respect to the relational context of abortion decisions: Abortions are more readily approved within the context of an unhappy relationship, and supportive views of partners and parents stimulates positive views toward the woman's abortion decision.

From this profile of abortion attitudes we conclude that variation in attitudes for the most part revolves around extenuating circumstances that lead to an abortion decision. Extreme poverty, poor health, pregnancy resulting in physical harm to the mother or the fetus are the conditions that trigger positive views toward an abortion. We also find that attitudes toward abortion are strongly affected by the stage of pregnancy when an abortion is contemplated, with greater approval of abortions in the first four months than in the fifth or later month of the pregnancy.

The preceding discussion, as well as prior research on abortion attitudes, focused on variance in abortion attitudes as a function of different pregnancy circumstances. The blank category within each vignette dimension provides an alternate way to assess the impact of particular pregnancy circumstances. We interpret the mean ratings associated with the blank levels as indicating the degree of support for abortions, when there is no information about the particular pregnancy circumstances. Table 3.3 ranks mean ratings that correspond to all the blank levels within the dimensions.

Table 3.3
Mean Ratings of Blank Levels within Dimensions

Dimension	Mean Rating
Phase of Gestation	5.8
Weekly Household Income	5.8
Number of Children	5.7
Quality of Relationship	5.6
Age	5.5
Marital Status	5.5
Partner-Parents' Views	5.5
Health Status	5.4
Reasons for Abortion	4.9

The lowest mean approval for a blank level is found on the dimension that describes overt reasons for an abortion (4.9 on a 9 point scale) where lack of any reason for an abortion depresses approval of abortion. Since this dimension showed the greatest variation in vignette ratings, we infer that respondents' judgments of abortion decisions is strongly influenced by the rationale provided by individual women; hence the absence of information regarding reasons for an abortion detracts from an unconditional approval of the woman's abortion decision. The highest approval ratings for the blank levels are on dimensions that describe the woman's financial standing and the phase of gestation (mean = 5.8). In both instances, respondents may assume that the woman faces no serious financial problems, and that an abortion is contemplated early in the pregnancy.

Much to our surprise, the analysis thus far does not show any significant impact of life-course attributes (age, marital status, or number of children) of vignette women on abortion attitudes. It is possible that these dimensions have mutually interactive effects that are not discernable at this aggregate level of analysis. For example, age, marital status, and parity might interact such that marital status and parity are more salient in approval of abortions among very young unmarried women (in their teens) than among older, largely married women (in their forties). So too, the importance of parental or spouse approval may vary as a function of the woman's age. Before we examine such interactions in greater detail, we estimate the combined contribution of all the situational dimensions to the structure of abortion attitudes.

Relative Influence of Situational Dimensions

Our discussion so far has been limited to the variation within dimensions of an abortion situation. With a regression analysis of vignette levels, we determine the independent effects of the situational dimensions, as well as the total amount of variance explained by all the dimensions in the vignette ratings. Table 3.4 presents the results of such an analysis in which all the vignette levels have been entered as dummy variables, with the 'blank level' of no information used as the deleted category in all dimensions. The coefficients attached to each of the levels may be interpreted as the relative increase or decrease in approval of abortion for a particular level, compared to no information on that dimension. Since the computer program randomly combines the vignette dimensions, the correlations among the independent variables are virtually zero, and the coefficients represent independent effects of each of the vignette levels.

Table 3.4
Regression of Vignette Ratings on Vignette Characteristics[1]

Levels	b coefficient (sig.)
Age 15	.189
18	.163
21	-.019
25	.079
30	-.097
35	.145
40	.050
45	.352 *
Marital Status	
Married	-.001
Unmarried	.097
Number of Children	
None	-.166
One	-.150
Two	-.185
Three	.219
Four	-.030
Five	.363 +
Six	.193
Weekly Household Income	
$1000	-.401 *
$800	-.114
$600	-.302 +
$300	.016
$100	.136
Quality of Couple's Relationship	
Happy	-.129
Unhappy	.159
	(contd.)

Table 3.4 (contd.)

Levels	b
Health Status	
Excellent	-.071
Average	.037
Very poor	.720***
Number of Months Pregnant	
Two	.156
Three	-.062
Four	-.172
Five	-.594***
Six	-.731***
Overt Reasons for an Abortion	
Rape by brother	2.04 ***
Rape by stranger	1.66 ***
Harm to mothers health	1.45 ***
Fetal deformity	1.76 ***
Financial problems	-.180
Extra-marital relationship	.187
Desire to limit family size	-.285
Woman does not wish to marry father	.287
Father does not wish to marry	.311
Woman wants to remain childless	-.241
Partner-Parent's Views	
All Approve	.315 *
All Disapprove	.044
Parents approve, partner disapproves	.279
Partner approves, parents disapprove	.453 **
Constant	4.71 ***

$$R^2 = .13 ***$$
$$N = 4315$$

(1) The deleted category for all dimensions is the blank level with no information on the particular dimension.

*** $p < .001$, ** $p < .01$, * $p < .05$, + $p < .10$

A significant, positive net increase in approval of abortions is found for women in their 40s, women in very poor health, pregnancies as a result of rape (by a brother or by a stranger), and pregnancies that would result in a deformed child or harm the mother's health. A significant decrease in approval is noted for women with very high household incomes ($1000 a week), and if an abortion would be performed beyond the fourth month of gestation. Strong approval is evoked only under extreme conditions: a pregnant woman suffering from extreme ill-health, a diagnosis of a deformed fetus, or impairment of the mother's health. While the social reasons for abortion trigger no significant variation in approval, the negative sign attached to betas replicate the pattern of mean ratings found in Table 3.2: Abortions based on financial problems, desire to limit family size, or remain childless are reasons that trigger a slight decrease in approval of abortions, whereas a pregnancy resulting from a pre-marital or extra-marital relationship, which challenges norms regarding the legitimate context of parenting, and evokes a higher approval of abortions.

The most salient indicators of increments in approval of abortion are the 'hard' reasons for an abortion, circumstances that have consistently elicited high levels of approval in national public surveys. The largest decrements in approval appear within the gestation dimension, with respondents disapproving of abortions performed past the fourth month of the pregnancy. Disapproval of late abortions is linked to concern for maternal health, as well as ambivalence regarding the moral status of the fetus. The significance of this dimension calls for an interpretation of abortion attitudes in the context of a developing pregnancy.

The remaining situational dimensions have a moderate and selective impact on abortion attitudes. Only women in the last phase of their reproductive life (45 years old) receive more sympathy for their decision to terminate the pregnancy. While very low income does not leave any effect on abortion approval, a very high income (over $50,000 a year) significantly decreases approval. We have collapsed the several combinations of spouse and parental approval, to represent four different instances of combined parent-partner approval of abortion. Clearly, support for the abortion decision by parents and partners leads to more sympathy for the woman's abortion decision. In the presence of conflicting responses of parents and spouses, respondents view partners' opinions as more salient than those of parents.[1]

The contribution of situational components to abortion attitudes is highly structured in that the reasons for an abortion, the woman's health status, and the timing of the abortion account for a large proportion of the variation in the judgments. Of secondary importance are age and economic circumstance of pregnant women, and the relational context within which abortion decisions are made. The total variation explained by all the vignette dimensions is a modest 13 percent. We decompose the explained variance (R^2) into independent contributions of each of the dimensions to compare the impact of all the vignette dimensions. This was done performing a regression analysis of vignette levels with a hierarchical inclusion of dimensions. A set of levels that comprise a dimension are entered as a block in a sequence of cumulative steps. Since the vignette dimensions are orthogonal by design, we can calculate the independent contribution of each dimension by examining the change in R^2 s with the addition of each dimension to the previous equation. In Table 3.5 we rank dimensions by the magnitude of their impact on abortion approval.

The reasons women provide for their abortion decisions alone account for more than two-thirds of the variation explained by all the situational factors together $(R^2 = .09$ compared to $R^2 = .13)$. Phase of gestation, economic status, and the woman's health condition account for the remaining four percent of variation in abortion ratings. This means that whatever the social characteristics of vignette women may be, abortion attitudes vary largely in response to reasons provided for an abortion decision. Conventional surveys usually measure abortion attitudes by varying the reasons for an abortion in the questions asked of respondents. The vignette data show the overwhelming importance of this substantive dimension, and so provide empirical evidence for the measurement approach taken by conventional survey research. These data also point to the significant contribution of additional situational dimensions, which have received only limited attention in previous studies of abortion attitudes. These include: the phase of gestation when an abortion is contemplated, the general health condition of the pregnant woman, and her economic status; situational traits that can modify levels of support indicated for the various health and social reasons for an abortion. An analysis of interactive effects of among these dimensions will illuminate

Table 3.5
Relative R^2 Contributions of Vignette Dimensions

Dimension	R^2
One Percent or More Explained Variance	
Reasons for Abortion	.093
Gestation	.012
Health	.013
Household Income	.005
Less than One Percent Explained Variance	
Age	.002
Marital Status	.000
Parity	.003
Quality of Relationship	.002
Parent/Partner Approval	.003
	Total R^2 = .133

departures from a general approval or disapproval of abortions, in response to complex combinations of situational characteristics.

But first we compare results from the vignette analysis with the most recent national survey data on abortion attitudes. For this purpose, we use the 1988 General Social Survey data on public support for abortion. Two purposes are served by this comparison. For one, the comparison will provide external validity to the results from our analysis; and second, comparison of abortion attitudes measured in a vignette design with measures in a conventional survey will indicate whether there are similarities in the profile of abortion attitudes that hold across methods.

A Comparison of Two Methods

The comparison of abortion vignettes and abortion survey items will proceed in three steps. First, we show similar support for the abortion circumstances in our sample and the GSS national sample of respondents. Second, we illustrate consistent approval or disapproval of abortion conditions across the two survey methods internal to the present study: vignettes vs. survey items in our telephone interview. Third, we examine context effects of particular vignette dimensions that amplify levels of approval of abortion for various reasons.

Attitude Profiles Across Samples

To demonstrate the external validity of results from this research, we look at the levels of support for abortion under each of the six conditions present in the GSS abortion questions and the two survey instruments used in this study(abortion vignettes and abortion items). In Table 3.6 the first two columns show the percentage of respondents who support abortions for six conditions in the GSS survey and our telephone survey.[2] The percentages are based on the proportion of respondents who think it is alright for a woman to have an abortion for a particular reason, compared to those who responded 'don't know' or 'no' to the same reasons. The third and fourth columns show mean and median ratings of vignettes (on the 9-point scale) in which the same six reasons characterized an abortion decision.

The ranked distribution of abortion approval within the GSS sample shows that more than 75 percent of the American public support abortion in the case of rape, harmful pregnancy, or if there is a strong chance of fetal deformity. Less than 50 percent of Americans support abortions if the woman is unmarried and refuses to marry the man, if she cites financial problems, or if she desires to limit family size as the reasons for an abortion. Our respondents show similar levels of approval for the six conditions: higher proportions (72 to 87%) who approve of an abortion for the three physical-health related conditions, and lower proportions (34 to 40%) who approve of abortions for the three social-personal circumstances. The largest difference (10 points) between the two samples emerges in a greater support for abortions in the case of rape among our respondents, compared to the GSS respondents.

A substantive interpretation of this difference is difficult to provide. Instead, we note that the difference could possibly be the result of differences due to samples and measurement. The GSS lead question asks for respondents approval of 'legal' abortion under each circumstance, whereas the lead question in this study omitted the

Table 3.6

Mean Vignette Rating and Percent of Respondents Who Approve of Abortion Under 6 Conditions in Greenfield 1987 Sample and GSS 1988 Sample

Conditions	% GSS	% Greenfield	Vignette Rating Mean/Median[1]
Health	80	82	6.3/7.0
Rape	77	87	6.5/7.0
Defect	76	72	6.5/7.0
Poverty	41	40	4.7/5.0
Family Size	39	42	4.6/4.0
Unmarried	38	34	5.2/6.0
	N=975	N=217	N=4315[2]

[1] Mean and median ratings are based on a scale of 1 to 9. High scores represent higher approval.

[2] The N for vignettes represents total number of vignettes rather than number of respondents.

term 'legal abortion.' There are also differences in order of items in the two surveys: The rape condition appeared first in a series of items in our telephone interview; in the GSS survey, this condition was preceded by four other conditions. Beyond this marked difference, the similarities in the profile of abortion attitudes are striking, with differences between the two samples that amount to only a few percentage points.

The mean and median ratings of vignettes where the six conditions were present also show a similar ranking of the justifications for an abortion: highest levels of approval of abortions are triggered by physical-health related conditions, and least approval by the discretionary circumstances surrounding an abortion decision. There is a different rank order of social reasons for an abortion in the single item responses versus the mean (or median) vignette ratings of abortion circumstances. Note that in the percent support distributions for the two samples, an abortion to prevent an illegitimate birth receives the lowest level of support (38% and 34%).

By contrast, this same reason evokes the highest mean and median rating among the three social conditions present in the vignettes; in fact, the median approval of abortions for unmarried women is two points higher than the median approval of abortions to limit the number of offsprings. We suspect that approval of abortions to prevent an illegitimate birth varies as a function of the social characteristics of the woman involved. Since we vary information about the social characteristics in the vignettes, a greater approval of abortions for women who wish to prevent an illegitimate birth may be linked to specific knowledge of the women's ages. If this is the case, we should find that exceptions are made in terms of higher approval of abortions premised on an unmarried status for women perceived as being too young to marry and raise children(15,18), and women who are too old to have children (40,45). We return to this issue in a later section.

Attitude Profile Across Methods

A detailed comparison of levels of support for abortion found in the vignette data with the conventional survey data is not possible, because we lack identical scales that measure abortion attitudes. The GSS and our own telephone instrument measure approval in terms of three categories of responses (yes, don't know, no), and abortion vignettes included a 1 to 9 rating scale with a wider range of values. Consequently, a greater variation in responses to the vignette ratings includes variation as a function of respondent's scale preferences.[3] With this limitation in mind, we focus the analysis on the general profiles of abortion approval that are consistent in our sample's responses to abortion vignettes and telephone interview items.

In Table 3.7 we distinguish mean ratings of seven pregnancy circumstances from the vignette data by responses to the telephone survey items. For instance, for all respondents who said they would approve of an abortion in the case of rape in the telephone interview, we calculate the overall mean rating for vignettes where rape appeared as a condition prompting an abortion decision.[4] If respondents are consistent across survey methods, we will find that those who approved of an abortion for a particular condition in the telephone interview would also provide high scores for the same condition when they rated the vignettes. As expected, for each of the seven conditions, the mean ratings for each type of abortion is

Table 3.7

Mean Vignette Rating by Responses to Seven Abortion Items
in Questionnaire (Greenfield Sample)

	Mean Rating *(N of vignettes)*	
	YES Response	NO Response
Matched Conditions		
Rape	7.0 (379)	2.6 (46)
Health	6.9 (404)	2.5 (37)
Fetal Deformity	7.4 (361)	3.5 (79)
Financial Problems	6.5 (188)	3.1 (220)
Family size	6.5 (137)	3.0 (163)
Unmarried Status	6.6 (90)	4.0 (118)
Childlessness	6.1 (53)	3.2 (68)

consistently high if respondents approved of the abortion in response
to a telephone interview. Similarly, respondents who disapproved of
an abortion are also consistent in providing low approval ratings for
the particular conditions involved. These findings provide further
evidence of the importance of reasons for an abortion, more than any
other situational dimension, in shaping moral responses to abortion.

The fluctuations observed in mean ratings within the two
response categories may be, partially due to the impact of other
situational dimensions present in the vignettes, and in part, due to
differences in scale preferences among respondents. Our expectation
was that various situational characteristics that provide a context for
the judgment of reasons for an abortion will modify acceptance or
rejection of the reasons for an abortion. An analysis of interactions
among vignette dimensions will determine if a combination of
situational factors modify approval of various reasons for an abortion
decision.

Context Effects of Vignette Dimensions

The regression analysis of the nine vignette dimensions showed
that apart from the overt reasons provided for an abortion, gestation
period and a woman's general health condition have the most impact

on abortion attitudes. Age and economic status have a moderate, but selective impact on abortion approval. First, we explore how the gestation phase and the pregnant woman's health modify approval of health-related and social justifications for abortions. Next, we analyze how respondents evaluate three types of personal reasons--- financial problems, family size limitation, and preference to remain unmarried--- when they have specific information about the pregnant woman's economic status, actual parity, and age. For instance, we check whether approval of abortions to limit family size varies by the number of children vignette women already have. The presence of interactions among these vignette dimensions will show that respondents are sensitive to nuances in abortion situations, and modify their attitudes in response to a combinations of situational factors.

Panels A through F of Table 3.8 present results of these analyses. We begin with Panel A, where mean approval of abortions within two categories of gestation and reasons for an abortion are presented. Approval levels reach a peak (6.8) for abortions that are premised on physical-health concerns, and if they are to be performed within the first four months of the pregnancy. By contrast, approval of abortions reaches very low levels if the woman is more than four months pregnant, and her decision to terminate the pregnancy arises from a variety of social-personal concerns. The impact of the gestation phase is very clear, since approval of abortions drops significantly (although only .6 points) even under extreme situations where a woman has been raped (by stranger or brother), or could suffer physical harm from carrying the pregnancy to term. Generally, lower approval of late than early abortions is linked to different views toward the fetus at early and later stages of a pregnancy. In the case of a pregnancy resulting from rape (especially incestual rape) most respondents may view an abortion as the most appropriate option to resolve the pregnancy, and hence a delay in the abortion decision might be seen as highly problematic. Furthermore, respondents may believe that health consequences of a pregnancy to the mother or the fetus can be diagnosed at an early stage today, with a pregnancy terminated within the first-trimester. It should be noted, however, despite significant decreases in approval of late abortions based on health concerns, such circumstances still elicit much higher approval than early abortions based on personal concerns (6.2 vs. 5.1).

Table 3.8
Mean Approval of Reasons for an Abortion by Gestation, Health Condition, Household Income, Marital Status, Parity, and Age in Vignettes

---

A. Reasons for an Abortion by Gestation

	Mean Rating (N)	
Gestation	Physical Health	Social-personal
2-4 months	6.8 (1041)	5.1 (1011) ***
5-6 months	6.2 (709)	4.4 (709) ***
	***	***

B. Reasons for an Abortion by Health Status

	Mean Rating (N)	
Health Status	Physical-Health	Social-Personal
Excellent	6.3 (579)	4.6 (545)
Average	6.6 (585)	4.5 (566)
Very Poor	6.7 (556)	5.6 (574)
	(*)	(***)

C. Approval of Financial Problems as Reason for Abortion by Income

Household Income of Vignette Women	Mean Rating(N)
$1000	4.1 (88)
$800	4.2 (87)
$600	4.6 (86)
$300	5.3 (89)
$100	5.1 (89)
	(*)

(contd. on next page)

Table 3.8 (contd.)

D. Family Size Limitation by Parity

Parity	Mean Rating (N)
1-3 children	4.5 (176)
4-6 children	4.6 (113)
	(N.S.)

E. Family Size Limitation by Age

Vignette Age	Mean Rating (N)
15,18	4.4 (62)
21-35	4.6 (163)
40-45	4.9 (77)
	(N.S.)

F. Abortions to remain unmarried by Age

Age	Mean Rating (N)
15,18	5.3 (118)
21-35	4.9 (191)
40,45	5.4 (113)
	(n.s)

There is a clear ranking of the most acceptable to the least acceptable abortion situations by these two factors: Highest approval is found for health concerns associated with an early abortion decision (6.8), followed by health concerns associated with a late abortion (6.2), followed by early termination of a pregnancy for a variety of social and personal reasons (5.1); and least approval is shown for a late termination of a pregnancy to avoid financial burden, or additional births, to remain childless, or unmarried (4.4).

The impact of the gestation dimension suggests ways in which respondents balance their concern for fetal life with a concern for the physical and social well-being of the pregnant woman. A tolerance for abortions that would prevent either harm to the mother's health or the birth of a deformed child, even in the second trimester, indicates a high value placed on a healthy life for the woman. This concern for the woman's health is not simply limited to the outcomes of a particular pregnancy; that is, whether, carrying the pregnancy to term endangers her health. Instead, a woman's extreme ill-health, independent of its effect on the pregnancy, results in a greater endorsement of various reasons individual women provide for their abortions.

In Panel B, we note very high approval of abortions, when a woman already suffering from very poor health is a victim of rape, or faces a pregnancy that could worsen her health ,or result in the birth of a deformed child. Sympathy for women in very poor health also extends to a greater acceptance of social-personal for their abortions. This is illustrated by a significant one-point increase in approval of social reasons for an abortion between women in very poor health (5.6) compared to those who enjoy excellent health (4.6).

The gestation dimension and the health dimension tap deeply held and sometimes conflicting values regarding preservation of life and compassion for physical suffering, which underlie support or opposition to abortion. While a concern for fetal life sets limits on an acceptance of late abortions, a high value placed on a prolonged healthy life for the woman leads to a tolerance of abortions, if they prevent physical suffering of women. On the other hand, life course attributes and social characteristics of pregnant women have only a selective influence on abortion attitudes, because they tap reproductive norms that vary among groups of respondents.

Age, marital status, parity, and social characteristics like economic status can inform judgments about abortions based on financial constraints, family size preference, or an unmarried status. For example, actual family income of vignette women might serve as a criterion for acceptance of abortion decisions based on financial problems. In Panel C. variation in mean approval within income categories provides evidence of such reasoning. Women with weekly household incomes between $100 and $300 are more apt to receive sympathy when they cite financial problems as a reason for an abortion, than women who enjoy higher household incomes in the range of $800 to $1000 a week. In other words, abortion approval varies not so much in terms of subjective financial constraints that individual women cite as bases for their decisions to abort; rather, respondents judge financial constraints as a valid reason only for very poor women.

Panels D through F show the impact of pregnant women's age and parity on approval of abortions intended to avoid additional births or a child outside of marriage. The number of children a woman already has makes no difference to the approval of abortions that would prevent additional births (Panel D). Women who have between four and six children do not receive greater sympathy for their decisions than women with one to three children. Nor does a woman's age make a difference, when the reason is family size limitation (Panel E) or to avoid a birth outside of marriage (Panel F). There is a slightly higher approval of abortions for unmarried women in their teens and in their forties, than for unmarried women in their prime childbearing years (early twenties to mid thirties). Even though differences are not statistically significant, there is some evidence that abortion as an option to prevent illegitimate births is endorsed selectively for very young women, and for women in the late years of their reproductive life. This also explains why among all personal reasons for an abortion, being single ranked higher in responses to vignettes than in responses to a conventional survey item.

The lack of any significant impact on the part of life course attributes of vignette women suggests possible interactions between the vignette dimensions and respondent characteristics. Family size preferences may reflect different ideological responses to fertility control. Individual respondents, based on personal experience and values, may believe that reproduction is a natural event that should not be controlled. For such individuals, the salience of parenting and children is very high, and an abortion to prevent additional births would be the least acceptable option, regardless of personal attributes of pregnant women. On the other hand, individuals who vary in their preferences for family size may show little consensus on what constitutes an ideal family size, or whether an abortion should be the preferred option to control fertility.

Unlike gestation and health, which tap universal concerns for human life, life course characteristics tap a host of fertility norms and preferences that vary over time and among individuals. Since the 1960s, challenges to traditional norms regarding sex and reproduction have taken a variety of forms. A higher incidence and exposure to pre-marital sex, pregnancy, and abortions; more openness as well as controversy surrounding sexual preferences and lifestyles, have all entailed a shift toward greater individual discretion in matters of sexuality and reproduction. But normative changes are very gradual and uneven in the short-run, so that responses among cohorts to sexual and reproductive issues will vary as a function of personal-historical experiences of individuals. Consequently, age, marital status, and parity, (characteristics which represent cohort, life course, and personal reproductive experience of respondents) may shape variation in responses to abortions among women who are in different stages of life. It is to such issues that we turn in the section to follow.

Respondent and Vignette Characteristics

We take up two issues in this section that pertain to the influence of respondent characteristics on abortion attitudes. We explore the reciprocal influences of life course attributes that respondents and vignette women share on abortion approval. Next, we estimate the combined contribution of respondent and situational dimensions to the variation in abortion approval. In conclusion, we review key findings from the analysis of the vignette data, and discuss their implications for the measurement of abortion attitudes

The vignette situations were designed to reflect the variety present in real life abortion situations, and included pregnant women who were at different points in their reproductive life. As a consequence, respondents may feel more empathy for abortion decisions made by women who are very much like them in age, marital status, and parity. For example, a 30-year-old respondent may feel more empathy for a 30-year-old woman described in the vignette than for a woman younger or older than herself.

We chose three characteristics - - - age, marital status, and parity - - - on which we can match women in the vignettes with our respondents. Age provides a first attempt to test interactions of this nature.

Impact of Age

Table 3.9 shows mean vignette ratings for each matched category of respondent and vignette age. Since the sample of respondents was chosen from a street census of adults, the youngest respondent in the samples is 19 years old, and the oldest respondents are in their 80s. The age of the women in the vignettes runs from 15 to 45, an age range spanning the reproductive years. Respondents were grouped into five age categories that closely approximated age in the vignette design. The differences in mean ratings across the rows represent the influence of respondent age within each vignette age category, whereas differences across the columns represent the influence of vignette age within a respondent age group.

The sharpest differences emerge between men and women over 60 years of age, and those under 25 years of age. Vignette age shows limited effects compared to respondent age. Only respondents over 60 years of age show a significant difference in approval, with greater

Table 3.9
Mean Ratings by Vignette Age and Respondent Age (N)

	Respondents' Age				
Vignette Age	*19-25*	*26-35*	*36-45*	*46-60*	*61-over*
15, 18	6.09	5.94	5.97	5.39	4.88 (***)
	(171)	(169)	(214)	(205)	(208)
21, 25	5.77	5.86	5.77	5.48	4.88 (**)
	(149)	(187)	(200)	(192)	(214)
30, 35	5.81	5.69	5.90	5.57	5.02 (*)
	(167)	(173)	(212)	(171)	(207)
40, 45	5.64	6.08	6.45	5.17	5.54 (***)
	(181)	(162)	(200)	(180)	(182)
	(n.s.)	(n.s.)	(+)	(n.s.)	(*)

support for abortions among women in their forties than for teenage women. The younger age groups are less likely to discriminate in terms of age of vignette women.

A closer inspection shows that respondents in each age group provide the highest approval for women who are either like-aged, or younger than themselves. Thus, respondents 25 years and younger show the highest mean rating for women in their teens (6.09); those between 26 and 45 years of age show the greatest approval of abortions for women close to their own age. The matching of respondent and vignette age points to a significant cohort effect in determining attitudes toward abortion. The trends within the youngest and oldest age group of respondents implies differences in their exposure to abortions. Today's elderly men and women experienced pregnancy and childbirth in the 1930s and 1950s, when abortions were viewed as the desperate last resort of a married woman, who wanted to prevent additional births, after she had had several children. In contrast, men and women in their early twenties have grown up in an era when abortions were both legal and openly discussed. Our respondents who are in their mid to late reproductive years straddled greater differences in their own life circumstance when abortion was legalized, and hence show no clear identification with particular age groups of vignette women. The cohort differences observed imply that over time, openness and greater exposure under legalization have led to more tolerance of abortions among young respondents, setting the stage for future trends in the direction of greater public support for abortions as today's young adults become older.

Impact of Marital Status

Marital status provides our second test of interaction between respondent and vignette variables. We had expected respondents to be more sympathetic to unmarried vignette women than to married women, but such a prediction was not sustained in the previous analysis of vignette dimensions. In Table 3.10 we once again test for interaction effects by matching respondents' marital status with vignette marital status. Like the previous analysis of age, marital status of vignette women has no effect but marital status of respondents does: Married and widowed men and women are much more conservative in their attitudes toward abortion than solo men and women.

Gender and marital status of the respondent show an interesting reversal of patterns. Unmarried women approve of abortions more than unmarried men, but among married respondents, the reverse is found: Married men are more tolerant of abortions than married women. Further, the peaks in approval within married and solo groups of respondents parallels similar marital status of vignette women. Single, female respondents are the most sympathetic toward an abortion among other single females. Marriage in general has a conservative influence on respondents' views toward abortion. The salience of children may increase within the context of a marriage, particularly for women.

Different life circumstances might explain higher approval of abortions among solo men and women. Abortions among unmarried young women are the result of a host of factors that spell social

Table 3.10
Mean Ratings by Vignette Marital Status and Respondents' Marital Status and Sex (N)

Vignette Marital Status		Respondent Marital Status	
		Soloa	Married-Widowed
Unmarried		6.39	5.40
	Male	6.09 (235)	5.62 (660)
	Female	6.65 (257)	5.20 (711)
		(*)	(**)
Married		6.33	5.40
	Male	6.24 (234)	5.58 (643)
	Female	6.41 (282)	5.25 (753)
		(*)	

a Solo=never married, separated, or divorced.

stigma, disruption of educational opportunities, and new responsibilities for which they are unprepared both emotionally and financially (Torres and Forrest 1988). It is particularly single women (divorced or never married), who face greater economic risks and disruption of life plans when they face an unwanted pregnancy.

Impact of Parity

The relative salience of actual and desired parity may vary as a function of an individual's position in the life course. Among young men and women who currently have no children, family size preferences may play a greater role than actual parity in determining their moral approval of abortions. By contrast, we believe that older individuals, whose childbearing is behind them, will be influenced by their actual parity in the attitudes they hold toward abortion.

In tables 3.11 and 3.12 we have matched vignette parity with respondents' actual and desired parity, respectively. Once again, differences in row means represent the impact of respondents family size, and column differences represent impact of vignette parity on abortion attitudes. As with marital' status, vignette parity has no effect, whereas respondents with large families are much less approving of abortions than childless respondents. This pattern holds for all levels of parity described for vignette women. Only respondents who have between one and three children show less approval of childless vignette women than women who already have a number of children. Respondents with fewer than three children may be at the threshold of a desired family size, and hence show greater tolerance of abortions for women whose parity exceeds their own.

Actual family size is only an indicator of current family size, and does not capture intentions to raise children. Preference for family size is a better indicator of norms regarding fertility limitation. Table 3.12 shows respondents' preferred family size by parity dimension in the vignettes. Sharp contrasts appear between individuals who desire to remain childless and individuals who cherish large families. Approval of abortions peaks among respondents who wish to remain childless, and declines linearly as desired family size increases. Once again, respondents who wish to have one to three children , discriminate approval by vignette age, showing highest approval of abortions for women with four or more children.

The three categories of desired parity may represent qualitatively distinct norms regarding family size limitation. The two extreme categories represent respondents who express low and high salience of children in personal life plans. Those who have raised a large family include individuals who wanted a large family , as well as individuals who wanted small families but resolved unwanted

Table 3.11
Mean Ratings by Respondents' Parity and Vignette Parity (N)

Vignette Woman's Parity	Respondents' Parity		
	None	1-3	4-more
None	5.90	5.46	5.30 **
	(398)	(782)	(260)
1-3	5.96	5.50	5.40 *
	(362)	(774)	(230)
4 or more	5.88	5.89	5.16 **
	(272)	(548)	(161)
	n.s.	*	n.s.

pregnancies in childbirth, putting other life demands aside to absorb an additional child. For these latter individuals, family size limitation may be the least acceptable reason for an abortion. Individuals most responsive to vignette parity are those who express a desire for children but still set limits on family size.

Our analysis so far has illustrated complex ways in which factors that define an abortion situation interact among themselves, and with important attributes of respondents in shaping moral responses to abortion decisions. Abortion morality is largely responsive to rationale provided by individual women for their decisions to terminate a pregnancy. Our respondents are most approving of abortions that prevent physical harm to the mother or fetus, and least approving of abortions for various social reasons that lead to real life abortion decisions of a majority of women. We also showed how these findings were highly consistent across samples and methods. The vignette analysis also illuminated two salient factors--- the duration of pregnancy and the woman's health condition---in shaping approval of various reasons for an abortion.

All of the situational dimensions together explained only 13 percent of the variation in vignette ratings. We interpreted this as indicating a greater impact of respondents' values and experiences on

Table 3.12

Mean Ratings by Vignette Parity and Respondent's Preferred
Parity (N)

Vignette woman's Parity	Respondents' Preferred Parity		
	None	1-3	4 or more
None	7.30	5.69	4.87 ***
	(43)	(972)	(327)
1-3	6.90	5.67	5.22 ***
	(41)	(935)	(299)
4 or more	7.48	6.03	4.67 ***
	(27)	(683)	(207)
	n.s.	*	n.s.

abortion attitudes. As a fitting conclusion this chapter, we pool all the situational factors with some important respondent characteristics, to determine their combined and separate contributions to the structure of abortion attitudes. Based on the preceding analysis, we include age, marital status, and family size of respondents, and add sex and personal exposure to abortions as additional predictors of abortion attitudes. Past studies have isolated church attendance, religious preference, education, family income, as important variables along which respondents vary in their support for abortion. Table 3.13 presents results from a regression analysis in which all the respondent variables were added to the vignette levels. Since vignette levels, by design, are not correlated with respondent variables, the inclusion of respondent characteristics does not change results that appeared in Table 3.4. Hence we show only the additional contributions of the respondent variables in Table 3.13.

Respondent characteristics more than double the explained variation in the vignette ratings, when added to situational characteristics ($R^2 = .29$ vs. $R^2 = .13$). All the respondent variables except education show a significant impact on abortion approval. Confirming our previous analysis, vignette ratings vary strongly in

Table 3.13

Regression of Vignette Ratings on Vignette and Selected Respondent Characteristics[1]

Respondent Characteristics	Beta
Catholic	-.204 ***
Protestant	-.110 ***
Other religion	.004
Church attendance	-.228 ***
Female	.028 *
Age	.098 ***
Solo[a]	.119 ***
Number of children	-.039 *
*Personal experience of abortion [b]	.103 ***
*Knowledge of friend or relative's experience of abortion[c]	.094 **
Education	-.012
Family Income	.106 ***

$$R^2 = .29 ***$$
$$N = 4002$$

[1] This equation includes the vignette levels reported in Table 3.4 Since vignette levels by design are orthogonal to respondent characteristics, the inclusion of respondent characteristics does not change the results from the previous regression. Given the large number of variables to be reported, only the contribution of the respondent characteristics are noted here.

[a] SOLO : 1=married and widowed 2=divorced and never married.

[b] Female respondents who have had an abortion and male respondents who's partners have had an abortion.

[c] Males and females who have had no personal experience with abortion but report knowledge of abortions experienced by friends or relatives.

* Comparison group for both b and c are respondents with neither personal experience of abortion nor exposure to others' abortion experience.

response to age, marital status and parity of respondents. The regression analysis suggests that age and abortion attitudes are positively related. But we noted in our previous analysis of age that the relationship is not linear, with sharp differences in attitudes that appear only among very old and very young respondents. The regression analysis masks such differences, since it seeks to present linear combinations of variables.

The strongest predictors of abortion attitudes are religious preference, church attendance, marital status, family income, and a personal experience with abortions. Catholics are more likely to disapprove of abortions than Protestants, but both religious affiliation groups show stronger disapproval of abortions than those with no religious affiliation. These differences among respondents of different religious affiliations appear even when we control for church attendance. Much of the literature in this area points to a declining Catholic-Protestant difference in attitudes toward pre-marital sex, contraception, and abortion. Put in the context of a cohort perspective, we would find that differences in religious affiliation may also include differences by age of respondents, with only older Catholics showing marked disapproval of abortions compared to older Protestants. The relationship between church attendance and abortion attitudes is as expected: support for abortions declines markedly with an increase in church attendance, suggesting the influence of frequent exposure to orthodox views of the church.

Personal reproductive experiences are closely linked to abortion views since they constitute an experiential basis from which to judge decisions to resolve a pregnancy by birth or abortion. Hence we find that a large family size has a negative impact on abortion attitudes, while past experience with an abortion has a positive impact on abortion attitudes. Abortion attitudes and reproductive experiences can have mutually reinforcing effects. For some respondents a positive disposition to abortions may have resulted in a personal choice to terminate an unwanted pregnancy. For others, the abortion experience itself could have resulted in shaping previously ambivalent views toward positive acceptance of abortions. Similar influences can illuminate the relationship between family size and abortion attitudes. Respondents who raised many children may have deliberately avoided decisions to abort a pregnancy. They may value large families or accept pregnancies in excess of their preferences simply because it is viewed as 'God's will' or nothing to interfere with. For these individuals few circumstances are likely to justify an abortion. It is not possible with our data to demonstrate the causal direction of the relationship between abortion attitudes and reproductive experiences. To do so would require longitudinal measures of attitudes and experience among respondents to show change in abortion attitudes over time.

The positive effects of family income on abortion attitudes, when we control for age and education, may imply changes in family size intentions as a function of increase in family income. A higher family income today is often attained by the employment of more than the adult male in the family. To maintain a higher standard of living requires that women be employed for longer periods of their lives. Families in which both spouses are employed have to reorganize their family plans by limiting the number of children, and investing in the education of a few.

Summary

The analysis presented in this chapter compared two sources of influences on abortion attitudes: situational factors and respondent characteristics. We isolated three key situational factors that impact on abortion attitudes, which in turn refer to the reasons individual women provide for their abortion decisions, the woman's health condition, and the duration of the pregnancy. These factors also interact in complex ways that both limit and encourage moral approval of abortions in general. These results confirm and extend previous research on abortion attitudes.

A comparison of patterns of approval for various reasons found in conventional surveys and the vignette survey showed that our respondents are consistent in their judgments across surveys methods internal to this study, and also share similarities with respondents in national surveys. The analysis of context effects of life course attributes of vignette women on levels of approval for relevant social reasons for an abortion did not show significant effects. This prompted us to look in the direction of possible interactions among life course attributes shared by respondents and vignette women. Age, marital status, parity, and desired family size of respondents do affect abortion attitudes.

The interpretation of age effects on abortion attitudes pointed to cohort differences among respondents in responses to abortion situations. There was also partial evidence of reciprocal influences of characteristics shared by vignette women and respondents. Lastly, when we compare the contribution of respondent variables and vignette dimensions, we note that characteristics of respondent account for a larger proportion of the variation in abortion approval.

Notes

1. A note of caution is in order: This dimension can have varying relevance depending on the age of the women involved. Hence, the significance of the partners' views over parents' views might reflect the composition of the vignette sample (where only 2 out of 9 vignettes included descriptions of teenage women).

2. Only 217 of the 291 respondents who completed both the telephone interview and the vignette instrument are included in this analysis. This allows us to compare individual responses to matched conditions in the questionnaire and vignettes in subsequent analysis.

3. In other words, if we present respondents with a wider range of options in scale values, they are more likely to respond to those options. Further, respondents may differ in the range of values used to indicate departures in approval or disapproval.

4. Vignettes were rated by respondents several days after they participated in the telephone interview, which also included a variety of questions on other issues. Hence we can assume that responses to abortion vignettes are independent of responses to the interview items on abortion.

4

The Ideational Context of Abortion

Perhaps it is fitting that abortion law at present should mirror our wonder as well as ignorance about the mystery of life, our compassion for women who may be frightened and lonely in the face of a major crisis, and our instinctive uneasiness at terminating a form of innocent human life, whether we call it a fetus, an embryo, a baby, or an unborn child. (Glendon 1987:46)

A critical and compassionate revaluation of abortion law and politics has emerged in response to the intense and polarized struggle that has persisted since abortion was legalized in the United States.[1] The critique is aimed at the legal and political language of abortion, which evokes irreconcilable differences in values by pitting the right-to-life of the fetus against the right of the pregnant woman to terminate a pregnancy. Such a polarized view of individual rights is deeply troubling for many who find themselves sympathetic to both the life preservation themes central to a pro-life stance, and the personal distress women face in resolving an unwanted pregnancy. In this context, Glendon's comment captures the moral ambivalence the public shows toward abortion, and suggests the interplay of strongly held values and beliefs that are at the core of abortion morality.

The view that abortion morality is embedded in a deeper structure of beliefs, norms, and values that constitute an individual's outlook toward many aspects of life has been central to the study of abortion activists(Luker 1984, Granberg 1987), and has received increased attention in contemporary studies of public attitudes toward abortion (Blake 1981, Deitch 1983, Granberg 1987). This is the issue we turn to in this chapter, by locating our respondents' attitudes toward abortion within the larger context of beliefs and values in closely related domains of life. Taking the lead from previous research on abortion activists, we focus on three important belief domains that overlap with abortion: sex and reproduction, human life, and gender roles. Each of these three areas span a broad spectrum of issues that touch upon many dimensions of personal and collective life, and we address a sample of topics in each domain that together tap values at the core of abortion morality.

Human life values are explored by linking attitudes toward abortion with three other life and death issues: attitudes toward euthanasia and suicide, as well as beliefs about the onset of human life. Second, in the area of sex and reproduction, we focus on a wide range of topics on which there is normative dissensus in contemporary society: pre-marital sex, homosexuality, extra-marital sex, minor's access to contraception, teenage parenthood, and various forms of artificial reproduction. And third, we examine the dimensions of gender role attitudes in the context of our respondents' views toward empowerment of women in politics, organization of domestic roles, and expectations concerning parenthood, motherhood, and marital relationships. From an empirical point of view our study measures attitudes and beliefs related to specific topics within each of the four domains. Underlying values are largely inferred when we attempt to correlate attitudes and beliefs across various domains in an effort to test whether there is a coherent structure of beliefs within which abortion attitudes are embedded.

A second important issue addressed in this chapter flows from the design features of this study. We utilized two different approaches to the measurement of abortion attitudes: a factorial survey that permits a detailed analysis of the abortion attitude structure, and a customary survey that includes broad measures of attitudes and beliefs in all the four domains investigated in this chapter. The analysis of abortion vignettes discussed in the previous chapter contributed to an understanding of the structure of abortion attitudes from the perspective of the dimensions of abortion situations. In this chapter, in which we shift attention to the larger ideational context of abortion attitudes, we utilize data from a telephone interview survey. Thus the study design allows us to compare two independent approaches to the empirical representation of the abortion belief structure, approaches that differ in their methodological and conceptual formulation; and we integrate attitudinal measures based upon responses to vignettes and survey questions at key points in our analyses.

The analysis of the belief domains is organized around two levels of conceptualization. At one level, we address the issue of dimensionality, and at another level we deal with the commonalities that underlie all attitude domains investigated in this study. Attitudes toward abortion, sexuality, human life, and gender roles reflect dimensionality in the extent to which specific issues within these domains evoke moral concerns that do not overlap, and attitudes also vary as a function of social-group characteristics of respondents. For example, in the abortion domain health grounds for abortion receive widespread support from the public, suggesting that a concern for maternal health overrides the value of fetal life, and the public shows high consensus in approving an abortion if a woman is raped, suffers from poor health, or is likely to deliver a deformed child. The consensus also minimizes significant differences in attitudes along social-group characteristics of individuals. On the other hand, abortions to prevent an unintended pregnancy for a variety of personal reasons receive only moderate support; and given the diversity of life circumstances these situations represent, moral approval of abortions will vary by sexual norms, centrality of human life values, expectations concerning parental obligations, and life course characteristics of respondents themselves. This point was illustrated in the previous chapter in the finding of significant interactions between respondents' and vignette women's age, marital status, and parity in shaping the moral judgments of abortion decisions. In other words, dimensionality reflects issue-specific moral concerns, and variation in attitudes and beliefs that are linked to the social-historical context of individual lives.

From the perspective of an individual's overall belief structure, views toward many domains of personal life interrelate in ways that suggest ideological coherence. Strong linkages across attitudes and belief in the areas of abortion, sexuality, reproduction, and gender roles suggest a deeper structure of values people bring to many life decisions. This was the thesis explored by Lesthaeghe and Surkyn (1988) in their European research on change in value orientation among successive cohorts of respondents. They conceptualized a continuum of high emphasis on 'institutional regulation' rooted in strong adherence to traditional religious beliefs to a high emphasis on 'individual discretion' that is the mark of a secular value orientation. This continuum reflected an underlying unity in the views expressed toward politics, work, family, sexuality, reproduction, and other aspects of personal and social life. In the American context, Judith Blake's research focused on the clusters of beliefs and attitudes that characterize the variety of positions Americans take on the abortion issue. We extend this line of research with an expanded set of attitudinal measures on topics of high salience to the current politics of abortion. Hence, the second stage of the analyses of the attitude domains moves beyond issues related to dimensionality of abortion attitudes to establishing significant linkages across the four belief domains.

We begin with the abortion domain and address three important issues. First, we show that two different approaches to the measurement of abortion attitudes capture a very similar structure of attitudes. A factor analysis of conventional survey items on abortion is used to determine the dimensions of abortion morality. These results are then compared to the findings from the analysis of abortion vignettes. In addition, correlations between similar scales of abortion attitudes from the two data sources are used to demonstrate the internal validity of our measures of abortion attitudes.

Second, we examine the moral and political implications of the abortion belief structure. Here, we wish to understand whether the different positions our respondents take on abortion represent a continuum of restricted to unconditional support for abortions. We also link the levels of moral approval of abortions to the degree of support for the pro-choice and pro-life positions on abortion. Third, we explain the dimensionality reflected in the abortion attitude structure as a function of key social-group differences in religion, life course position, and personal reproductive experiences of our respondents.

Abortion Attitudes: Two Approaches to Measurement

The concept of dimensionality is central to the design of factorial surveys. The thousands of abortion decisions rated by respondents include unique combinations of life course characteristics, pregnancy circumstances, gestation phase, economic and health characteristics of pregnant women, and the views of significant others involved in the abortion decisions. The vignette analysis linked the variation in responses to abortion decisions to the variation in dimensions of abortion situations. We now explore this dimensionality with a different and familiar set of measures of abortion attitudes.

Conventional surveys measure variation in responses to abortion decisions through several items, each of which focuses on a single dimension of an abortion situation. As survey experts often point out, the mark of poor measurement is an item that offers multiple stimuli such that responses of all individuals cannot be meaningfully linked to a single construct of interest. Hence, customary questions on abortion capture the variation in responses to abortion situations through individual items for every relevant dimension. Our telephone interview began with a series of questions each of which dealt with a particular reason for an abortion, or the marital status of the woman involved, or the age of the fetus, or the views of parents, spouses and partners. The point of the analysis undertaken here is to show that the structure of attitudes toward abortion is similar across the two measurement designs, despite the fact that the analysis of the structure itself uses different statistical approaches.

Abortion Factor Structure: Conventional Survey Items

Sixteen different questions related to abortion were included in an exploratory factor analysis. Eight of the survey items measure approval of abortion under a variety of health and social-personal conditions familiar from the previous chapter. Another four questions focused on the salience of the views of parents, partners and spouses to the approval of adult and minor women's decisions to have an abortion. The remaining four questions asked respondents whether they would support access to legal abortions if the pregnant woman was an unmarried minor and her parents and partner expressed approval or disapproval; if she was an adult married women and her husband was against the abortion; and if she was more than three months pregnant. The last set of eight questions that focused on the views of others toward the woman's abortion decision did not specify any particular reason for an abortion.

A factor analysis of these 16 items resulted in four distinct factors as shown in Table 4.1. There is little significant sharing across the four factors which greatly reduces the problem of index construction. Factors 1 and 2 show a structure that has been in place for many years in national polls - the clustering of abortion situations that relate to social-personal and physical/psychological health. The first factor contains eight items that measure approval of abortions under a variety of discretionary circumstances, in the presence of couple consensus, and if the woman alone desires an abortion for unspecified reasons. The second factor taps broad health concerns related to abortion, and the four items that load high on this factor measure approval of an abortion if the woman is raped, if she suffers from AIDS, if her health is endangered, and if the fetus will be born deformed. We label these two factors : *Social-Personal* and *Health* indicators of abortion attitudes, and interpret health to include both physical and psychological concerns that underlie the four situations presented.

All four items that load on the third factor measure abortion attitudes in the context of the relative rights of husbands, parents, and fetuses. Conditional approval of abortions if husbands and parents oppose them, and if the fetus is more than six months old point to the salience of rights of others in abortion decisions made by individual women. A high score on the *Rights* index represents the acceptance of an individual woman's right to abortion over the rights of fetuses (in the case of late abortions), husbands and parents.

Factor 4 captures a unique phenomenon - that of abortion attitudes in the presence of *couple dissensus*. The questions related to this construct asked respondents if they would approve of an abortion if a woman's partner or husband favored an abortion, but the pregnant woman herself was opposed to it. Less than 8 percent of our respondents approved of an abortion under these circumstances, indicating a strong disapproval of abortion if the pregnant woman wanted to continue the pregnancy. Had we included a question that asked respondents to indicate their approval of a woman's refusal to bear any children at all for her husband, we may have found greater variation in responses. Viewed another way, husband's or partner's involvement in an abortion decision receives greater recognition if they express a desire to parent, or concur with the woman on her independent decision to abort.

The abortion factor structure using the survey data closely approximates the structure of attitudes found in the analysis of

Table 4.1
Factor Analysis of Abortion Items

	Factor			
Abortion Items	1	2	3	4
Social-Personal				
Financial Constraints	**.82**	.25	.22	.04
Does not want anymore children	**.80**	.26	.17	.16
Voluntary childlessness	**.80**	.26	.21	.15
Does not want to marry the man	**.80**	.18	.26	-.01
Married: Both want abortion	**.71**	.31	.35	.13
Wife wants abor. husband does not	**.60**	.08	.46	.16
Unmarried: Both want abortion	**.68**	.34	.37	.16
Woman wants abor. partner does not	**.65**	.22	.47	.16
Physical-Psychological Health				
Woman suffers from Aids..	.19	**.83**	.10	.01
Woman has been raped	.16	**.79**	.19	.07
Fetus may be deformed	.31	**.78**	.17	.11
Harmful to mothers health	.27	**.70**	.10	.02
Rights of Others				
Minor, parents disapprove	.21	.19	**.78**	.04
Minor, parents approve	.35	.33	**.67**	.10
Husband against abortion	.42	.19	**.64**	.09
More than 3 months pregnant	.19	.05	**.67**	.03
Couple Dissensus				
Unmarried partner wants abortion, woman does not	.10	.07	.06	**.84**
Husband wants abortion, woman does not	.16	.04	.09	**.80**
EIGENVALUE	8.56	1.65	1.25	1.01
Pct of Variance	47.5	9.2	7.0	5.6

abortion vignettes. The distinctions between the four factors represent variation in the approval of overt reasons put forth to justify an abortion decision (health vs. social-personal distinction in factors 1 and 2), and the relational context of abortion decisions (rights of parents, spouses, fetuses in Factors 3 and 4). In the case of the vignette data, we relied upon a multiple regression analysis to depict the abortion belief structure in terms of the relative salience of situational dimensions. The responses to abortion vignettes varied in large part as a function of the types of reasons given for an abortion decision, the phase of gestation, and maternal health. The interactions among these dimensions in turn suggested the following calculus of judgments: The highest level of approval emerged for an early termination of a pregnancy based on health reasons, and the lowest level of approval was found for an abortion past the fourth month of pregnancy, especially if it was based on discretionary reasons. Thus the factor structure and the regression analysis of the vignette ratings suggest that abortion attitudes revolve around a creative tension between a compassion for the hardship faced by women who wish to abort, and a respect for the preservation of fetal life which assumes greater salience as a pregnancy progresses.

Attitude scales were constructed by summing scores on items that showed high loadings on a factor, with high scores indicating approval of abortion under the specified conditions. Figure 4.1 shows the distributions of scores on the four scales from the survey data (Panel A), and the distribution of the Mean Vignette Rating (Panel B), which is the mean score on all 20 vignettes rated by each respondent. The mean scores in relationship to the median and range on the scale tell us the extent to which variation in these indices is skewed toward the liberal or conservative end of the continuum, a point to keep in mind in interpreting results throughout the chapter. A significant negative or positive impact of social characteristics of respondents on abortion approval can imply a substantive change in the direction of approval or only a shift in the degree of approval. Among the five abortion indices, skewed distributions in opposite directions are apparent in the high mean approval of abortions under health grounds (median score of 9 on the 9-point scale), and in the very low approval of abortions in the context of Couple Dissensus (a mean score of 1.5 on the 5 point scale). The skewed distribution on the Health Index indicates a saturation of public approval of abortion for health reasons. The variation in the 'disapproval' of abortions in

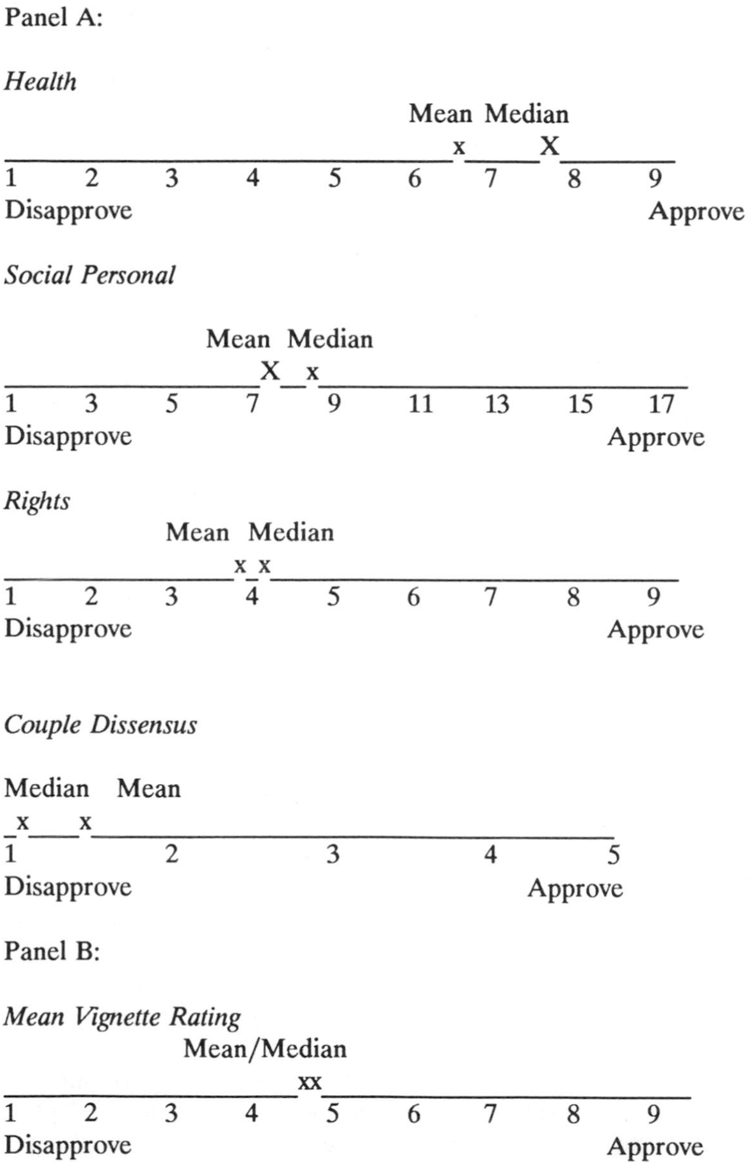

Panel A:

Health

```
                                        Mean Median
                                      x         X
_____
1       2       3       4       5       6       7       8       9
Disapprove                                              Approve
```

Social Personal

```
                        Mean  Median
                          X   x
_____
1       3       5       7       9       11      13      15      17
Disapprove                                              Approve
```

Rights

```
                Mean  Median
                  x x
_____
1       2       3       4       5       6       7       8       9
Disapprove                                              Approve
```

Couple Dissensus

```
Median    Mean
  x       x
_____
1                 2               3               4               5
Disapprove                                      Approve
```

Panel B:

Mean Vignette Rating

```
                        Mean/Median
                           xx
_____
1       2       3       4       5       6       7       8       9
Disapprove                                              Approve
```

Figure 4.1 Distribution Characteristics of Abortion Indices

the context of Couple Dissensus is too small to be attributed to significant social or ideological differences among respondents.

The Social-Personal index, the Rights index,(Panel A) and the index of Mean Vignette Ratings (Panel B) show a wide spread of scores with mean and median ratings that fall closer to the mid-point of the scale. The mean score on the Social-Personal Index is 9 with a scale range of 1 to 17 points; on the rights index the mean and median scores are between 4 and 5 on the 9 point scale; and the mean of Mean Vignette Ratings is 5.6 on a 9 point scale. These three scales measure attitudes in areas that span many different pregnancy circumstances that have been the focus of longstanding moral debate. We now turn to an examination of the relationship among these different measures of abortion attitudes, and pinpoint the similarities in the attitude structure captured by the two methods.

Inter-Index Correlations: Vignette and Survey Scales

The distinctions revealed in the factor structure do not necessarily mean that the Health, Social-Personal, and Rights dimensions of abortion attitudes are unrelated. The factor structure implies two things. First, the four measures of abortion attitudes draw upon different concerns as shown in the labels we attributed to them: physical-psychological health, social-personal factors, competing rights of others, and couple dissensus. Second, at least the first three indices may represent a continuum of restricted to unconditional support for abortion that has emerged historically with changes in the legal and social climate surrounding the abortion issue.

Public support for abortion has varied as a function of the health and social-personal factors for a very long time; the terms 'therapeutic abortions' (for health reasons narrowly defined) and 'criminal abortions' (all other, largely social-personal reasons) were the basis of common law regulation of abortions late into the 19th century, and regulation of abortions by the State until the mid-half of the 20th century. If a continuum of restricted to unconditional support exists among the public, then we expect to find a higher correlation between the two liberal measures of abortion attitudes (social-personal and rights). With the polarization of abortion politics, we expect to find a close relationship between moral approval of abortions and support for the pro-choice position on abortion.

We include two additional indices in these analyses that are based upon vignette ratings, and constructed to approximate the Health and Social-Personal indices drawn from the questionnaire data. These two indices are referred to as the Vignette Health Index and the Vignette Social-Personal Index, to distinguish them from the Health Index and the Social-Personal Index that are based upon responses to the survey items. Each respondent rated some abortion decisions that were based on health reasons and some that were based on social-personal reasons. The random assignment of vignette levels within each dimension of the factorial survey theoretically results in each respondent receiving a random sample of 20 vignettes, in which the appearance of a particular level is proportional to the total number of levels within a dimension.[2] In order to correlate comparable sets of measures across the two data sources, we calculate the mean scores for each respondent based upon the number of situations in which either a health condition was present as the reason for an abortion, or any one of the personal reasons were cited as the reason for an abortion. Hence the Mean Vignette Health Rating is the mean of ratings on all vignettes that contained any one of four health reasons; the Mean Vignette Social-Personal Rating is the mean of ratings for all vignettes in which any of the 6 social-personal reasons appeared as a condition prompting an abortion.[3] From the point of view of interpretation, a critical difference between the vignette and survey indices is that questionnaire indices measure attitudes along a particular dimension, and vignette indices measure the same attitudes in context - the context is variation in background information regarding other characteristics of an abortion situation. Thus a high correlation across indices from the two data sources will show that respondents are consistent and focus attention on the types of reasons behind an abortion decision both in the presence and absence of contextual information. For the sake of clarity we present correlations between indices internal to the vignette and questionnaire data sets in panels A of Table 4.2, and show the correlation between indices across the two data sets in Panel B.

Three of the four survey indices share a significant and high correlation with each other. Note that the highest correlation (.72) is found between approval of abortions on social-personal grounds and the view of abortion as the pregnant woman's prerogative, regardless of the circumstances or the views of others involved in the decision. This relationship indicates that the acceptance of abortion under

Table 4.2
Correlations among Abortion Indices

---

*Panel A: Correlations between Abortion Indices within Survey
        and Vignette Data Sets*

	Survey Indices (N=291)			Vignette Indices (N=217)
	Soc.Per.	Rights	Coup.Dis.	Social Personal
Health	.58 ***	.47 ***	.18 ***	.71 ***
Social-Pers.		.72 ***	.32 ***	
Rights			.23 ***	
Couple Dissensus			---	

---

*Panel B Correlations between Indices across Vignette and Survey
        Data Sets. (N=217)*

	Vignette	
Survey	Health	Social-Personal
Health	.73 ***	.58 ***
Social-Personal	.61 ***	.74 ***
Rights	.58 ***	.64 ***

*** p < .001

many discretionary circumstances is closely linked to a broader view of abortion as ultimately a woman's private right that transcends the rights of others. We cannot empirically demonstrate a causal direction in these data, but it seems more plausible that the majority of respondents who approve of abortion under unspecified circumstances even when the woman's husband or parents oppose the decision, will also approve of a variety of specific reasons women provide for their abortions. The reverse situation may not hold true for most individuals, as suggested by the finding that even staunch supporters of legal abortions restrict their moral approval to first-trimester abortions, and remain undecided about the role of parents and spouses in pregnancy resolution decisions.

By comparison, the Survey Health index of approval is only moderately correlated with the Survey Social-Personal index (.58), and shows an even lower correlation with the Survey Rights index (.47). The lowest coefficients are found in the correlation of the Couple Dissensus index with all the other three abortion indices (.18 to .32). These correlations indicate a greater independence between a view of abortions as a solution to extenuating circumstances that portend harm to the mother's health and a view of abortion as a solution to an unintended pregnancy, or as the uncontested reproductive right of women. Individuals who tolerate an abortion if it is required to prevent extreme harm to the mother's physical and psychological health are expressing a deep concern for life of the mother. Those who draw the line on health reasons for abortion are least apt to support abortion as the private right of women. Furthermore, the acceptance of abortion on health grounds is only moderately related to an approval of abortion based on a variety of personal reasons (.58): poverty, family size limitation, and postponement of marriage and childbearing. The strength of relationships between the Health index and the two liberal measures of abortion attitudes, underscores the compromise position the public takes toward abortion. There is no indication in these data that the public is polarized in support of the right of the fetus versus the woman's right to abortion. Instead, respondents weigh these rights in favor of the woman only when they are forced to choose between preserving the life and health of the pregnant woman and the life of the fetus. There is greater variation among respondents in the extent to which they define 'life' to include the quality of life in a broader context of the social, economic, and personal circumstances that lead to an abortion decision; and in whether these decisions can preclude the rights of others. The lower correlation between the Health index and the Rights index of abortion (.47) shows that a view of abortion as a personal right of individual women is least compatible with a tolerance of abortion that arises from a balance of concerns related to fetal life and women's health.

In contrast to these findings with the survey data, the correlation between the Vignette Health Index and Vignette Social-personal Index is higher (.71), than that found between the two similar survey indices (.58). The higher correlation in the case of the vignette indices is to be expected, because the two scales measure responses to various reasons for an abortion in context. The influence of background dimensions such as gestation phase and maternal health that were found to have independent effects in the vignette analysis are also implicated. And in this sense the individual mean rating of all vignettes is a composite measure of a respondent's attitudes toward abortion.

Having established the relationships between the three dimensions of abortion attitudes (Health, Social-Personal, Rights), we turn to a comparison of similar indices across the two data sets. The first striking result in Panel B is that abortion indices that represent similar conditions are highly correlated across the two methods: .73 on the Health indices and .74 on the Social-Personal indices. In other words, the responses to the types of reasons are highly consistent and similar in the two data sets.

The correlation between two different indices (Health and Social-Personal) each drawn from a different data set show a pattern that is similar to that found between the Health and Social-Personal measures within the questionnaire data (see Panel A). The correlation between the Vignette Health Index and Survey Social-Personal Index is .58, and between the Vignette Social-Personal Index and Survey Health Index is .61. These figures are almost identical to the correlation between the Health and Social-Personal Indices when both are drawn from the survey data (.58 Panel A.). Similar patterns are found when we compare the correlations between the two vignette indices and the Rights Index from the survey data. The Vignette Social-Personal index shows a slightly higher correlation with the Survey Rights Index (.64), as compared to the correlation observed between the Vignette Health Index and the Survey Rights Index (.58).

In sum, the high correlations between comparable indices based on vignette and questionnaire data show that the two methods capture the same structure of responses to abortion situations. The structure of abortion attitudes revolves around distinctions drawn among justifiable grounds for an abortion, and hence indices that mirror this distinction across the two data sources are highly correlated. We can use measures from either data source as equivalent indicators of abortion attitudes in the analysis that follows. Since the major goal of this chapter is to place the abortion attitudes within the broader context of a belief structure, we rely upon the data from the telephone survey. This also maximizes our sample size for the individual level analysis undertaken in this chapter.[4] The preceding analysis has shown that our Massachusetts community sample, like the general public in national surveys is not polarized on the abortion issue. A logical next step is to show how the dimensionality of abortion attitudes translates to political support for the two abortion activist groups.

Abortion Morality and Political Support

Every year since abortions were legalized, pro-choice and pro-life supporters have rallied in Washington to demonstrate public support for their respective positions, an event that carried special significance in 1989 with the largest turnout ever of pro-choice supporters in defense of the present abortion law. In the backdrop of the highly polarized abortion politics, public support for abortions is best characterized as paradoxical. The preceding analysis showed that our respondents, like the general public, straddle a middle course on abortion. A very small portion of our respondents have ever attended a pro-life meeting or contributed time or money to the cause (5.8%); an even smaller proportion have participated in a pro-choice meeting or contributed money or time to pro-choice activities (4%). In light of these small proportions of direct political involvement, we define political support more broadly, based on the following questions concerning their political views:

Pro-Life Support

On a scale of 1 to 10, where 1 means a 'Very Strongly Oppose' Pro-Life position on abortion and 10 means a very strongly support the Pro-Life position, what number between 1 and 10 best describes your views?

Pro-Choice Support

On a scale of 1 to 10, where 1 means a 'Very Strongly Oppose' Pro-Choice position on abortion and 10 means a very strongly support the Pro-Choice position, what number between 1 and 10 best describes your views?

General Political Orientation

How about your political views in general? Would you say you are very liberal, liberal moderate, conservative or very conservative?

The measure of liberal-conservative political orientation (item 3, above) is included here to compare its relationship to abortion attitudes and the two more issue-specific measures of political support for pro-life and pro-choice political groups.

The correlations between the four abortion attitude measures and the three political attitude scales are shown in Table 4.3. Health, Social-Personal, and Rights indices of abortion attitudes share a high positive correlation with support for the pro-choice platform (.55, .68, .56), and a very similar level of negative correlation with support for the pro-life position on abortion (-.60, -.66, -.59). The direction and strength of these relationships are quite revealing, and suggest that the level of support for the two political groups varies with the level of moral approval of abortion. In other words, ideological coherence may characterize the two ends of the spectrum of moral and political support for abortion. Those who show ambivalent approval of abortions are also likely to be fence sitters when it comes to political support for the two groups.

Respondents who identify themselves as holding liberal political views are more likely to support the pro-choice position (.28), and are also more likely to oppose the pro-life position on abortion (-.24) But this relationship is clearly quite weak. Furthermore, similar weak correlations are found between each of the three indices of moral approval of abortion and the index of conservative-liberal political

Table 4.3
Correlations between Abortion Indices and Political Support Indices

	Abortion approval				Political Support		
	Health	Soc.Per.	Rights	Dissen.	Pro-Life	Pro-Choice	Political Orientation
Health		.58 ***	.47 ***	.18 ***	-.60 ***	.55 ***	.29 ***
Social-Personal			.72 ***	.32 ***	-.66 ***	.68 ***	.27 ***
Rights				.24 ***	-.59 ***	.56 ***	.25 ***
Dissensus					-.16 ***	.13 ***	.04
Pro-Life Support						-.71 ***	-.24 ***
Pro-Choice Support							.28 ***
Political Orientation							

*** $p < .001$

orientation (.29, .27, .25). In other words, support for pro-choice and pro-life groups is more closely tied to moral approval of abortions than to a general orientation toward politics measured along a liberal-conservative continuum. Abortion attitudes and support for pro-choice or pro-life groups are not strongly structured by our respondents' general orientation to politics: Pro- and anti-abortion views may be well represented among both liberals and conservatives. Respondents can view themselves as liberal on many political issues unrelated to abortion, and still show only moderate approval of abortions and moderate political support for the pro-choice groups. In a provocative analysis, Blake (1983) has demonstrated why the most 'logical' or 'natural' political constituency in support of legal abortion, namely women, becomes 'short-circuited' simply because compounding influences of higher church attendance, traditional views toward pre-marital sex, and lower educational attainment enhance moral disapproval of abortions among women.

Within the context of abortion politics, we note a high negative correlation (-.71) between support for pro-choice and pro-life groups. This means that respondents translate their own views on abortion to a consistent support for either the pro-choice or pro-life positions. This also suggests that many respondents see a simultaneous support for the positions articulated by the two groups as highly incompatible. Respondents may perceive the pro-choice and pro-life ideologies as sharply polarized, presenting no middle ground even on the health issues related to abortion. In sum, the extent to which respondents support the two political groups is reflected in their moral views toward abortion. We turn next to an examination of the abortion factor structure from one additional perspective: We explain the dimensionality found in the domain of abortion attitudes as a function of social-group differences among respondents.

Dimensionality and Social-Group Differences

The analysis of social-group differences in abortion attitudes focuses on three sets of variables: religion, life course position, and personal reproductive experiences of respondents. Our measures of religion are limited to religious affiliation and frequency of church attendance. Age and marital status are used as indicators of respondent's life course position, although age can also represent cohort differences in attitudes toward abortion. Respondent's family size and personal experience with abortion are used as indicators of past reproductive experiences.

Religion is an important variable in our analysis for two reasons. First, past studies have consistently found church attendance to be the single most important discriminator of liberal-conservative attitudes in the areas of sex, contraception, and abortion. Second, abortion continues to be one of these three areas in which Catholic-Non-Catholic differences remain significant. The fact that our study was conducted in Massachusetts means our survey sample contains equal proportions of Catholics and Protestants, which permits us to compare the joint effects of religious affiliation and church attendance. We did not inquire into ethnic background, Protestant denomination, or specific tenets of religious faith. Hence we rely on religious affiliation using a simple Catholic-non-Catholic dichotomy, and church attendance. Respondents' educational attainment is used as a proxy measure of secular influences. Previous studies have reported no gender differences in abortion attitudes. However, we include gender as a control so that we can isolate the independent effects of marital status.[5] The nine social-group variables were entered in multiple regression equations with the Health, Social-Personal, and Rights indices as dependent variables.[6]

Table 4.4 shows the regression results for the three abortion indices. Frequency of church attendance as an indicator of commitment to religious identity emerges as the most consistent predictor of abortion attitudes in all three equations. Individuals who attend religious services regularly are more likely to disapprove of abortions under all of the specified conditions. The negative effects of church attendance indicate a very high salience of traditional religious beliefs that are reinforced through frequent exposure to religious teachings and participation in a social community of individuals who share similar values. If we remember that the variation in approval on health grounds for abortion is highly skewed toward positive approval, then it is particularly interesting that the single best predictor of deviation toward a conservative stance on abortion is frequent participation in religious services. As expected, respondents show no differences by age, marital status, sex, parity, or personal experience with abortions in their support of physical and psychological health reasons for an abortion. Catholics are significantly more opposed than non-Catholics to abortion for social-

Table 4.4

Regression of Abortion Indices[a] on Social-Group Characteristics (Unstandardized Coefficients)

Social-Group Indicators	Health	Social-Personal	Rights
Catholics[1]	-.25	-2.76 ***	-.71 *
Church Attendance[2]	-.60 ***	-.90 **	-.60 ***
Education3	-.09	.18	.02
Female[4]	.20	-.05	.13
Age [5]	-.00	.03	-.00
Solo [6]	-.18	1.90 +	.22
Number of children [7]	-.10	-.48 +	-.13
Personal exp. of abortion[8]	5.69	4.49 ***	1.02 *
Knowledge of Friend/Relative's[9] experience with abortion	.26	2.33 **	.86 *
Constant	9.56 ***	10.07 ***	6.36 ***
	$R^2 = 18$	$R^2 = .26$	$R^2 = .21$

[a] Hi scores on abortion indices indicate high approval.

[1] 1 = Catholics 0 = non-Catholics (includes Protestants, Jews, and those with no religious affiliation)

[2] 1 = never or hardly ever 2 = once or twice a year 3 = once a month 4 = once a week 5 = several times a week

[3] 1 = Less than High school 2 = High school 3 = some college 4 = 4-year college 5 = graduate school

[4] Male = 1 Female = 2

[5] Age lo = 19 hi = 87

[6] Solo 1 = married or widowed 2 = never married or divorced.

[7] Number of children: lo = 0 hi = 8

[8] Women who report a personal experience with abortion and men who report exposure to abortion experience of wife or sex-partner. Deleted category is respondents with neither personal experience nor exposure to abortion experience of friends and relatives.

[9] Respondents who report knowledge of abortion experiences of friends and relatives, but report no personal experience of abortion. Deleted category same as in 8.

*** $p < .001$, ** $p < .01$, * $p < .05$, + $p < .10$

personal reasons and , to abortions as the autonomous right of women. The negative impact of a Catholic affiliation on abortion attitudes is independent of the impact of church attendance on both the Social-Personal Index and the Rights Index of abortion attitudes.

Greater conservatism among Catholics is likely to be rooted in strong ties to ethnic community traditions, rather than an adherence to the official teachings of the Catholic Church. In other words, the differences between Catholics and Non-Catholics cannot be simply attributed to differences in theological beliefs. It has been amply documented that most Catholics depart from the Church's stance on abortion, pre-marital sex, and contraception, by showing no difference in their personal behavior on these issues as compared to Protestants. Catholics who show greater conservatism on the Rights Index may be more opposed to an abortion because it goes against the views of parents and spouses, reflecting their concern for harmony in family relationships, a sentiment that may be rooted in strong ties to ethnic traditions and communities (D'Antonio 1985). Second, despite the fact that the age of respondents has no significant impact on abortion attitudes, it is not clear at this juncture to what extent Catholic-non-Catholic differences in attitudes are related to age.

Personal exposure to an abortion and knowledge of the experiences of close friends and relatives has a significant positive impact on the approval of abortions in the case of the two liberal measures. In the absence of attitude measures at various points across the life span of respondents, it seems likely that there are reciprocal influences between abortion attitudes and reproductive experiences. The decision to have an abortion may be based upon a positive disposition toward abortions prior to the pregnancy. On the other hand, a personal experience of abortion can also redirect ambivalent views toward a positive acceptance of abortions.

The interplay between personal reproductive experiences and abortion attitudes is also suggested by the moderate impact of respondents' family size on abortion attitudes. Respondents who have many children are more likely to be opposed to abortions to limit or postpone births. A large family size among some respondents may have resulted from desires to have many children, and their opposition to abortions may arise from the high salience of parenthood and children to them. And for those individuals who desire fewer children than they actually have, it may be hard to view any one of the pregnancies as unwanted in retrospect. Whether a pregnancy is welcomed or viewed as unwanted is closely related to how individuals resolve their pregnancies and the values they bring to reproductive decisions. This point is eloquently illustrated by one pro-life activist in Luker's study:

> I never wanted to have a baby, I never planned to have five children...I mean my general attitude was, "Hell, I am pregnant again." But I thought pregnancy was a natural part of marriage, and I believed so much in the word *natural*, and so I loved the babies when they were born...you see a lot of unwanted pregnancies, but you almost never find an unwanted baby...(p.169).

Of the two life course indicators, age and marital status, only marital status has a moderate impact on abortion attitudes. Unattached solo individuals (divorced or never married) are more likely to approve of an abortion if the woman cannot afford a child at the present time, if she is unmarried and wishes to prevent an illegitimate birth, or if she is married and does not want any more children. All these circumstances are specific to the marital status, age, and family size of pregnant women, and we find that respondents' own marital status and family size have a significant impact on approval of abortions. Unmarried or divorced men and women are probably more vulnerable to the variety of contexts in which a pregnancy may be viewed as problematic, and hence they sympathize with the life circumstances of unmarried, poor, and minor women. Unplanned parenthood will be perceived as incompatible with other life options, as many single men and women seek higher levels of educational attainment, expect to be employed for longer periods of time, and postpone marriage and childbearing. A similar economic rationale may operate when divorced women face a loss of economic and emotional support to accommodate an unexpected pregnancy. By contrast, children and parenthood assume greater salience within the normative context of marital relationships, which set the tone for the emotional resources men and women bring to an unintended pregnancy.

Religion and personal exposure to abortions are the two significant predictors of attitudes in the case of the Rights index of abortion. Women who have had an abortion, and men who have shared an experience with their spouse or partner are more likely to respect women's autonomy in abortion decisions. But this relationship is only marginally significant. The majority of individuals who experience an abortion today rarely seek an abortion beyond the 12th week of gestation, and so they may feel ambivalent about a woman's right to abortion beyond the first trimester. Moreover, consultations with friends and relatives about the abortion decision may have resulted in positive experiences for some, and negative experiences for others. The diversity of these experiences is perhaps reflected in the weak impact of this variable on the Rights index.

The lack of significant differences by age of respondents in the case of the multiple regression analysis may point to interactive effects between age and other respondent characteristics. As noted in the previous chapter, the impact of age may be selective to the characteristics of abortion situations. Older respondents show greater support for abortion decisions made by vignette women in their 40s, while young respondents show greater support for abortion decision made by women in their teens.

Thus far our analyses have explored the dimensionality of abortion attitudes from a variety of standpoints. We have shown that two different approaches to the measurement of abortion attitudes essentially capture the same structure of beliefs. We have also linked moral views toward abortion to political support for abortion activists. The correlation among the three abortion indices were high enough to suggest an underlying continuum of restricted approval based on human life values, to an unconditional acceptance of abortion as a woman's personal right. The different positions our respondents take on abortion was in part explained by social-group differences that pertain to religious commitment, life course position, and reproductive experiences. Conservative views on abortion are rooted in a strong commitment to religious activities, while permissive views are best predicted by personal experience or exposure to abortions. In the next section we explore the structure of attitudes toward two other human life issues: euthanasia and suicide

The Domain of Human Life Values

The measurement of human life attitudes consisted of three sets of questions that focused on respondents' beliefs about when human life begins, approval of euthanasia for a terminally ill patient, and approval of suicide under three different circumstances. The questions were framed as follows:

Beginning of Life
People vary in when they think human life begins. Some think human life begins at conception and others think it begins at birth. When do you think human life begins? (At conception, very early in the pregnancy, late in pregnancy when fetus can survive outside the woman's body, only at full-term birth, or don't know?)

Euthanasia
When a person has a painful disease that cannot be cured, do you think doctors should be allowed to withhold treatment that is prolonging a terminal illness if the patient and his/her family want the treatment to be stopped?
(Rating Scale: (5) Definitely Yes ... Definitely Not (1))

Suicide
People sometimes decide to end their lives for various reasons. Do you approve or disapprove of a person ending their life under each of these following circumstances:
a. The person has a painful incurable disease...
b. The person has become bankrupt and sees no way to become financially solvent again...
c. The person is tired of living and feels ready to die...

The singular focus on 'life' in the recent wave of anti-abortion politics has forced into the open a serious consideration of the legal and moral rights of fetuses, and made abortion itself a sanctity of life issue. The pro-life challenge has spread beyond abortion to include opposition to euthanasia and various forms of reproductive research and technology. The three topics considered in this study -- abortion, suicide, and euthanasia -- share a common focus on the values we bring to the preservation of human life. However, there is a crucial difference between abortion and other situations that involve the termination of human life. Abortion morality revolves around the relative rights of fetuses and pregnant women, and this issue is further complicated by first having to decide whether the fetus can be considered a human being with the full rights of personhood enjoyed by the pregnant woman. The moral dilemma in the case of euthanasia and suicide centers around whether individuals have the right to terminate their own lives, when they decide that the continuation of life is physically and psychologically intolerable.

In the analysis presented here we consider three issues. First, we explore the structure of attitudes toward euthanasia and suicide, and show that views toward euthanasia and suicide rest upon the same moral calculus that underlies attitudes toward abortion. Second, we describe the different beliefs respondents bring to the definition of human life, which provide an insight into why attitudes toward abortion vary to a great extent. Third, we link measures of human life attitudes to abortion attitudes in order to test for a coherent belief structure that characterizes moral responses to abortion, euthanasia, and suicide.

Views Toward Euthanasia and Suicide

The factor analysis of human life attitudes included four items that relate to euthanasia and suicide. The results of this analysis, shown in Table 4.5, reveal a structure of attitudes that is very similar to the abortion belief structure. Two factors distinguish between approval of euthanasia and suicide for individuals suffering from a terminal illness, and approval of suicide for social-personal reasons. We label the two constructs Terminal-illness Suicide- Euthanasia, and Personal-Social Suicide. As with abortion, health concerns predominate when individuals exempt incurable illness as justifiable grounds for euthanasia or suicide. By contrast, suicide is not considered a justifiable solution to the despair faced by individuals in the midst of an economic or personal crisis. This distinction is further illustrated by the distribution of scores on the two indices shown in Figure 4.2. The scores on the Terminal-Illness Suicide-Euthanasia Index show more variance, and the median is closer to the positive end of the scale (median of 5 on 7 point scale).

The Social-Personal Suicide index shows a highly skewed distribution in the opposite direction, suggesting overwhelming opposition to suicide when a person could presumably lead a healthy life (a median of 1 and a mean of 1.5 on a 5 point scale). The very small minority who expressed approval of suicide under all

Table 4.5
Factor Analysis of Euthanasia-Suicide Items

	Factor	
Suicide/Euthanasia Items	1	2
Suicide (Tired of living)	.85	.09
Suicide (Bankruptcy)	.78	.02
Euthanasia (Terminal illness)	-.12	.88
Suicide (Terminal illness)	.39	.62
EIGENVALUE	1.62	1.05
Proportion of Variance:	40.4	26.2

Panel A. Terminal Illness Euthanasia-Suicide

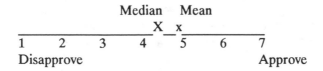

B. Personal-Social Suicide

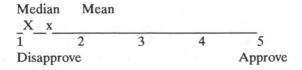

Figure 4.2 Distribution Characteristics of Euthanasia-Suicide Indices

circumstances were not significantly different in their social-group membership from the majority who oppose suicide for social-personal reasons. On the other hand, attitudes toward terminal illness euthanasia and suicide divide along the same set of social-group differences that were found to be significant for approval of abortion on health grounds.

Table 4.6 shows the regression of seven social-group predictors on attitudes toward terminal illness euthanasia-suicide. As expected, opposition to euthanasia and suicide increases with greater participation in religious services. Catholics show slightly more opposition to euthanasia and suicide, but the results do not suggest a sharp difference on the basis on religious affiliation. In addition, education is positively related to approval of euthanasia and suicide. The positive impact of education suggests that higher levels of education lead to a secular-relativistic view of human life as worth protecting only if it involves the nurturance of a painless, healthy life.

Table 4.6

Regression of Terminal Illness Euthanasia-Suicide Index[b] on Social-Group Characteristics[a] (Unstandardized Coefficients)

Social Group Indicators	Terminal Illness Euthanasia/Suicide
Catholic	-.33 [+]
Church Attendance	-.33 [***]
Education	.25 [*]
Female	.09
Age	-.01
Solo	.07
Number of Children	-.02
Constant	5.74 [***]
	$R^2 = .14$ [***]

[a] Variable direction and deleted categories for predictor variables appear in Table 4.4

[b] High scores on Terminal-Illness Euthanasia/Suicide Index refer to high approval.

[***] $p < .001$, [**] $p < .01$, [*] $p < .05$, [+] $p < .10$

Thus far the negative impact of church attendance on attitudes toward abortion, euthanasia, and suicide has been consistent: Those who are regular participants in institutional religion share a view that all human life is sacred including that of the fetus, and the termination of human life is never justifiable.

Views Toward Fetal Life

For centuries American women and midwives associated pregnancy with quickening, and the morality of abortions became questionable only past the point of quickening. For other individuals even a range spanning conception to birth may be restrictive in capturing the essence of human life, if they consider life to be a continuous process of transmission of genetic traits and capacities from one generation to another. Because abortion is the termination of a particular pregnancy, views toward fetal life and personhood are particularly salient to moral approval of abortions.

Table 4.7
Distribution of Responses to Beginning of Life Question

Life Begins at:	*Percent*
Conception	36
Very early in the Pregnancy	15
Viability	29
Full-term birth	13
Not Sure	7
	N = 291

As shown in Table 4.7, 36 percent of our respondents reported that human life begins at conception, 15 percent reported 'very early in the pregnancy,' 29 percent reported viability, and 13 percent believe that human life begins at full-term birth.[7] The spread of responses to this question suggests that our respondents do not agree upon a single definition of the beginning of human life, a matter that is at the heart of the abortion controversy. Furthermore, the diversity of opinions on this issue is a clear indication that moral pluralism, rather than medical 'facts', is at the heart of the debate over fetal life and personhood. Despite the lack of consensus, the majority of our respondents view human life as beginning before birth (87%), and a substantial number of them believe that human life begins at conception (36 %) or when the fetus is viable (29%). One major implication of this finding is that our respondents' views are clearly at odds with the view of human life implied in the laws regulating abortion, which have hitherto avoided the question of when human life begins, precisely on the grounds of moral pluralism. Another implication is that to the extent that moral views toward abortion are closely tied to views toward fetal life, support for abortion among those who view human life as beginning at viability is highly tenuous, in light of the fast-paced technologies that have made it impossible to anchor fetal viability at any definite point in the pregnancy. Presently, viability is variously defined as between 20 and 24 weeks of pregnancy. As ever younger fetuses can be sustained outside the womb, fetal viability is being pushed closer and closer to conception.

An interesting range of social-group differences explain whether respondents view the beginning of human life closer to conception or full-term birth. Table 4.8 shows the results from a regression analysis in which the same set of variables used in the earlier analysis of attitudes toward euthanasia and suicide are used to explain differences in beliefs about the onset of human life. As expected, respondents who participate frequently in religious services are more likely to view human life as beginning closer to conception. Interestingly, more women than men believe that human life begins early in pregnancy. This gender difference is probably rooted in women's unique experience of motherhood, which Adrienne Rich has described as the potential relationship of any woman to her powers of reproduction and to children (1977:xv). Women are genetic, carrying, and nurturing parents, while men are genetic and nurturing

Table 4.8

Regression of Beginning of Life Index[b] on Social-Group Characteristics[a] (Unstandardized Coefficients)

Social Indicators	Beginning of Life
Catholics	-.23
Church Attendance	-.26 ***
Education	-.05
Female	-.35 *
Age	-.00
Solo	.22
Number of Children	-.12 +
Constant	4.49 ***
	$R^2 = .14$ ***

[a] Variable direction and deleted categories for predictor variables appear in Table 4.4.

[b] 1 = conception 2 = early pregnancy 3 = not sure 4 = viability 5 = full-term birth.

parents. Given this difference, men's experience of a pregnancy is gained vicariously through the experiences of their wives and partners, and their first physical contact with a child occurs after birth.[8] Or as Elshtain (1982:59) states, mothering requires that 'the reality of a single human child be kept before the mind's eye'. For those women who have not yet experienced a pregnancy, the menstrual cycle is itself a constant reminder of the potential for motherhood, resulting in a more closely integrated view of sex, pregnancy, and its consequences, that is uniquely different from men's experience. However, we cannot then conclude that this gender difference leads to greater opposition to abortions among women than men. It suggests that women bring a different moral vision to the abortion issue than men do.

Note also that respondents who have had many births are more likely to view human life as beginning closer to conception. This finding further informs the link between family size and attitudes toward abortion: Opposition to abortions among those who have many children is in part rooted in the centrality of children in personal lives, and the sanctity of human life assumes salience for these individuals early in pregnancy. In sum, moral views toward fetal life are grounded in religious and reproductive values, which in turn provide meaning to sexual and reproductive aspects of life.

As a fitting conclusion to this discussion of human life values, we examine the relationship among all of the human life issues discussed above. Such an analysis will help us place the abortion issue within the context of other human life issues, and simultaneously show that our respondents' attitudes toward various human life issues are interrelated.

Links between Abortion and Human Life Issues

The correlations among the three measures of human life attitudes, Terminal-illness Euthanasia-Suicide, Personal-Social Suicide, Beginning of Life and the three measures of abortion attitudes are shown in Table 4.9. The first three columns show the relationships among the three human life indices discussed above. All correlations are significant, but none of the relationships appear particularly strong. The strongest relationship is found for approval of euthanasia and suicide under terminal-illness conditions and a view of human life as beginning at later stages of a pregnancy (.29). The correlation between the two measures of attitudes toward euthanasia and suicide is very low (.19). This means that not only are the two dimensions of attitudes toward euthanasia and suicide distinct, but they are also weakly related. Widespread, deeply felt opposition to suicide and euthanasia is relaxed only to alleviate extreme suffering involved in prolonging the life of a terminally ill patient. In comparison to the value dissensus we have found within the abortion domain, moral sanctions against suicide are much more firmly entrenched and less amenable to change.

The Terminal-Illness index of suicide and euthanasia, and the index of beliefs about fetal life are closely related to all three indices of abortion attitudes. Those who approve of suicide and euthanasia in the case of terminal illness are also likely to approve of abortion for a variety of reasons (.31, .40, .36). Similarly, a gradualist perspective on human life leads to support for abortions in many situations (.41, .51, .51). These findings point to a cluster of values related to human life issues, where a secular developmental view of life is conducive to a liberal acceptance of abortions. An absolutist view of human life as beginning at conception as opposed to a view

Table 4.9

Correlations among Human Life Indices and Correlations with Abortion Indices

	Human Life Indices			*Abortion Indices*	
	Per.Soc. Suicide	Beg.Life.	Health	Soc.Per.	Rights
Terminal Illness Euthanasia/Suicide	.19***	.29***	.31***	.40***	.36***
Personal-Social Suicide		.11*	.13**	.24***	.18***
Beginning of Life			.41***	.51***	.51***
N=291					

*** p < .001, ** p < .01, * p < .05, + p < .10

that defines the fetus as an emerging, potential human being is less likely to lead to a support for abortion for many reasons.

Two important issues emerge from the above analysis of human life values. First, we have shown that an absolutist view of human life is embedded in a traditional religious outlook that is characteristic of those who show a strong commitment to institutional religion. Secular values arising from exposure to higher education facilitate a tolerance of euthanasia and suicide as the right of individuals who face a life of pain and misery. Second, views toward abortion are particularly influenced by views toward fetal life and personhood. The variation in when individuals believe human life begins is significantly related to exposure to religious beliefs, gender, and salience of children in personal lives. In this context both human life values and reproductive values shape moral responses to abortion. The section that follows places abortion attitudes within the context of reproductive values through a detailed focus on respondents' views toward many aspects of sex, contraception, and pregnancy.

The Domain of Sex and Reproduction

Current trends in sexual behavior, marriage, divorce, and parenting indicate a break from traditional patterns of sequencing sexual and reproductive behavior within the context of marriage, and the emergence of greater diversity in sexual and reproductive lifestyles outside the context of marriage. As sex became separated from marriage, with a rise in pre-marital sexual activity, parenting is now being separated from marriage, with an increase in out-of-wedlock births, decline and delay in marriage, and an increase in divorce rates (Rossi 1983). More recently, artificial insemination has made possible reproduction without sex. These developments have also entailed a shift in value orientation toward sexuality and reproduction, with an emphasis on 'choice', planning, and control over sex and fertility.

However, the concepts of choice, planning, and control assume varied meanings in the lives of women as a function of their age, marital status, social class, and personal circumstances. For example, the perception that teenage pregnancies present a social problem arises from ambivalent views toward the rights of minors, and a concern that premature parenthood can harm the health, economic, and social well being of teenagers. In short, the tremendous diversity in who parents, when, and how, has made marriage an inadequate reference point from which to examine emergent norms and behavior in the domain of sex and reproduction. To some of our older respondents, the changing patterns of sexual, marital, and family life styles will represent a fundamental challenge to their own experiences of sex , marriage, and procreation. To others, largely young respondents, pre-marital sexuality, cohabitation, contraception, and planned parenthood will represent normative patterns of sex and reproduction within their own peer groups.

Our analysis in this section attempts to provide a coherent picture of the views our respondents bring to bear upon many contemporary issues related to sex, contraception, and pregnancy. First, we show that moral views toward many aspects of sex and reproduction reflect multi-dimensional concerns related to sexual morality, health, individual rights, and sexual identity. Second, conservative and liberal views toward sex, contraception, and pregnancy are linked to social-group differences in religiosity, education, gender, and age. Third, we show that despite the dimensionality reflected in the structure of attitudes toward sex and reproduction, individuals' attitudes toward many different topics are both internally consistent and significantly related to attitudes toward abortion.

Four of the six topics to be investigated in this section focus on our respondents' attitudes toward sex and contraception: pre-marital sex, minors' access to contraception, homosexuality, and extra-marital sex. Two other questions focus on attitudes toward teenage parenthood and artificial reproduction. We review the attitudinal items to be discussed in this section, and provide the exact wording of a question where necessary.

Measures on Sexual Behavior

All questions on sexual behavior specified both a male and a female subject. For example, the questions on pre-marital sex asked respondents if they 'approve or disapprove of an unmarried woman having sex with a man ' in the context of four types of relationships: if she was engaged to the man, if she was in love with him, if she had strong affection for him, and if she was sexually attracted and wanted a casual relationship. This same question was repeated with the focus on approval of pre-marital sex for an unmarried man. Similarly, the questions related to homosexuality and extra-marital sex were also gender specific. Preliminary results showed that respondents did not differentiate their moral acceptance of pre-marital, extra-marital and homosexual behavior on the basis of whether a male or female subject was involved.

The questions on teenage contraception and parenthood also included a relational component. Of the three questions that focused on contraceptive access, two asked respondents whether they think retail stores should sell contraceptive devices to boys and girls under 16 years of age. The issue of parental consent was limited to the third question, concerning the availability of birth control pills for minor women, and this was worded as follows:

Do you think contraceptive pills should be available to girls under 16 years of age: with parental consent, without parental consent, or should they not be available at all to teenage girls?

On teenage parenthood, four different combinations of parents' and partner's views were specified:

If an unmarried woman (under 18 years of age) becomes pregnant would you approve of her decision to have and rear the baby, without getting married, if...

a) Her boyfriend and her parents support her decision.....
b) If her boyfriend supports her decision, but her parents oppose it...
c) If her parents support her decision, and her boyfriend opposes it...
d) If both her parents and her boyfriend oppose her decision....

Hence a liberal approval of contraceptive access for teenagers should be interpreted as the endorsement of free access to contraceptives without parental consent. An unconditional support for a pregnant teenager's decision to remain unmarried and raise the child should be interpreted as a support for the parenting rights of teenagers, even if parents and partners express disapproval.

The focus on artificial reproduction was restricted to married couples facing infertility problems, as we were interested in tapping views related to natural vs. artificial reproduction, and individual choice in fertility decisions. Artificial reproduction can also apply to unmarried, fertile, and homosexual couples, but such an extended focus would detract from the themes that are central to the abortion question. The specific item asked for respondents' approval of four different forms of artificial reproduction: 1) artificial insemination using husband's sperm, 2) artificial insemination using donor's sperm, 3) laboratory conception using sperm and ova from biological parents, 4) surrogate motherhood.

Dimensions of Attitudes Toward Sex and Contraception

The factor analysis of the 17 items related to sex and contraception resulted in five distinct factors as shown in Table 4.10. The first two factors tap attitudes toward pre-marital sex; the third, extra-marital sex; the fourth, minors' access to contraception; and the fifth, homosexuality. All factor loadings are high with very little overlap across the five factors. A general implication of these results is the multi-dimensional nature of moral responses to sex and contraception. The key distinction in the first two factors is the degree of commitment implied in pre-marital sexual relationships. Items related to the first factor measure tolerance of pre-marital sex if the man and woman are engaged to be married, or in love; the second factor represents approval of pre-marital sex if the man and woman share affection, or desire a casual relationship. Hence factors 1 and 2 are labelled Pre-marital Sex with Commitment and Casual Pre-marital sex. Note that minors' access to contraceptives emerges as an attitude domain distinct from pre-marital sex, which suggests that contraceptive issues elicit moral concerns that go beyond sexual morality. A permissive view toward minors access to contraception implies multiple concerns related to minor's rights, their health, consequences of unprotected sexuality, and a general permissive attitude toward sexuality.

Extra-marital sex and homosexuality draw upon additional concerns that are distinct from those evoked by pre-marital sexuality. Homosexual relationships violate cultural norms regarding same sex relationships along with the heterosexual basis of gender role identities. On the other hand, extra-marital sex threatens existing heterosexual relationships which involve dependent others such as spouses and children. Blumstein and Schwartz (1983) conclude that monogamy in relationships is a strongly held ideal, even when couples do not adhere to it.

Figure 4.3 shows the distribution of approval scores on the five sex and contraception indices, and two additional indices based upon responses to teenage parenthood and artificial reproduction. High scores on all indices mean high approval. Among the five indicators of attitudes toward sex and contraception (Panels A through E), attitudes toward pre-marital sex with commitment, homosexuality, and extra-marital sex show the least variation in scale scores due to widespread acceptance in the case of pre-marital sex with commitment, and widespread opposition in the case of homosexuality and extra-marital sex. The median score on Pre-marital Sex with Commitment is 9 points, which is the scale maximum. The median score on the Homosexuality and Extra-Marital Sex indices is 1, which is the lowest possible score on both scales. By contrast, we detect much variation among our respondents on the Casual Pre-Marital Sex and Minors' Access to Contraception indices, which show mean scores that are closer to the mid-point of the scale.

Table 4.10

Factor Analysis of Items measuring Attitudes Toward Sex and Contraception.

			Factor		
Sex/Contraception Items:	*1*	*2*	*3*	*4*	*5*
(Approval of)					
A.Pre-marital sex with Commitment					
Female engaged to the man	**.91**	.22	.09	.19	.10
Male engaged to the woman	**.91**	.23	.10	.20	.11
Male in love with woman	**.88**	.29	.12	.21	.10
Female in love with man	**.86**	.33	.13	.18	.11
B.Casual Pre-marital Sex					
Male wants casual relsp.	.21	**.90**	.17	.12	.10
Female wants casual relsp.	.22	**.87**	.18	.16	.08
Male has affection for woman	.34	**.81**	.22	.11	.15
Female has affection for man	.37	**.78**	.20	.14	.15
C.Minors' Access to Contraception					
For boys under 16 (retail stores)	.22	.16	.08	**.92**	.06
For girls under 16 (retail stores)	.22	.16	.08	**.92**	.06
Availability of Pill (with or without parental consent)	.15	.09	.04	**.71**	.25
D.Extra-marital Sex					
Married female partner	.11	.20	**.93**	.08	.14
Married male partner	.14	.17	**.92**	.04	.15
Both partners married	.10	.21	**.92**	.08	.13
E. Homosexuality					
Male	.14	.12	.18	.16	**.93**
Female	.14	.20	.21	.18	**.91**
EIGENVALUE	7.67	2.33	1.78	1.30	1.23
Proportion of Variance:	48.0	14.6	11.1	8.1	7.7

The Artificial Reproduction and Teenage Parenthood indices are summated responses to all four conditions included in each of the related items. There is moderate to high approval of various forms of Artificial Reproduction for couples facing infertility problems (Panel F), and close to absolute approval of a pregnant teenager's decision to raise the baby (Panel G). The mean and median scores on the Artificial Reproduction Index fall between 6 and 7 points on the 9-point scale; the median score on the Teenage Parenthood Index is 9 on the 9-point scale!   We are aware of few surveys of public attitudes toward artificial reproduction to provide a context for interpretation. Our data indicate that a very high proportion of our respondents approve of artificial insemination and laboratory conception, if these two methods involve only natural parents (87% and 81%). The proportion who approve of the use of an unrelated donor's sperm in artificial insemination is somewhat lower (63%). The lowest approval is found for surrogate motherhood (32%). Two implications emerge from these findings. First, the majority of our respondents are sympathetic to certain forms of artificial reproduction, when a married couple faces infertility problems. Second, the distinctions between acceptable and unacceptable methods of artificial reproduction center around the involvement of strangers - either a male donor, or a surrogate mother, because these individuals share an ambivalent relationship to the biological family unit. During the course of our telephone interviews several respondents made reference to the 'Baby M' case to justify their ambivalence or disapproval of surrogate mothering.

With regard to teenage parenthood, we were surprised at first to find very high levels of approval. We had expected much dissensus in the approval of unmarried motherhood, especially if the pregnant woman was a minor. Fifty percent of our respondents are likely to approve of a teenager's decision to parent, even if her partner and parents disapprove of her decision to continue the pregnancy to term.

It is important to recall that the question on teenage parenthood included the views of parents and partners toward the minor woman's decision to parent, and that we asked this question in the context of an abortion survey. A disapproval of the unmarried teenager's decision to have and raise the baby leaves respondents with the option of endorsing abortion, and this may be especially problematic if the pregnant minor and all others involved support her decision to parent. Among those who show support for abortions, a high

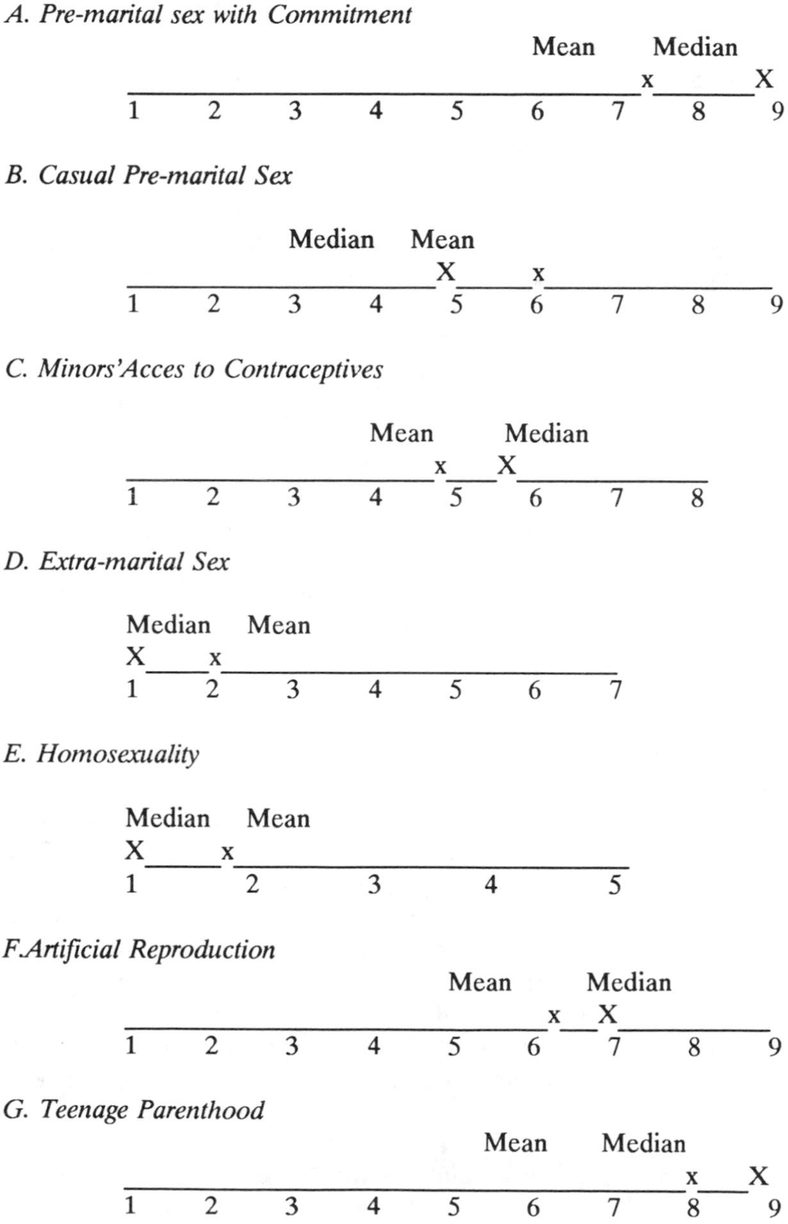

A. Pre-marital sex with Commitment

```
                                        Mean        Median
                                              x          X
  _____
   1     2     3     4     5     6     7     8     9
```

B. Casual Pre-marital Sex

```
                      Median   Mean
                         X        x
  _____
   1     2     3     4     5     6     7     8     9
```

C. Minors'Acces to Contraceptives

```
                            Mean        Median
                               x    X
  _____
   1     2     3     4     5     6     7     8
```

D. Extra-marital Sex

```
     Median    Mean
       X         x
  _____
   1       2     3     4     5     6     7
```

E. Homosexuality

```
     Median    Mean
       X         x
  _____
   1         2         3         4         5
```

F.Artificial Reproduction

```
                               Mean        Median
                                  x    X
  _____
   1     2     3     4     5     6     7     8     9
```

G. Teenage Parenthood

```
                                     Mean        Median
                                           x    X
  _____
   1     2     3     4     5     6     7     8     9
```

Figure 4.3 Distribution of Sex and Reproduction Indices

emphasis on 'choice' may result in a respect for the teenager's decision to parent.

Another question on teenage pregnancy asked respondents to suggest the best option to resolve a pregnancy when the woman is unmarried, under 18 years of age, and does not think it is the right time to have a child. Here, the question did not indicate the woman's personal preference or the views of significant others. The majority - 58 percent suggested adoption, 20 percent cited abortion, and only 8 percent said the woman should have and raise the baby. In other words, many of our respondents may consider adoption as an alternative to endorsing abortion or teenage parenthood, but faced with the woman's decision to parent, and the complexity of responses of her parents and partner to the decision, they are more likely to support parenthood. In her study of abortion counsellors, Joffe (1986) reports that counsellors are constantly aware of the autonomy of the pregnant woman, and at the same time doubt the motives of teenagers who wish to parent. As one counsellor states, " Our basic task is to lay the 'I' of that woman out there - to have her get in touch with what she wants, rather than what her husband or mother wants.' (p. 101). Despite this philosophy, one of the most wrenching situations faced by abortion counsellors was to support a teenager's decision to continue a pregnancy to term, when her own parents were opposed to it.

To summarize, the domain of sex and reproduction shows a multi-dimensional character which suggests that many competing values influence individuals' views toward sex, contraception, pregnancy, and its resolution. This dimensionality may in part reflect significant differences in the religious background and life course characteristics of our respondents. The topics investigated involve issues that affect men and women at different points in their lives, and the moral concerns these issues evoke have become increasingly complex over the course of history, rather than less so. As the next logical step we determine the common and unique social-group predictors of attitudes toward the six topics in the domain of sex and reproduction.

Sex, Reproduction, and Social-Group Differences

In Table 4.11, panels A and F show six regression equations in which the two measures of attitudes toward pre-marital sex, the index of Minors' Access to Contraception, Artificial Reproduction, Extra-Marital Sex, and Homosexuality were used as dependent variables. In Panel A, we find that three respondent characteristics have a significant impact on permissive views toward pre-marital sex. In light of the fact that the majority of our respondents approve of pre-marital sex in the context of a committed relationship, a conservative view is found among older respondents and those who are frequent participants in religious services. Age and church attendance have a similar, highly significant, negative impact on attitudes toward casual pre-marital sex (Panel B). The negative impact of age in both instances is likely to reflect both cohort and life course effects. Younger respondents are more liberal in their views toward pre-marital sex due to the fact that they are more likely to have engaged in pre-marital sex, in an era in which sex before marriage is increasingly the norm. Older respondents may retain conservative views toward pre-marital sex that were customary when they were young. The fact that disapproval of pre-marital sex increases with age also suggests a change in values that arise from the duties, concerns, and responsibilities of parenthood.

In Panels C through F, we find that age continues to show a consistent negative impact on attitudes toward minors' access to contraception, artificial reproduction, and homosexuality. All three of these issues have assumed complex moral dimensions only in the past few decades, and liberal views are found among younger cohorts of respondents. Church attendance also has a consistent negative impact on attitudes toward all six indices of sex and reproduction. The lack of significant differences between Catholics and non-Catholics on all indices confirms evidence from other studies that religious affiliation is no longer a salient predictor of views toward sexual and contraceptive issues. On the other hand, the continued salience of church attendance as the best predictor of traditional values in this domain leads us to conclude that a deep commitment to traditional religious beliefs, among both Protestants and Catholics, is found only among those who are frequently exposed to these values. Those who never, or only rarely attend religious services are more likely to have distanced themselves from the views espoused by traditional religious institutions on matters related to personal morality.

Respondents' level of educational attainment is positively related to permissive views toward pre-marital sex, teenage contraception, artificial reproduction, extra-marital sex, and homosexuality. The

Table 4.11

Regression of Sex and Reproduction Indices[b] on Social-Group Characteristics[a] (Unstandardized coefficients)

	Panel A	Panel B
Social-Group Indicators	*Pre-marital Sex with Commitment*	*Casual Pre-marital Sex*
Catholic	.21	.09
Church Attendance	-.82 ***	-.90 ***
Education	-.02	.41 +
Female	.55 +	-.12 ***
Age	-.08 ***	-.05 ***
Solo	-.12	-.64
Number of Children	.11	-.04
Constant	11.57 ***	9.82 ***
	$R^2 = .31$	$R^2 = .26$ ***

	Panel C.	Panel D.
Social-Group Indicators	*Teen Access to Contraception*	*Artificial Reproduction*
Catholic	-.24	-.38
Church Attendance	-.57 ***	-.34 ***
Education	.33 *	.50 ***
Female	.51 +	.06
Age	-.05 ***	-.04 ***
Solo	-.67 +	-.05
Number of Children	.09	-.03
Constant	7.50 ***	.23 ***
	$R^2 = .21$ ***	$R^2 = .21$ ***

(Continued)

Table 4.11 (contd.)

	Panel E	Panel F
Social Group Indicators	*Extra-Marital Sex*	*Homosexuality*
Catholic	-.21	-.08
Church Attendance	-.26 **	-.20 **
Education	.32 **	.34 ***
Female	-.25	.44 **
Age	-.01	-.02 **
Solo	-.11	.07
Number of Children	-.01	.01
Constant	2.71 ***	1.42 **
	$R^2 = .12$ ***	$R^2 = .18$ ***

[a] Deleted categories for predictor variables shown in Table 4.4
[b] High scores on dependent variables indicate high approval.

effect of education points to the influence of secular values on attitudes, which may in part be related to social-class differences. The positive impact of education is particularly significant in the approval of minors' access to contraception without parental consent, various forms of artificial reproduction, extra-marital sex, and homosexuality - issues on which there is clearly a great deal of variation in public attitudes.

Significant and opposite effects of gender are found for attitudes toward casual pre-marital sex and attitudes toward homosexuality. Women show less approval of casual pre-marital sex than men, (Panel B) and men show less approval of homosexuality than women (Panel F). Women may be more reluctant to approve of casual pre-marital sex because sexual freedom has mixed implications for their lives. They may perceive fewer emotional rewards, greater risk, and a devaluation of their status in casual sexual relationships. Women's greater approval of pre-marital sex in the context of committed relationships provides further evidence of different needs men and women bring to sexual relationships. On the other hand, men are more opposed to homosexuality, as their own masculine identity is grounded in heterosexual relationships.

In sum, the key social-group differences in our respondents' views toward sex and reproduction emerge along the lines of religion, age, education, and gender. The consistent, opposite effects of religion and education on liberal views toward sexuality and reproduction suggest that a religious-secular orientation underlies respondents' moral views. Further, the negative relationship between age and permissive attitudes toward sexuality underscores the historical context of respondents' exposure to issues related to sex, contraception, and pregnancy. More important, attitudes toward different dimensions of sexuality and reproduction may show a cohesive structure of relationships within these social groups. This issue is dealt with in greater detail in the chapter to follow. But first we will establish the strength of the relationships among all indicators of attitudes toward sex and reproduction, and determine whether attitudes toward these issues are related to abortion attitudes.

Links Between Abortion and Sex/Reproduction

Table 4.12 shows the matrix of correlations among the seven indices of attitudes in the domain of sex and reproduction in Panel A. The first striking result is that all attitudinal measures, except for teenage parenthood, share moderate to high correlations with each other. Attitudes toward Pre-marital Sex with Commitment and Casual Pre-marital Sex are very closely associated (.60), indicating that a very permissive view toward pre-marital sex is inclusive of an acceptance of pre-marital sex in the narrower context of committed relationships. That a continuum of liberal-conservative views underlies moral responses to many dimensions of sexuality is suggested by the highly significant correlations among all indices. The lowest correlations are found between approval of teenage parenthood and all other indices. Support for a teenager's decision to carry the pregnancy to term and raise the baby is greatly enhanced due to family involvement in the decision-making process, and because respondents may view an abortion as a less desirable solution.

Panel B shows the relationship between all the sex and reproduction indices and the three abortion indices. The highest correlations are found between approval of pre-marital sex (.29 to .47), support for teenage contraception (.29 to .32), approval of artificial reproduction (.30 to .33) and all three indices of abortion. Somewhat lower, but significant correlations are found between

Table 4.12

Correlations among Sex and Reproduction Indices and Correlations with Abortion Indices.

A. Correlations among Sex and Reproduction Indices (All high scores indicate high approval)

	Pre-Marital Casual Sex	Contraception Access	Artificial Reprod.	Homosexuality	Extra-marital Sex	Teenage Parenthood
Pre-Mar Sex (Commitment)	.60 ***	.49 ***	.43 ***	.34 ***	.31 ***	.12 *
Pre-mar Sex (Casual)		.38 ***	.34 ***	.40 ***	.45 ***	.21 ***
Contraceptive Access			.41 ***	.34 ***	.22 ***	.19 ***
Artificial Reproduction				.34 ***	.25 ***	.17 **
Homosexuality					.42 ***	.16 **
Extra-Marital Sex						.11 *

N = 290

(continued)

Table 4.12 (contd.)

B. Correlations between Sex and Reproduction and Abortion Indices

---

Sex and Reproduction:	Health	Abortion Social-Pers.	Rights
Pre-marital sex with commit.	.47 ***	.31 ***	.33 ***
Casual Pre-marital sex	.29 ***	.33 ***	.37 ***
Access to Contraceptives	.32 ***	.29 ***	.32 ***
Artificial Reproduction	.32 ***	.30 ***	.33 ***
Extra-marital Sex	.18 ***	.23 ***	.23 ***
Homosexuality	.24 ***	.28 ***	.27 ***
Teenage Parenthood	-.03	-.05	-.05

*** p < .001, ** p < .01, * p < .05, + p < .10

approval of homosexuality, extra-marital sex, and abortion (.18 to
.28). A permissive view toward sexual behavior, and a respect for
choice in reproductive decisions leads to an acceptance of abortions
for a variety of reasons. The only index unrelated to abortion
attitudes is teenage parenthood, which shares very low correlations
with the three indices of abortion attitudes that are not statistically
significant (-.03 to -.05).

These results confirm our expectation that attitudes toward
various aspects of sex, contraception, and procreation share a strong
core of overlapping moral concerns, and are also significantly related
to abortion attitudes. We turn next to an examination of abortion
attitudes within the domain of gender role attitudes.

The Domain of Gender Roles

The most interesting turning point in the history of abortion
politics was the change in the constituency and issues that dominated
abortion reform until the mid 1960s. A male dominated professional
elite was replaced by women from various feminist organizations who
not only called for the repeal of all abortion laws, but defined

abortion as a woman's rights issue. Today the legality of abortion is premised upon a woman's right to privacy in reproductive decisions.

Abortion became linked to feminist politics precisely at the time when significant structural changes in gender roles began to emerge in the larger society. These changes indicated that women were entering institutions of higher education and the work force in increasing numbers, and intending to stay attached to their jobs with only short interruptions during and after childbirth. The inclusion of abortion on the agenda of organized feminist politics also suggested the shift from a earlier focus on economic issues to a consideration of sexual and reproductive issues. Today the politics of female sexuality is central to both the political and scholarly focus of feminism.

From a feminist, pro-choice perspective, the right to abortion is central to defining a woman's control over her body, and in facilitating the full participation of women in both the public and private spheres of life. It flows from this argument that those who espouse gender equality in the work place, in politics, and in the home will also affirm women's autonomy in sexual and reproductive matters. It is not clear to what extent the general public shares this sentiment. Previous studies have reported that gender role ideology is only weakly related to public attitudes toward abortion (Deitch 1983).

In the analysis that follows, we link our respondents views on various gender role issues to their attitudes toward abortion. We examine whether a liberal orientation toward women's political and economic roles, and an egalitarian view of domestic role sharing results in greater moral support for abortions. Nine statements related to contemporary gender roles were given to respondents. They were asked how strongly they agreed with each of the characterizations of gender roles and responsibilities. The exact wording of these statements appears below:

1. *There is more satisfaction in marriage and having a family than in jobs or careers.*
2. *It is all right for married women to have full time jobs as long as they do most of the housework and caring of children.*
3. *Every healthy married couple should have at least one child.*

4. *Men should share equally in all family chores, whether or not*
   their wives are employed.
5. *More women should be elected to office in the U.S.*
   Congress.
6. *Fathers and mothers should share equally in the daily*
   care of young children.
7. *Women should leave their husbands if they are*
   physically and sexually abused by their husbands.
8. *Young children develop best when they are cared for*
   only by their parents.
9. *Most pre-school children suffer emotional damage if*
   they attend day care centers while their mothers work
   full time.

These statements concern empowerment of women in national politics, salience of family life over work life, women's work roles and family responsibilities, the importance of children in marriage, parental involvement in child care, and equal sharing of childcare and domestic chores between married couples.

Preliminary findings indicated that a substantial majority of our respondents expressed liberal views toward many indicators of gender roles. Sixty-three percent of all respondents disagree that women should have primary responsibility for housework if they are employed outside the home; 62 percent disagree that every married couple should have at least one child; 77 percent agree more women should be elected to office in the U.S. congress; 88 percent agree that mothers and fathers should share equally in daily child care; 75 percent agree that men should share equally in all family chores whether or not their wives are employed; and 94 percent think that women should leave husbands who abuse them.

The two items on which there was much more variation in respondents' attitudes focused on their views toward the impact of mother's work on children's emotional development, and parents as primary caretakers of children. Nearly half of the respondents (47.5 %) agreed that children develop best only when they are cared for by their parents, and 42 percent agreed that pre-school children suffer emotional damage if they attend day care, while their mothers work full-time. In short, there is much more disagreement among respondents when they face the issue of the impact of non-traditional female roles on the welfare of children. Woolsey (1977) states that only a minority of employed mothers utilize institutional care, and most families prefer to have children cared for in their homes by relatives or non-relatives. It is interesting that a similar preference for parental control over childcare arrangements, rather than day care centers has also been found in Sweden (Popenoe 1988).

Dimensions of Gender Role Attitudes

A factor analysis of the nine items yielded three distinct factors with eigenvalues greater than 1, as shown in Table 4.13. The item loadings indicate some amount of overlap across factors 1 and 2, with factor 2 tapping a wide variety of issues that do not easily indicate a clear attitudinal construct. The items that load high on Factor 1 measure attitudes toward domestic role sharing between husbands and wives. The four items that load on Factor 2 relate to many different issues: women's primary responsibility for housework, importance of children in a marriage, empowerment of women in politics, and women's right to leave husbands who abuse them. The last two issues show negative loadings on this factor, indicating traditional views on all four issues. Factor 3 shows high loadings for two items, both of which relate to parental primacy in child care. Those who think that children develop best when they are cared for only by their parents are also likely to view women as primary parents, as they see women's work as detrimental to very young children. In response to the last item which was included as a measure of family salience, respondents stated their views on whether marriage and raising a family were more satisfying that a job or career. This item shows very low coefficients and also overlaps with factors 2 and 3. This finding has the following implication: Respondents may not rank family and work life as mutually exclusive sources of life satisfaction; rather, they are likely to consider both family life and work life as equally important. When made to choose 70 percent agreed that they would derive more satisfaction from marriage and parenting than from jobs or careers. Given very low coefficients, this item was excluded from the three indices that were constructed to represent the three dimensions of attitudes toward gender role and parenting.

We have labeled these factors Domestic Role Sharing (Factor 1), Gender Role Integration (Factor 2), and Parental Primacy (Factor 3), while acknowledging that there is a great gap between the construct

Table 4.13

Factor Analysis of Gender Role Items

	Factor		
Gender Role Items	*1*	*2*	*3*
A. *Domestic Role Sharing*			
Equal sharing of childcare	**.83**	-.17	-.07
Equal sharing of domestic chores...	**.82**	.11	-.07
B. *Gender Role Integration*			
Women primarily respon. for housework....	.04	**.74**	.15
Children must in marriage	.37	**.62**	.31
More women in Congress	.47	**-.58**	.08
Women should leave husbands who abuse them	.36	**-.56**	-.02
C. *Parental Primacy*			
Pre-school Children suffer in day care	-.03	.02	**.85**
Children should be cared for only by parents	-.12	.08	**.80**
More satisf. in marriage and family than in jobs	.06	.30	**.37**
EIGENVALUE	2.26	1.73	1.18
Proportion of Variance:	25.0	19.2	13.1

labels and the items that represent them. The factor structure indicates that attitudes toward many different issues in the domain of gender roles do not represent a single underlying construct that captures a liberal-traditional continuum. Respondents simultaneously hold liberal views toward some domains of gender roles, and more traditional views in other domains. An emphasis on egalitarian relationships in the domestic sphere is distinct from an acceptance of greater involvement of women in the public sphere (Factors 1 and 2). The index of Gender Role Integration contains items that measure a wide range of issues which do not show a clear and consistent relationship: More than three-fourths of our respondents agree that more women should be elected to national political office, and an even higher proportion agree that women should leave husbands who abuse them. Hence a traditional view as represented in this index captures views in transition. A minimal pro-natalism ('every married couple should have at least one child), and support for women's participation in the labor force as long as they also assume domestic responsibilities is found in conjunction with support for the political empowerment of women and a respect for their autonomy over the stability of marital relationships when they are physically and sexually abused by their husbands.

Where necessary, scores were reversed so that the three gender role indices show high scores in the direction of liberal views toward non-traditional gender roles and responsibilities; i.e. support for gender role integration, support for equal participation in domestic and child care activities, and low emphasis on parental/maternal primacy in child care.[9] The distribution on these scales appears in Figure 4.4. The index of Gender Role Integration and the index of Parental Primacy show considerably more variation in attitudes than the index of Domestic Role Sharing. The mean and median scores are close to the mid-point on the Gender Role Integration and the Parental Primacy indices: a median of 8 on a 13-point scale, and a median of 6 on a nine-point scale. The distribution of scores on the Domestic Role Sharing Index represents a skew toward egalitarian views. The fact that most of our respondents approve of equal involvement of couples in domestic chores and childcare, but vary to a greater extent on issues related to women's employment and parental responsibilities indicates that an ideology of equality is more easily accepted within the context of domestic relationships. Greater participation by males in domestic chores and childcare will be welcomed because it enhances the quality of marital and family relationships. On the other hand, views toward women's relative responsibilities toward work and family may evolve only gradually, because women continue to be viewed as primary parents, and the home remains the primary locus for the care of young children.

Panel:

A. *Gender Role Integration*[a]

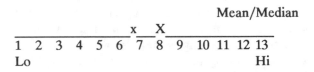

```
                                   Mean/Median
                        x    X
1   2   3   4   5   6   7   8   9   10  11  12  13
Lo                                      Hi
```

B. *Domestic Role Sharing*[b]

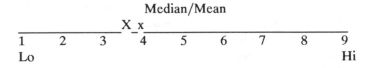

```
                  Median/Mean
                X x
1       2       3       4       5       6       7       8       9
Lo                                                              Hi
```

C. *Parental Primacy*[c]

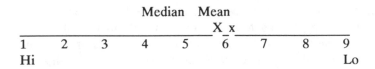

```
                  Median   Mean
                            X x
1       2       3       4       5       6       7       8       9
Hi                                                             Lo
```

Figure 4.4 Distribution Characteristics of Gender Role Indices

[a] High scores indicate high support for Gender Role Integration.
[b] High scores indicate high support for Domestic Role Sharing.
[c] High scores indicate low emphasis on Parental Primacy.

Table 4.14

Regression of Gender Role Indices[b] on Social-Group Characteristics[a]
(Unstandardized Coefficients)

Social Indicators	Gender Role Integration	Parental Primacy	Domestic Role Sharing
Catholic	-.26	-.35 [+]	.01
Church Attendance	-.05	-.20 [*]	-.01
Education	.53 [***]	.13	-.16
Female	.98 [***]	.67 [***]	-.46 [*]
Age	-.05 [***]	-.02 [**]	-.01 [*]
Solo	-.26	.15	.80 [**]
Number of Children	-.00	.12 [+]	.07
Constant	7.36 [***]	5.41 [***]	8.12 [***]
	$R^2 = .20$ [***]	$R^2 = .12$ [***]	$R^2 = .09$ [***]

[a] Variable direction and deleted categories appear in Table 4.4
[b] High scores on Gender Role Integration, Domestic Role sharing, and Parental Primacy indicate high support for non-traditional gender roles.
[***] $p < .001$, [**] $p < .01$, [*] $p < .05$, [+] $p < .10$

Social-Group Differences in Gender Role Ideology

We now examine whether a common set of social-group variables help explain the variation in attitudes toward the three dimensions of gender roles. Table 4.14 shows the three regression equations in which religion, education, gender, and life course characteristics of respondents have been entered as predictors of attitudes toward gender roles and parenting. The two most important predictors of gender role ideology are gender and age. The negative impact of age on gender role attitudes indicates that older respondents hold a more traditional perspective on the relationships between married couples, and the roles they assume as parents, spouses, and breadwinners.

Older respondents emphasize greater parental involvement in raising young children, and prefer gender role segregation in domestic and child rearing activities.

Gender differences on these issues indicate that women are more liberal than men on two of the three dimensions of gender roles. Women hold less traditional views toward women's public and political roles, are less likely to emphasize parental primacy in child care, but more likely to detract from an emphasis on egalitarian sharing of domestic roles. These findings indicate the salience of both work and family roles in women's lives, such that women may welcome greater opportunities for participation in the economic and political sphere, while still wishing to maintain their autonomy and status within the family. By contrast, single men and women are apt to reject role segregation and support more egalitarian sharing of domestic responsibilities between couples. This emphasis on gender equality among single and divorced men and women may result from their own life circumstances that involve dual responsibilities of both work and family life. Several studies have noted that couples revert to traditional roles in child care and house care responsibilities when they become parents, even when they come to these relationships with egalitarian expectations (LaRossa and LaRossa 1980).

Another important point to note is that religion has a minimal relationship to gender role attitudes. A high frequency of church attendance is positively related to an emphasis on parental involvement in child socialization. In other words traditional religiosity is more likely to influence values individuals bring to child socialization rather than gender roles. But the overall relationship between religion and gender role attitudes is quite weak, compared to the significant influence of religious views on attitudes in the domain of human life values, and sex and reproduction.

Links between Abortion and Gender Roles

In concluding our analysis we explore the relationship among the three dimensions of gender role ideology, and determine the strength of relationships between a liberal sex-role ideology and support for abortions. Table 4.15 shows the correlations among all the gender role and abortion indices. First, all three indices - Parental Primacy, Gender Role Integration, and Domestic Role Sharing show very low correlations among them (.25, .10, .12). A moderate positive

Table 4.15
Correlations among Gender Role Indices and Correlations with Abortion Indices

	Gender Roles			Abortion		
	Parental Primacy	Role Integration	Domestic Sharing	Health	Social Personal	Rights
Parental Primacy[a]		.25***	.10*	.17**	.09	.17**
Gender Role Integration[b]			.12*	.16**	.18***	.20***
Domestic Role Sharing[c]				.14*	.07	.02

N = 284

[a] High scores indicate low emphasis on Parental Primacy.
[b] High scores indicate high support for Gender Role Integration.
[c] High scores indicate high support for Domestic Role Sharing.

*** p < .001, ** p < .01, * p < .05, + p < .10

relationship is found between support for gender role integration and a lower emphasis on parental primacy in childcare (.25). Those who support women's autonomy and involvement in the public spheres of work and politics are also more apt to recognize advantages of non-familial care of children.

All of the gender role indices show significant, but very low correlations with abortion attitudes (.02 to .20). In other words, support and opposition to abortion is largely independent of our respondents views toward women's public and political roles. The direction of these associations is as expected: The positive correlations imply that a support for gender equality in both public and private spheres is positively linked to greater support for abortions. But there is no strong evidence in these data that our respondents' position on gender roles shapes their position on abortion. In concluding this chapter we will show that abortion morality overlaps to a greater extent with human life values, and norms concerning sexuality and reproduction, and only marginally with gender role ideology.

The Ideational Context of Abortion

Our analysis so far has shown the dimensionality of attitudes and beliefs in four major domains: abortion, human life, sex and reproduction, and gender roles , and demonstrated the ways in which the dimensionality of beliefs and attitudes are linked to social-group characteristics of respondents. The factor structure of beliefs and attitudes in each domain also indicated non-overlapping moral concerns that relate to specific issues. From another perspective various dimensions of attitudes and beliefs within each of the four domains showed an underlying ideological coherence. Furthermore, specific indicators of human life values, sexual and reproductive norms, and gender role ideology relate significantly to abortion attitudes. All of the analysis was aimed at placing abortion attitudes within the context of an individual belief structure. As a fitting conclusion to this chapter, we pool significant and relevant indicators of attitudes within each domain, and show the correlations between summated indices that capture the variation in beliefs in the four domains.

We used two criteria in selecting indices to construct the final summated index of all four domains. The first concerned a significant moderate relationship between a particular dimension and all other dimensions of attitudes within a belief domain. The second concerned significant correlations between an attitudinal index and the three abortion indices. Two attitudinal scales were dropped on the basis of these criteria: The Personal-Social Suicide index and the Teenage Parenthood index. Both indices showed highly skewed distributions, and very low correlations with abortion attitudes. Clearly, the relationships among all the gender role indices were quite low, which suggested that this domain as represented by our measures does not relate to abortion attitudes. But for comparative purposes we include a summated scale of the three gender role indices in the analysis that follows.

A second goal of our analysis of the abortion belief structure concerned the relationship between two different measures of abortion attitudes based upon survey and vignette data. Hence we pool all three survey indices (Rights, Social-Personal, and Health) to represent the Survey Abortion Index, and use the Mean Vignette Rating to represent the Vignette Abortion Index. We show that these two measures of abortion attitudes are highly correlated at this aggregate level, and also share a similar relationship to the three other attitudinal domains.

Table 4.16 shows the correlations between five summated indices that represent the Survey Abortion Index, the Vignette Abortion index, the Human Life Attitude Index, the Sex and Reproduction Index, and the Gender Role Index. The first striking result is that the relationship between the Survey and Vignette abortion indices is very strong (.80). Both indices are rich measures of abortion attitudes in a wide variety of contexts, and the high correlation demonstrates the internal validity of responses to abortion vignettes and abortion items. Note also that the two abortion scales share a very similar relationship to all other attitude domains: the correlations with the Human Life Index is .61 and .56; the correlations with the Sex and Reproduction Index is .48 and .44; and the correlations with the Gender Role Index is .23 and .22. In short, two independent measures of abortion attitudes that are based upon a different methodological and conceptual formulation capture the essence of the abortion belief structure. Second, the correlations show strong linkages between abortion attitudes and attitudes in the domains of

Table 4.16
Correlations among Abortion, Human Life, Sexuality, and Gender Role Domains

Domain Indices[a]	Abortion(S)	Abortion(V)	Human Life	Sexuality	Gender Roles
Abortion (Survey)		.80 ***	.61 ***	.48 ***	.23 ***
Abortion (Vignette)			.56 ***	.44 ***	.22 ***
Human Life				.42 ***	.24 ***
Sex and Reproduction					.40 ***

*** p < .001

Human life, and Sex and Reproduction, and weak linkages between abortion attitudes and gender role ideology. The strength of relationships among all four belief domains also suggests a greater overlap between abortion and other human life issues, followed by strong links between abortion and the domain of sexuality, and only a moderate overlap between abortion morality and sex role ideology. But note that the index of gender role attitudes shares the strongest relationship with attitudes toward sex and reproduction (.40). Hence it is possible that abortion morality and gender role ideology share an indirect relationship: A non-traditional view of gender roles may facilitate greater tolerance of abortions when individuals also hold liberal views in the domain of sex and reproduction. Among the three domains of abortion, sex and reproduction, and human life, highly significant inter-correlations point to an underlying unity to the values our respondents bring to issues within these domains.

A secular, relativistic view of human life, a permissive orientation to sexuality, and an emphasis on individual discretion in parenting and abortion decisions are internally consistent. On the other hand, a respect for the absolute value of human life, and a closely integrated view of sex and procreation leads to an opposition to various forms of non-traditional sexuality, reproduction, and is also expressed in a moral opposition to abortions. The analysis of social-group differences among respondents throughout this chapter indicated that our respondents' life course position, past reproductive experiences, and religiosity explain significant variation in the views they express toward many topics within the four major domains. The variation in beliefs and attitudes along social group characteristics of respondents also provides a clue to the interaction of social-structural factors, historical changes, and abortion values. The influence of two social-group variables is of particular interest to an interpretation of the belief structure underlying abortion attitudes.

Age and church attendance showed a significant and consistent relationship to many of the topics investigated in this chapter. The influence of church attendance, which is used as a proxy for religiosity, implies that opposition to abortion, euthanasia, suicide, a respect for fetal life, and an opposition to sexual promiscuity are rooted in the salience of religious values which provide an overarching framework for the values and beliefs individuals bring to bear upon many life decisions. A traditional value orientation, based upon the salience of religion cuts across religious affiliation. A key finding in our analysis is that Catholics continue to differ from Non-Catholics only on the abortion issue, but not on a number of other issues related to sex, contraception, and pregnancy. In other words, a conservative morality on abortion, sex, reproduction, and gender roles may characterize a homogenous core of individuals who continue to adhere to traditional religious practices.

Age differences were significant in respondents' perception of various issues related to sexuality, gender roles, and reproduction. Greater conservatism among older respondents compared to younger respondents suggests cohort differences in their exposure to changes in gender roles and sexual behavior. Abortion morality varied less as a function of respondents' age, and more as a function of their past reproductive experiences. In light of our findings in Table 4.14, the centrality of human life issues to abortion morality leads to less significant differences in moral views as a function of respondents' historical position. Human life values are deeply entrenched and are more resistant to change, whereas norms in the domains of sexuality and gender roles have undergone dramatic changes in recent decades. Another implication of the patterns of age effects found for the four belief domains is that the ideological coherence of abortion, sexuality, human life values, and gender role ideology will be stronger among younger cohorts of respondents than older cohorts of respondents.

The political-ideological links among the four domains have surfaced over the course of the history of abortion politics. Human life values have been central to abortion morality for a much longer period of time, just as sexual and reproductive norms have shaped reproductive experiences. It is only in recent times that an ideological link has been forged between the politics of abortion and the politics of women's rights within the context of a feminist movement. The link between gender ideology and abortion morality also rests upon structural changes in the experiences of work and family life, and normative expectations individuals bring to marriage, parenthood, and gender roles. Favorable views toward women's autonomy and control over reproductive decisions will arise from a perception of the links between changing gender roles and their consequences for sexual and reproductive lifestyles. However, abortion attitudes are embedded in a complex and sometimes competing set of beliefs about the value of human life, the meaning of sexuality and procreation, and the rights and obligations individuals bring to intimate relationships. A very high value placed on human life is relaxed only to avoid pain and suffering of a terminally ill patient, or out of a compassion for a variety of stressful situations faced by pregnant women, when their lives take precedence over fetal life at least in the early stages of pregnancy. In this sense our respondents are not split between a pro-choice and a pro-life view of abortions - they are both pro-choice and pro-life when they express an 'instinctive uneasiness at terminating a form of innocent human life', as well as 'compassion for women who may be frightened and lonely in the face of a major crisis.' (Glendon 1987:46).

Summary

Two issues were central to the analysis of this chapter. In the first major part of this chapter, the analysis centered around the abortion belief structure, the relationship between abortion morality and political views, and the social bases of variation in abortion attitudes. In the second part of this chapter, we shifted attention to three other belief domains to explore the links between abortion, human life values, sexual and reproductive norms, and gender role ideology. The analyses of the four belief domains centered around both the dimensionality and ideological coherence that underlies beliefs and attitudes in each of the four domains. We summarize the highlights of the preceding analysis and trace the implications of selected findings for the issues that will be addressed in the next chapter.

Abortion Belief Structure

Two different methodological approaches were used to represent the abortion belief structure, and a comparison of the results from the vignette and conventional survey approaches showed a very similar structure of attitudes toward abortion. Approval of abortions vary in response to reasons women provide for their abortion decisions, and the abortion belief structure revealed distinctions in moral positions based upon Health, Social-Personal, and Rights dimensions of abortion situations. Respondents who limit their tolerance of abortion on health grounds are least apt to view abortions as the uncontested right of individual women. On the other hand, a highly individualized perspective of abortion as the right of pregnant women facilitates a tolerance of a variety of pregnancy circumstances as justifiable grounds for abortion.

Our analyses also revealed an interesting pattern of relationships between abortion morality and political support for abortion groups. Moral approval of abortions was consistently linked to a high positive support for the pro-choice position on abortion, and negatively linked to support for the pro-life position on abortion. Support for the pro-choice and pro-life positions on abortion showed a very high negative correlation, suggesting that a support for the two political groups is perceived as highly incompatible when they present no middle ground even on health grounds for abortion. A liberal political orientation was only weakly related to abortion views and to support for abortion groups: In other words, pro-life and pro-choice support, and moral approval of abortions is   represented among both liberals and conservatives. The chapter that follows examines the abortion belief structure within sub-groups of respondents defined by age, religious affiliation, and gender, using the age of respondents primarily as a marker of the social-historical context of their exposure to the abortion issue.

The Ideational Context of Abortion

The second major section of this chapter was devoted to the analysis of both the dimensionality and ideological coherence that characterizes the four belief domains: abortion, sex and reproduction, gender roles, and human life issues. Attitudes toward euthanasia and suicide showed a belief structure that was very similar to the abortion belief structure: tolerance of euthanasia and suicide are distinguished on the basis of health versus social-personal factors just as moral approval of abortions vary by health and social-personal factors surrounding a pregnancy. Second, abortion attitudes were significantly related to views toward Terminal-illness suicide and euthanasia, but showed stronger links to respondents' beliefs about fetal life and personhood. We found that there is very little consensus among respondents' in when they define the beginning of human life, and this variation is crucial to understanding the variety of beliefs individuals bring to the abortion issue.

Within the domain of sex and reproduction, we found that attitudes toward pre-marital sex, minors' access to contraception, extra-marital sex and homosexuality project distinct dimensions of sexual morality, and at the same time beliefs and attitudes on each of these topics overlap significantly to suggest ideological coherence within the domain of sex and reproduction. Another important finding was the very high level of support for teenage parenthood and the lack of any significant relationship between support for teenage parenthood and support for abortions. When the issue of teenage parenthood is posed within the context of the competing views of parents and boyfriends, and when the alternative to parenthood is perceived as abortion, many respondents are willing to tolerate unmarried parenthood. This also implies that normative departures from the sequencing of marriage and parenthood may be more easily tolerated than attempts to prevent parenthood once a pregnancy is in progress.

Our findings on the domain of Gender Roles showed weak relationships between abortion attitudes and attitudes toward female empowerment, gender role integration, domestic role sharing, and parental primacy. The majority of our respondents showed liberal views on many contemporary issues related to empowerment of women in politics, work, and the family. On the other hand, respondents were divided on their views concerning parental control and primacy in childcare activities. There is some suggestion in our data that the relationship between abortion attitudes and gender role ideology may be mediated through the values in the domain of sexuality and reproduction. The concluding analysis of this chapter showed that abortion values are embedded within a larger framework of an individual belief structure such that an individuals' views toward abortion are meaningfully linked to their views toward the sanctity of human life and values toward sex and reproduction. In the next chapter we show that the links between the four belief domains varies as a function of respondents' age, and hence reflects the historical changes in the politics of abortion.

Social-Group Bases of Value Dissensus

At various points throughout this chapter we explained the dimensionality of belief domains through a focus on selected social-group characteristics of respondents. Religion, church attendance, and education were used as indicators of religious and secular value orientations, and age, marital status, and parity were used to show the influence of life course position, and personal reproductive experiences on beliefs and attitudes. In abortion domain, the variation in respondents' views were significantly related to religious affiliation, church attendance, personal exposure to abortions, and parity. On topics related to sex and reproduction, value dissensus for the most part reflected the influence of age, religion, education, and gender. And in the domain of gender roles, age and gender were the two most significant predictors of a liberal-conservative sex-role ideology. Based on these findings we shift our analyses in the next chapter to sub-groups of the sample defined by age, religion, and gender and explore both the variations in the abortion belief structure, and the larger belief structure within which abortion values are embedded.

Notes

1. For an excellent collection of critical pro-choice and pro-life perspectives on the politics of abortion see Callahan and Callahan, 1984.

2. Four levels describing health reasons, 6 describing social-personal conditions, and one blank level was included in the vignette dimension. So we expect each respondent to receive approximately 7 of 20 vignettes that included health grounds for abortion, 11 that relate to social-personal reasons, and the remaining 3 vignettes where no particular reason was mentioned.

3. Vignettes with blank levels were omitted from this analysis. The analysis in the previous chapter did indicate that the level of approval for vignettes where no reason was provided for an abortion was low but not significantly different from the level of approval found for the discretionary reasons for abortion.

4. The telephone survey preceded the mailing of vignettes. Hence the completed sample for the telephone survey is larger ($n = 291$) than the sample for the vignette survey ($n = 217$). We also found no systematic bias in terms of sex, age, or religion, among those who did not complete the vignette surveys compared to those who did.

5. The interaction between gender and marital status was discussed in the previous chapter, where we found that solo women are more approving of abortion decisions made by solo women than solo men. In contrast to this pattern, married men are more liberal toward abortion decisions made by married women than married women themselves are.

6. We do not include the fourth index of Couple Dissensus. This index showed a highly skewed distribution and abortion attitudes measures by this index did not differ significantly by any of our social-group indicators. Hence the regression equation with this index showed no statistical significance on any independent predictor variable.

7. Only 7 percent said "don't know" and they were placed between early pregnancy and viability on the scale.

8. The terms 'genetic', 'nurturing', and 'carrying' parent are used by Snowden, Mitchell, and Snowden (1983) in their attempt to construct a terminology to understand the social implications of artificial reproduction: 'For a woman to be called a 'mother', for example, we would usually expect her to be responsible for the production of the ovum which provides half the germ cells of the child, the pregnancy and birth of the child and the care of the child after its birth....In the usual situation the male who produces and delivers the sperm and who cares for the resulting child after its birth is the same person, and fulfills the role of 'father"(1983:31). With the exception of adoption, and now artificial reproduction, mothering has involved genetic, carrying, and nurturing functions; fathering has involved genetic and nurturing functions.

9. It is difficult to view a high emphasis on parental control over childcare versus control by others (day care centers, non-relatives) as fitting into a traditional-liberal view toward parenting. Presently, a dissatisfaction concerning cost and quality of available childcare arrangements may influence preference for parental control over the care of young children. Second, it is not clear to what extent the recent concern over child abuse has influenced a strong preference for not involving strangers in unsupervised care of young children. The correlations among all three gender role indices suggest that an emphasis on parental primacy is positively correlated with a traditional view of gender role integration (.25). Hence we reversed this index to conform in direction to the two other gender role indices.

5

Age, Religion and Gender

I was talking with my niece and her friend -- both of them
are professionals in their mid-twenties -- about the changes
that have occurred in the past twenty years. I was
describing how painful it was for me when I was nineteen
and had to get married. They both looked at me as if I
had two heads and said, 'Why didn't you get an abortion?'
I said, 'Because it was illegal!' and they both just sort of
stared at me. Then they said, 'Oh...yeah...' (quoted in
Messer and May 1988:xi).

Within their life time our oldest respondents have witnessed the
transformation of abortion from a private, illegal experience to one
that is a topic of public, political debate. From their perspective,
many aspects of contemporary abortion decisions are likely to reflect
significant changes in values concerning marriage, sex, parenthood,
and gender roles. A whole generation of Americans reached sexual
maturity in the aftermath of the legalization of abortions in 1973. To
these young men and women, a safe, legal abortion has always been
a readily available option - but an option that has become fraught
with complex moral and political concerns.

In this chapter, we attempt to place our respondents' views
toward abortion within the historical context in which they attained
sexual maturity and faced personal decisions concerning sex,
contraception, and pregnancy. We examine age differences in
attitudes toward abortion to index the differential impact of historical
changes in the abortion issue on respondents' views, as a function of

the intersection of respondents' age and historical time. The study sample was stratified into four age groups: 19-25, 26-40, 41-60, and 61-over to facilitate the analysis of age differences in attitudes toward abortion. Respondents in these four groups straddle much variation in their current life course position and in their exposure to past historical events. The reproductive years from 15 to 45 represent a crucial period in the life course of individuals when their attitudes toward marriage, sex, contraception, abortion, and related issues are formed, and perhaps are most amenable to change as a result of life experiences. By anchoring our adult respondents' sexual and reproductive lives in historical time, we can examine the impact of social change on their attitudes toward abortion.

A second topic explored in this chapter concerns the interaction of age and religious affiliation to test for cohort differences in the attitudes of young and old Catholics and non-Catholics. The comparison of belief structures between the two groups will further illuminate the ways in which Catholics and non-Catholics responded to changes in the moral and political issues related to abortion.

A third topic deals with the views men and women bring to the abortion issue. In the analysis of gender differences in abortion attitudes in the previous chapters, we found that men and women do not differ in the extent to which they approve of abortion decisions based on a variety of life circumstances. On the other hand significant gender differences in views found in other closely related belief domains can result in different ways in which men and women link their position on abortion with their position on sexuality, reproduction, human life issues, and gender role ideology.

Ideally, an analysis of cohort effects requires repeat measures of attitudes at many points in time for different birth cohorts. The absence of such data complicates the interpretation of age differences in attitudes: Observed differences across age groups at any one point in time suggest multiple effects of maturation, life course position, and cohort composition. Hence we begin our discussion in this chapter with a review of key areas of change in the abortion issue, and provide a conceptual framework that facilitates the interpretation of cohort differences using cross-sectional data. Within the backdrop of this conceptual framework, we sketch the profile of the four age groups of respondents used in the analyses that follow.

Age, History, and Attitudes Toward Abortion

Three areas of change in the abortion issue spanning the past three decades are particularly relevant to the analyses in this chapter: 1) change in the characteristics of women experiencing abortions, 2) the shift from an emphasis on health issues to moral concerns, 3) the legalization of abortion, followed by the incorporation of a highly polarized moral issue into mainstream politics.

The Experience of Abortions

An important demographic shift triggered the emergence of abortion politics in the late 19th century: a change in the characteristics of women having abortions. According to Mohr(1978), estimates of abortion during the 1850s and 1860s range from 1 in 5 pregnancies to 1 in 4 pregnancies: These figures were in sharp contrast to an estimate of 1 abortion in every 25 pregnancies during the early decades of the 19th century. From an experience that involved unmarried women who wished to prevent an illegitimate birth, abortions became increasingly used by married women who wished to limit births beyond their desired family size. This shift in the characteristics of women who had abortions resulted in an increased demand for abortions. Subsequently, the campaigns for professional legitimacy on the part of 19th century physicians centered around efforts to regulate legal access to abortions.

For centuries abortion had remained a private decision made within the context of the immediate family, and no laws regulated the performance of abortions. Public opinion on abortion was not an issue that concerned professional physicians who campaigned for restrictive abortion laws in the late 19th century. In fact, physicians argued that pregnant women who sought abortions were ignorant about the scientific facts related to pregnancy and fetal development, because women identified the onset of a pregnancy with 'quickening'. In other words, physicians based their opposition to abortions on claims to scientific knowledge of pregnancy and fetal development. The focus on technical issues thus discouraged public involvement in the abortion issue in the 19th century (Luker 1984).

Table 5.1
Abortion Trends and Percent Distribution of Legal Abortions by Age,
Marital Status, and Parity: United States, 1973, 1978, 19831

	1973	1978	1983
% *Distribution by Age*[2]			
13-14		1.1	1.0
15-17	32.8	12.0	10.6
18-19		17.7	15.5
20-24	32.3	34.7	34.8
25-29	17.4	18.9	20.8
30-34	9.7	9.5	10.9
35-39	5.5	4.6	5.0
40-44	2.3	1.5	1.4
% *Distribution by Marital Status* [3]			
Married	29.0	23.5	18.7
Solo	71.0	76.5	81.3
% *Distribution by Parity*			
None	55.2	56.7	56.5
One	15.4	19.2	20.9
Two	13.9	14.0	14.4
Three	8.1	5.9	5.3
More than three	7.4	4.2	2.9

[1] Source: Tables 32.1, 32.3, 32.4, 32.5 International Handbook on Abortion. Sachdev (1988).
[2] 1973 data shows combined percentage of abortions among women 19 years or less.
[3] Solo=Never married, divorced, widowed, separated.

On the other hand, the 19th century abortion laws that distinguished between therapeutic (abortions to save the life of the mother) and criminal abortions (all other reasons for abortion) had little impact on the actual incidence of abortions (Luker 1984). Abortions to limit family size or prevent births during harsh economic times (such as the Depression) were key factors behind illegal abortions during the first half of the 20th century. Hence the strict laws against abortion, which resulted in increased medical control over legal access to abortions, shaped public perception of permissible and criminal abortions for almost a century, until the dramatic change in the 1970s culminating in the 1973 Supreme Court decision.

A second significant demographic shift in the characteristics of women who obtained abortions became evident in the 1970s with much attention focused on the prevention of births outside of marriage and toward the postponement of first births by married women. National trend data on the incidence of abortions, collected annually since the legalization of abortions in 1973, reveal significant information about women who have abortions. Table 5.1 shows the trends in legal abortions by age, marital status, and parity of pregnant women in five year intervals from 1973 to 1983.

In 1973, 71 percent of all women who had an abortion were unmarried; a decade later, more than four-fifths of all women who had an abortion were unmarried. The age distribution in all three time periods shows that the majority of women who have abortions are in their teens or early to mid-twenties. In 1983, 27.1 percent of all women obtaining abortions were under 19 years of age; 35 percent were between 20 and 24 years of age; 21 percent were between 25 and 29 years of age; 11 percent in their early thirties, 5 percent in their late thirties, and 1 percent over forty years of age. Over two-thirds of abortion clients are under 24 years of age, less than a third in their prime childbearing years, and an overwhelming majority are unmarried.

The average parity of women at the time of an abortion is even more revealing. More than 50 percent of all women who have abortions have had no previous births. In 1973, only 15.5 percent of all women who had an abortion had three or more children - This figure declined to 8.2 percent by 1983. These figures suggest that family size limitation as a reason for abortion characterizes only a smaller percentage of all women who currently seek abortions. Many women resort to abortions to postpone parenthood or to space the desired number of childbirths - reasons that are in sharp contrast to the experiences of earlier reproductive cohorts who were more apt to have sought an illegal abortion to prevent additional births, when they had already given birth to three or more children. During these same years an increasing proportion of women who achieved their desired family size resorted to sterilization, thus undercutting the probability of further unwanted pregnancies and any need for abortion as a solution.

In summary, the age, marital status, and parity characteristics of abortion clients convey two important messages about the sexual and reproductive experience of contemporary American women. First, the proportion of abortion clients beyond age 35 tapers to a small minority due to increased reliance on sterilization by married couples who have achieved their desired family size (Sachdev 1988). Second, the increases in pre-marital sexual activity and in delayed marriage and childbearing since the 1960s have resulted in a significant proportion of women who have abortions in the early phase of their reproductive lives. Prevention of pre-marital births and postponement of first births emerge as significant reasons behind contemporary abortion decisions. The implication of these trends for our analyses is as follows: Our elderly respondents who completed their childbearing in the 1940s and 1950s are more apt to recall illegal abortions experienced by married women in their later years of childbearing. By contrast young respondents in their twenties in 1987 are more likely to have been exposed to legal abortion experiences of peers in high school or college. A first glimpse of these cohort differences was provided in Chapter 3, where we showed that respondents over 60 years of age were more approving of abortion decisions made by women in their forties, while respondents in their early twenties were most approving of abortion decisions made by teenage women.

Abortion Morality and Abortion Politics

In addition to the changes in the legal status and the personal experience of abortions, the moral concerns central to the abortion issue have also changed during the past few decades. Long-term shifts in patterns of sex, marriage, and childbearing which became apparent in the 1960s set the stage for the consideration of abortion as an issue involving sexual and reproductive rights. Critical events surrounding the abortion debate took place during the years when the oldest age group of respondents (60 and over) had already completed their childbearing, and the youngest age group (19 through 26) attained sexual maturity. Efforts to reform abortion laws, spearheaded by professionals in law and medicine in the 1950s, centered around health risks of illegal abortions (Rossi and Sitaraman 1988). By contrast, in the mid 1960s the abortion issue became a women's rights issue.

The involvement of the National Organization for Women in the 1960s resulted in strengthening the view of the right to abortion as an integral part of the political, economic, and reproductive rights of individual women. Feminist involvement in the abortion issue also had the effect of moving the abortion issue into the realm of popular political discussion. But the shift from an exclusive focus on maternal health to reproductive rights has also encouraged the consideration of other moral issues. At present, support for abortions is cast within the framework of sexual and reproductive freedom, while opposition to abortions centers around issues related to the sanctity and protection of fetal life, and the relative rights of parents and spouses in abortion decisions. The focus on rights of unmarried women and minors has evolved in response to the fact that the majority of women who resort to abortions today are unmarried and/or minors.

Legalization of abortions in 1973 is a historical benchmark from which to assess the above mentioned changes. First, the proportion of pregnancies ending in abortions increased in all age groups of women between 1973 and 1985 from 19 percent to 30 percent (Sachdev 1988). This increased incidence may have contributed to heightened public knowledge of abortions as more friends, lovers, wives, and daughters resorted to abortions. Second, the abortion issue set the precedent for the resolution of other moral issues through legal and political channels. Lifestyle and personal morality issues have played an important role in mainstream politics throughout the 1980s. Candidates for elective office as well as appointive posts are judged in terms of personal ethics in addition to their formal positions on matters they may legislate on. Hence the definition of political liberalism or conservatism in the 1980s includes an individual's stance on marriage, family, and morality along with political positions on such issues as defense spending, social welfare, and domestic economic affairs. In the abortion context, this trend has actually intensified with the Supreme Court decision in the Webster Case that shifted greater control over abortion laws to the states.

The mayoral elections in many cities across the nation, and the elections for the governors of New Jersey and Virginia became test cases for the political salience of the abortion issue. Candidates who hold moderate positions on the issue are now forced to take a stand, as many local pro-choice organizations are attempting to show that the young and women are willing to vote on the abortion issue. According to some political analysts, abortion is to the youth of the 1980s what the Vietnam War was to the youth of 1960s (New York Times 1989). The importance of the abortion issue in mainstream politics points to broader changes in the definition of political liberalism and conservatism. These will be reflected in the ways in which young and old respondents incorporate their moral views toward abortion, sexuality, human life, and gender roles into their overall political orientation. Today, a permissive view toward sexual matters and life style issues among young respondents is more likely to coincide with a liberal political orientation. By contrast, older respondents who reached adulthood in an earlier era are more likely to exempt their moral views on issues such as abortion, pre-marital sex, homosexuality, euthanasia, and women's rights from their overall political orientation.

Empirical Evidence on Cohort Effects

To our knowledge, there are no empirical studies to date that deal with age differences in abortion values from a cohort perspective. But there is some evidence from those that focus on a number of other social and political issues, which show that attitudes and values are shaped during an individual's adolescence and youth, and tend to remain stable thereafter. In other words, "cohorts develop distinctive meaning-giving universes early in life and seem to maintain them throughout their adulthood". (Lesthaeghe and Surkyn 1988:40). Of particular relevance to us is the recent analysis of European Value Studies by Lesthaeghe and Surkyn (1988). They relate shifts in fertility patterns to long-term secular trends in value orientation among successive birth cohorts in Western Europe. Their work suggests that secularization (measured in terms of declining adherence to institutional religion) and individuation (an emphasis on individual discretion in personal morality) are two facets of long term changes in value orientations. Young respondents emphasize greater individual discretion in matters related to family, religion, morality,and politics; whereas older respondents show more conservative views on many issues in these same domains.

In another study of collective memories of a sample of the American population, Schuman and Scott(1989) asked their respondents to recall two important national and world events that took place during the past 50 years. Respondents were more likely to mention events that happened during their adolescence or youth: Respondents who are currently 60 years of age or older were more likely to mention the Depression and World War II, while respondents in their thirties and forties recall the Vietnam War. Their findings point to early adulthood as the critical point in the life course of individuals, when historical events have an important impact on their orientation toward social and political issues.

The rationale for viewing adolescence and youth as developmental stages holding the maximum potential for attitude formation and change is as follows. During adolescence and youth individuals are inducted into the larger world of school, work, and politics. During this same period they also experience a close timing of critical life events: school completion, moving out of parents' home, taking up the first full-time job, marriage, and parenthood. Within the domain of sexual and reproductive issues, we suggest that attitudes are most likely to be shaped in adolescence and youth as individuals reach sexual maturity and face decisions regarding sex, pregnancy, contraception, and abortion. These are also issues that they are less likely to communicate with parents, and so more open to influences from peers and the larger society. The personal salience of these issues will be heightened during the reproductive life span of individuals. The values they bring to these decisions, and the decisions they form set the stage for further changes in their attitudes and values. By contrast topics such as national security or defense spending are less likely to be bound by personal position on the life course. Change in attitudes may occur as much in one age group as another.

For example, Thornton, Alwin, and Camburn(1982) trace trends in sex role attitudes among women and their children from 1962 to 1980 and show that while mothers and daughters shifted toward more egalitarian views over time, the change was greater among daughters

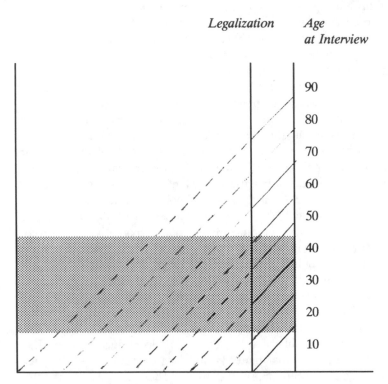

Adapted from Riley(1987) and Rossi(1990).

Figure 5.1 : Age and Historical Time: Cross-sectional Analysis versus Cohort Analysis

than mothers. In short, the potential for attitudinal change may exist at all ages, but personal experiences relevant to such changes will play a role, such that the potential for change in beliefs and attitudes concerning sexual and reproductive matters is greatest among those who are themselves in the early reproductive phase of the life course.

Profile of Age Groups

In Figure 5.1 we map the conceptual framework that will facilitate an interpretation of cohort differences with cross-sectional data. The horizontal axis in Figure 5.1 represents historical time over the decades from 1900 to 2000. The extreme far right vertical axis presents the age of respondents in ten year intervals at the time of interview (Year = 1987). A second vertical axis runs through the year 1973 marking the legalization of abortion, and provides an historical date to assess the experiences of respondents both before and after legalization. The shaded area across the graph shows the reproductive phase spanning ages 15 to 45 for various birth cohorts. Using the current age of respondents as a reference point we can project back to the historical era during which they spent their childbearing years. The bold diagonal lines represent age after legalization, and the dash lines represent age prior to legalization. The following profile of the four age groups in terms of their historical exposure to social changes and their current life course position is based upon this conceptual scheme.

60-89:

Respondents now in their sixties were born during the Depression of the 1930s. Those in their seventies and eighties were adolescents during that same period, and suffered the most impact of the economic depression. A significant minority remained unmarried or childless, and may have experienced illegal abortions to postpone or prevent the birth of a child. Many later benefitted from the post war prosperity and contributed toward the baby boom of the 1940s and 1950s. All of these individuals were well past their reproductive ages when the turbulent 60s challenged their values and beliefs on topics such as marriage, sexuality, gender roles and parenting. Ten percent of our sample in this age group report either a personal experience of abortion or knowledge of the experience of a friend or relative.

41-60:

Men and women now in their forties were born in the 1940s during or after World War II. Those in their fifties were born between the boom and bust cycle of the 1930s. Respondents who are now between 41 and 60 were between 27 and 46 in 1973 when abortion became legalized. Some were actively involved in the campaign for the rights of racial minorities and women during the 1960s. In contrast to the older age group, 35 percent of respondents in this age group report a personal experience of abortion or knowledge of the abortion experience of friends and relatives.

26-40:

Respondents in this age group are currently in different phases of their reproductive lives. Those in their thirties were in their teens when abortions were legalized and have spent much of their prime child bearing years since legalization. Born during the boom of the 1950s, this age group came of age during the economically difficult times of the 1970s. Close to half of all respondents in this age group report an abortion experienced by themselves, or a friend, or a relative.

19-25:

The youngest respondents were born in the post baby boom era. Many are still in college or working adults who have not yet married. Currently, 83 percent of our respondents in this age group are still childless and 72 percent have not yet married. This group attained sexual maturity in the aftermath of legalization, and show a similar profile of exposure to abortions as those in their late twenties and thirties. They were between 5 and 11 years of age when abortion was legalized: Hence as they became sexually mature, legal abortions were readily available.

The four age groups of respondent have spent their reproductive years during different historical phases of the abortion debate. While the sharpest distinctions in historical backgrounds emerge between the very young respondents and the oldest respondents, all respondents under 60 years of age have spent some portion of their childbearing years during a time when abortions for a variety of personal-social reasons were legal and easily available. We now turn to the first set of analyses that show differences in the abortion belief structure between our young and old respondents.

Age and the Ideational Context of Abortion

We investigate three topics in this analysis of age differences in the abortion attitudes: 1) the dimensionality of abortion attitudes 2) the link between abortion attitudes and respondents' political orientation, and 3) the larger ideational context within which abortions attitudes are embedded. The earlier empirical chapters discussed the dimensionality of abortion attitudes in two contexts: first, in the case of the dimensions of hypothetical abortion situations; and second, in terms of the distinctions drawn between the health, social-personal, and rights issues involved in abortion decisions. We concluded that the health, social-personal, and rights dimensions of abortion attitudes represented a liberal-conservative continuum of moral views toward abortion. Respondents who approved of abortions, even if the woman's parent or spouse was against the abortion decision, were also likely to endorse a wide variety of social-personal circumstances as valid justifications for an abortion. By contrast, respondents who restricted their approval of abortions to rape, fetal deformity, or harm to the mother's health were least likely to support a woman's abortion decision, if it went against the views of partners, parents, and spouses. We now explore the change in the abortion belief structure over time by examining the structure of relationships among the health, social-personal, and rights dimensions of abortion attitudes within the four age groups of respondents.

Panels A through D of Table 5.2, show the correlations among the Health, Social-Personal, and Rights Index of abortion within each age category. The most striking result is that the pattern of relationships found for the whole sample is replicated in each of the four age groups. Approval of abortion under health circumstances is strongly linked to approval of abortion for a variety of social-personal reasons (.61, .54, .59, .56). Second, support for the abortion rights of minor and adult married women when their parents or spouse disapprove of their decision is very highly correlated with approval of abortions under many discretionary circumstances (.66, .74, .72, .72). Both young and old respondents who support a pregnant woman's autonomous rights in an abortion decision endorse abortions for a variety of social-personal reasons.

However, among the oldest age group of respondents, those who restrict their support for abortions to health related concerns are

Table 5.2

Correlations among Abortion Indices within Four Age Groups of Respondents

	Panel A Under 25(N = 54)		Panel B 26-40 (N = 92)	
	Soc.Per.	Rights	Soc.Per.	Rights
Health	.61 ***	.52 ***	.54 ***	.45 ***
Soc.Per.		.66 ***		.74 ***

	Panel C 41-60 (N = 78)		Panel D 61-over (N = 67)	
	Soc.Per.	Rights	Soc.Per.	Rights
Health	.59 ***	.58 ***	.56 ***	.29 ***
Soc.Per.		.72 ***		.72 ***

*** p< .001

least likely to view abortion as the uncontested right of the pregnant woman (.29). By comparison, the three younger age groups show much higher correlations between the Health index and the Rights index of abortion (a range of .45 to .58). The issue of relative rights of pregnant women, parents, and spouses has emerged in recent years, when the majority of legal abortions involve unmarried minors. Our young respondents are sensitive to the fact that the issues of rights concerns themselves, their peers, or their adolescent children. They became exposed to abortions at a time when a typical abortion experience involved teenagers or young adults like themselves, who wished to postpone parenthood to continue schooling or maintain a job. Older respondents did not face such issues in their youth. An abortion was an alternative considered by married couples who had already had two or three children, and it remained an unsafe, criminal, and private option throughout their childbearing years. Hence support for the rights of wives and minor women is more likely to resonate with the reality of abortions today for our young respondents than for our oldest respondents.

In sum, the abortion belief structure shows both stability and change over time. The distinction between health and social-personal grounds for abortion is an important axis along which young and old respondents demarcate their approval of abortions. In addition to this, a concern over the relative rights of parents and spouses has been added to the abortion belief structure: This dimension is an integral part of the structure of abortion attitudes expressed by young respondents who have spent part or all of their reproductive years since the legalization of abortions.

Age, Religiosity, and Political Support for Abortions

One retrospective measure of attitudinal change used in our study helps to illustrate the ways in which both young and old respondents reacted to political developments since the legalization of abortion. We asked our respondents to report whether they had changed their position on abortion in the past five years, and if so, to indicate the direction of change in terms of greater support for either the pro-choice position on abortion, or the pro-life position on abortion. The distribution of responses by age is provided in Table 5.3.

Very young respondents (19-26) are most likely to report any change at all (51%), while the oldest age group of respondents provide the greatest proportion of ambivalent 'don't know' responses (15%). Adults under 40 years of age are twice as likely as those over 40 years of age to report a shift in attitudes favoring the pro-choice position on abortion. Adults over 40 years are evenly divided in the change in support for the pro-choice and the pro-life position on abortion (18.2% vs. 13% and 18.5% vs. 21.5%). In short, young respondents are more likely to report attitudinal change over the past five years, and the change is toward greater support for the pro-Choice position on abortion. While these figures indicate the direction of change in abortion attitudes among different age groups of respondents, they do not show the nature of change. For example, we do not know whether a shift favoring a pro-choice or pro-life position represents polarization of views, or a shift toward a more

Table 5.3
Change in Support for Pro-Choice/Pro-life Position on Abortion by Age groups

Panel A.		19-26	26-40	41-60	61-89
More Favorable to Pro-Choice		34.0	34.8	18.2	18.5
More Favorable to Pro-Life		17.0	13.0	13.0	21.5
No change in Attitudes		45.3	51.1	64.9	44.6
Dont Know		3.8	1.1	3.9	15.4
Percentage reporting any change		51.0	47.8	31.2	40.0
	N =	53	92	77	65

Panel B	Abortion Index		
% Reporting Change	LOW	MEDIUM	HIGH
Favorable to Pro-Choice	6.6	18.3	41.4
Favorable to Pro-Life	36.8	19.7	2.1
No change in attitudes	56.6	62.0	56.4
	----	----	----
% Distribution of Approval Scores	26.5	24.7	48.8
	P = .001	N = 287	

moderate position among those who previously held extreme positions on abortion.

The measures we have available are self-reports of change over the past five years, and a measure of *current* support for the two political groups and approval of abortion. These measures allow a modest test of the nature of change in support for abortions. We relate current attitudes toward abortion to the reported change in views over the past five years. Panel B. of Table 5.3 shows the percent reporting change in attitudes over the past five years within three categories of current level of approval of abortion. The column percentages indicate the direction of change in attitudes among those who show high, medium, and low support for abortions.

Those who now show extreme positions on the abortion index are slightly more likely to report a change in support for the pro-choice or pro-life position over the past five years. The direction of change itself suggests polarization of views. Note that among those who are low in their support for abortion, 37 percent report that they shifted to favor the pro-life position over the past five years. Similarly, among those who are currently high in their support for abortion, more than 41 percent have moved to such a position over the past five years. In contrast to these two extreme positions, respondents who indicate moderate approval of abortion have moved to a position favoring either the pro-choice or the pro-life position on abortion. In other words, change is more evident in the direction of strengthening extreme views. To put these findings in context, we note that 49 percent of all respondents in our sample currently show high support for abortion, and the remaining 51 percent are split between low and medium approval of abortions.

As a next logical step in these analyses we examine the strength of relationships between abortion attitudes, political orientation, support for the pro-choice and pro-life positions, and the frequency of church attendance. We are particularly interested in addressing two issues. First, we wish to know whether the relationship between abortion attitudes and a liberal-conservative political orientation has strengthened over the years, such that younger respondents show a strong correlation between their position on abortion and their overall political orientation. Second, we wish to compare the strength of the relationship among abortion views, political orientation, and religiosity across the four age groups. We predict that the relative salience of political views and religiosity will differ across the four age groups: Among older respondents, abortion attitudes will be closely tied to religiosity; by contrast, young respondents will show a strong relationship between a liberal political orientation and attitudes toward abortion, as a consequence of secular trends in value orientations having a much greater impact on the young compared to the old.

Table 5.4 shows the results from a test of these hypotheses. Within all four age groups, high approval of abortion is strongly correlated with high support for the pro-choice position on abortion, and low support for the pro-life position on abortion. By contrast, a

Table 5.4

Correlations among Abortion Approval, Support for Pro-Choice and Pro-Life Groups, Political Orientation, and Church Attendance within Age Groups.

	Panel A Under 25 (N=54)				*Panel B* 26-40 (N=92)			
	Pro-C	Pro-L	Polit. orient.	Church attend.	Pro-C	Pro-L	Polit. orient.	Church attend.
Abortion	.64***	-.72***	.41**	-.40**	.64***	-.54***	.25**	-.37***
Pro-choice		-.70***	.42*	-.30**		-.57***	.15+	-.27**
Pro-life			-.28*	.37**			-.08	.36***
Political Orientation				-.43***				-.33***

	Panel C 41-60(N=78)				*Panel D* 61-over (N=67)			
	Pro-C	Pro-L	Polit. orient.	Church attend.	Pro-C	Pro-L	Polit. orient.	Church attend.
Abortion	.75***	-.79***	.34***	-.46***	.74***	-.78***	.16	-.33**
Pro-choice		-.82***	.29**	-.35***		-.66***	.23+	-.15
Pro-life			-.44***	.48***			-.07	.35***
Political Orientation				-.20*				-.02

liberal political orientation reveals a moderate to strong relationship with abortion attitudes that is significant for all age groups, except those who are over 60 years of age(.16 vs. .41, .25, .34 for the three younger age groups). In other words, political orientation plays little role in how our elderly respondents feel about the abortion issue.The strongest positive relationship between abortion attitudes and a liberal political orientation emerges among the youngest group of respondents who are currently in their early twenties (.41). These young adults also draw strong significant links between a liberal political orientation and support for the pro-choice position on abortion. By contrast, both abortion attitudes and support for abortion groups are unrelated to the political orientation of older respondents.

Another important finding that illuminates a shift in the relationship between political orientation and abortion politics is the strong negative correlation between a liberal political orientation and frequent church attendance. The strength of this relationship increases in a linear fashion with each younger age group of respondents from -.02 among the oldest to -.43 among the youngest respondents. In light of the finding that religiosity is a strong and consistent predictor of abortion attitudes among all age groups of respondents, the strong negative relationship between a liberal political orientation and religiosity has the following implication. A strong adherence to institutional religion (as measured by frequency of church attendance) continues to shape attitudes toward abortion, but among young respondents today, a liberal-conservative political orientation is an equally important predictor of attitudes toward abortion. Furthermore, a high commitment to organized religion also suggests a conservative political orientation, and in turn conservative views on abortion. By contrast, older respondents exempt their stance on abortion from their overall political orientation. These finding makes sense when we note that the today's elderly reached adulthood in the 1920s to 1940s, when issues such as abortion, homosexuality, sex education were rarely topics of political debate as they are today. Hence for the oldest respondents religion and politics represented distinct, unrelated domains of life.

On the other hand, young men and women who have come of age in the aftermath of legalization and in the midst of highly polarized political debate over abortion show signs of a different outlook toward politics. Within this group, a secular outlook indexed by low participation in organized religion is closely related to a liberal outlook on political issues. We explore this further in the overall belief structure underlying attitudes toward abortion, which reveals a similar pattern of cohort influences.

Age and the Ideational Context of Abortion Attitudes

A major area of change on the abortion issue in the past few decades concerns the shift from a focus on medical issues to moral concerns related to sexuality, human life values, and women's rights. These three belief domains were found to be significantly correlated with abortion attitudes in the previous chapter. Here we explore the relationship among these domains across the four age groups of respondents to test for change in the belief structure underlying abortion attitudes over time.

Table 5.5 shows the correlations among four indices that represent attitudes toward abortion, sex and reproduction, gender roles, and human life issues. Across all age groups, abortion attitudes are significantly related to human life values, and to attitudes toward sexuality and reproduction, and the strength of these relationships are also quite similar in all four age groups. Second, within each age group human life values show a much stronger relationship to abortion attitudes (.58, .49. .62, .68) than to attitudes and beliefs in the domain of sex/reproduction or gender roles. The index of gender role attitudes shows a significant relationship to abortion views only within two age groups: very young respondents and the mature middle aged in their forties and fifties (Panels A and Panel C). The two groups which show no significant links between gender role ideology and abortion attitudes are respondents in their twenties and thirties, and those who are over 60 years of age.

A convenient way to summarize the comparison of the four groups is to inspect the mean of all the correlation coefficients in each of the four groups. The mean correlations shown below are a descriptive representation of the internal coherence of all the different belief domains within each age group.

Age	Mean Correlation
19-25	.39
26-40	.21
41-60	.37
61-over	.35

Table 5.5

Correlations among Abortion, Sex and Reproduction, Human Life and Gender Role Attitudes within Age Groups.

Panel A Under 25 (N=54)

	Hum.life.	Sex.Rep	Gen.Role
Abortion	.58 ***	.44 ***	.24 *
Human Life		.43 ***	.29 *
Sex.Reprod.			.35 **
Gend.Roles			

Panel B 26-40 (N=92)

	Hum.Life.	Sex.Rep.	Gen.Role
Abortion	.49 ***	.38 ***	.02
Human Life		.20 *	.15 +
Sex.Reprod.			.10
Gend.Roles			

Panel C 41-60 (N=78)

	Hum.life.	Sex.Rep	Gen.Role
Abortion	.62 ***	.45 ***	.31 **
Human Life		.33 **	.15 +
Sex.Reprod.			.38 ***
Gend.Roles			

Panel D 61-over (N=67)

	Hum.Life.	Sex.Rep.	Gen.Role
Abortion	.68 ***	.53 ***	.09
Human Life		.54 ***	.11
Sex.Reprod.			.14
Gend.Roles			

*** $p < .001$, ** $p < .01$, * $p < .05$, + $p < .10$

Note that the means are quite similar in three of four groups. Only respondents in the age group 26 to 40 show a mean that is more than ten points lower than any other group. In other words, respondents in the 26 to 40 age range show less cohesive system of attitudes and beliefs compared to all other age groups of respondents. Furthermore, with the exception of this group, each younger age group shows a progressively higher mean correlation among the four belief domains. The values that young respondents bring to the abortion issue represent more integrated set of views in the domains of sexuality, gender roles, and human life values than the two oldest age groups.

Two points need to be emphasized with respect to these findings. First, the strong positive correlations among three of the four belief domains (abortion, human life, sex/reproduction) in each of the four age groups points to the continuity of core values over time. While young and old respondents differ in the degree to which they hold permissive views in the domains of sexuality and human life values, they define their views toward abortion with a similar set of beliefs and values. Among individuals who were raised at different points in historical time we find that human life values and sex/reproductive norms are central to defining their views toward abortion.

Second, the lack of a linear trend in the relationship between gender role attitudes and abortion attitudes does not fit well with a prediction that younger respondents will show progressively stronger links between a liberal gender role ideology and permissive acceptance of abortions. Instead, our findings indicate a significant relationship between gender role ideology and abortion attitudes for two non-adjacent age groups: those under 25 and those in the 41 to 60 age range. By contrast, respondents in their late twenties and thirties are similar to those over sixty, in that their views on gender role issues are unrelated to all other belief domains.

We can explain the fact that older respondents do not relate their position on gender roles to their position on abortion, since abortion was not a women's rights issue during their youth. Neither was the experience of abortions premised upon conflicting obligations toward work, schooling, and family, reasons that now characterize the abortion decisions made by women in the early phases of their reproductive life. Laws that made it criminal to seek an abortion unless a woman's health was harmed had not been challenged until the 1960s, when many of our older respondents had already completed their childbearing. The experience of abortion during their childbearing years represented a desperate last resort of women who could not accommodate additional children in the late years of childbearing. By contrast, young respondents attained sexual maturity after abortions were legalized and view abortion as a legal right that is based upon an integrated view of women's political, economic, and reproductive opportunities. The question remains as to why young respondents in their late twenties and thirties do not show a similar profile.

One interpretation of this finding is that the 26 to 40 age group represents a very diverse group of adults, some of whom are currently beginning families, while others are close to the end of their childbearing years. Hence the variation in where they are in the reproductive life span may influence the values they bring to the abortion issue. Our age categories are not fine-tuned enough to detect subtle changes in attitudes and beliefs at different points in the reproductive life span of individuals, or to distinguish differences that are due to current life course position, as opposed to those due to differences in cohort membership.

A second possibility concerns differences in religious composition of the four age groups. This interpretation was quickly ruled out when we found that the proportion of Catholics to non-Catholics was not markedly different across the four age groups. Whether this age groups's (26-40) departure from a linear pattern reflects sampling error or some regional peculiarity cannot be ascertained internal to our western Massachusetts sample. Hence we chose to explore this issue by comparing our results with results from a similar analysis of a more representative national data set. We chose the 1985 NORC General Social Survey data set since it contains the most number of items that approximate our own measures. The data for this study was collected between September 1987 and March 1988. In the analysis that follows we compare the pattern of intercorrelations among the four belief domains in the national or regional data sets.

1985 General Social Survey Data

A major challenge was to find sufficient items in another data set to construct measures that approximate the indices used in our analyses. A comparative analysis was not a central component of our study design when we decided to collect original data. Our interest in

Table 5.6
Items and Indices: General Social Surveys (1985) and Greenfield (1987)

Domain	GSS 1985	Greenfield 1987
Abortion	Health Reasons Social-Personal	Health Social-Personal Relative rights of parents/spouses
Human Life	Euthanasia Suicide	Euthanasia Suicide Onset of Human Life
Sex/Reproduction	Pre -marital sex Extra-marital sex Homosexuality	Pre-marital Sex Extra-marital sex Homosexuality Teenage contraceptive access Artif.Reproduction
Gender Roles	Sex Role Index[*]	Gender Role Integration Parental Primacy Domestic Role Sharing

[*] a) Working mother can establish warm secure relationship with her children as a mother who does not work.
 b) Women are much happier if they stay at home and take care of their children
 c)It is much better for everyone if the man earns the main living and the woman takes care of the home.
 d)It is more important for a wife to help her husband's career than to have one herself.

analyzing the contemporary structure of abortion attitudes with sensitivity to changes in the abortion issue over time provided the rationale for collecting primary data rather than analyzing existing data sets. The downside of this choice is a lack of a perfect match in measures across data sets.

However, we were fortunate to find sufficient number of items to match our own for at least three of the four domains. A check list of items and indices that appear in both our data set and the 1985 General Social Surveys is shown in Table 5.6. Additional items found in our own indices but not in the GSS are also noted. A quick glance will indicate that we are able to match most of the measures on the index of Human Life Values, Sex/Reproduction, and Abortion. On the Gender Role Ideology index, an initial search resulted in only two items that were at least approximately close to those in our data set. Instead of using these two items, we decided to construct an index based on four items that have been used in previous analyses of sex role attitudes. As shown in Table 5.6 these four items measure attitudes toward women's family roles relative to their work roles, which have been used in the Home Orientation Index by Thornton and Camburn (1979) and in the Sex Roles Scale by Mason and Bumpass (1975). The correlations among the four attitude indices derived from the GSS items are shown in Table 5.7 Alongside these results we also reproduce Table 5.5 for the purpose of comparing our findings with the findings from the GSS data analysis.

Several similarities and differences can be found in results from the two data sets. First, the strength of relationships among the three major domains: abortion, sex/reproduction, and human life values are remarkably similar across the two data sets. As with our own data, these three domains are strongly intercorrelated in all age groups showing a continuity in the values that are at the heart of the abortion issue. Variations across age groups are once again found with respect to the relationship between gender role attitudes and attitudes in the three other domains. The GSS results show the highest correlations between gender role ideology and attitudes toward abortion, human life, and sexuality among respondents over 40 years of age, while those who are forty and older show lower correlations. Similar to our own findings, respondents over 60 years of age show the weakest relationships between gender role attitudes and all other belief domains.

Table 5.7

Correlations among Attitudes Toward Abortion, Sex, Human Life, and Gender Roles By Age: General Social Surveys, 1985 and Greenfield, 1987

	GSS 1985			Greenfield 1987		
	Under 25 (n=189)			Under 25 (n=54)		
	Hum.Life	Sex	Gen.Role	Hum.Life	Sex	Gen.Role
Abortion	.55 ***	.48 ***	.32 ***	.58 ***	.44 ***	.24 *
Human Life		.38 ***	.20 **		.43 ***	.29 *
Sex.Rep.			.45 ***			.35**
Gender Role						
	26-40 (n=510)			26-40 (n=92)		
	Hum.Life	Sex	Gen.Role	Hum.Life	Sex	Gen.Role
Abortion	.54 ***	.54 ***	.39 ***	.49 ***	.38 ***	.02
Human Life		.45 ***	.25 ***		.20 *	.15 +
Sex.Rep.			.43 ***			.10
Gender Role						

(continued on next page)

Table 5.7 (contd.)

	GSS 1985						Greenfield 1987					
	41-60 (n=415)			*over 60 (n=336)*			*41-60 (n=78)*			*over 60 (n=67)*		
	Hum.Life	Sex	Gen.Role	Hum.Life	Sex	Gen.Role	Hum.Life	Sex	Gend.Role	Hum.Life	Sex	Gend.Role
Abortion	.53 ***	.47 ***	.22***	.50 ***	.44 ***	.12 *	.62 ***	.45 ***	.31**	.68 ***	.53 ***	.09
Human Life		.47 ***	.15 **		.38 ***	.05		.33 **	.15+		.54 ***	.11
Sex.Rep.			.27 ***			.22 ***			.38***			.14
Gender Role												

*** p<.001 ** p<.01 * p<.05 + p<.10

In contrast to our findings we note that respondents in the 26-40 age range in the national survey show a very coherent structure of beliefs that embraces views toward abortion, human life, sexuality, and gender roles. A quick summary comparison of the two data sets is facilitated by the absolute mean correlation of the matrices shown in Table 5.8. The mean of the correlation matrices show a linear pattern of increasing coherence among younger age groups, with a slight decline in the youngest age group (.28, .35, .43, .40). The pattern also suggests a distinction between those over 60 years of age and all other younger age groups.

Table 5.8
Mean of Correlations within Four Age Groups: GSS 1985 and Greenfield 1987

	GSS 1985	Greenfield 1987
Under 25	.40	.39
26-40	.43	.21
41-60	.35	.37
60 -over	.28	.35

Overall the GSS results point to clear differences in belief structures between the oldest respondents and those under 60 years of age. These results also confirm the general pattern of age differences found in our data. On the other hand, the non-linear patterns of relationships found in our own data are not replicated in the GSS analysis: Respondents in the 26 to 40 age range show the most coherent set of beliefs and attitudes in the GSS data, while our own data set showed the opposite. These differences in the findings across the two data sets limit firm conclusions regarding a linear pattern of greater coherence in the belief structures of younger cohorts of respondents. The regional peculiarities of our sample may also underlie differences in findings across the GSS and Greenfield data sets. Furthermore, a test of cohort differences in belief structures would require repeat measures of attitudes and beliefs over time for different birth cohorts. The composition of our Massachusetts sample differs in important ways from a national representative sample of Americans, particularly with respect to religious representation. Compared to a majority Protestant representation in the national sample, our sample contains a 50-50 ratio of Catholics to Protestants in all age groups. If religious composition has any direct bearing on the patterns of relationships found in our data then we expect the relationship between religion and age to suggest a differential impact of social change on the structure of beliefs Catholics and non-Catholics bring to the abortion issue. It is to this issue that we turn to in the discussion that follows.

Differences among Catholics and Non-Catholics

Since the 1960s differences between Catholics and Protestants in attitudes and behavior in the areas of sex, contraception, and fertility have declined and gradually disappeared. As many young Catholics as Protestants engage in pre-marital sex, use birth-control pills, and perhaps resort to an abortion to prevent an unwanted pregnancy. Despite the lack of significant differences in the sexual and reproductive practices of contemporary Catholics and Protestants, many studies continue to pinpoint significant differences in attitudes toward abortion between Catholics and Protestants. Unfortunately most of the studies take the Catholic-Protestant difference in abortion attitudes as given, and fail to interpret this lingering difference within the context of historical change on the abortion issue. Social change in often gradual and has a differential impact on individuals as a function of their social group membership and related experiences. Furthermore, the impact of these changes may be manifested more rapidly in some groups as compared to others. In the broader context of secularization (defined in terms of a declining adherence to organized religion) Lesthaeghe and Surkyn (1988:10) comment that "Secularization takes place within each denomination, and if the Catholic-Protestant duality had any statistical relevance in the past, it is because secularization generally occurred faster among most mainstream Protestants than among . . . Catholics."

Table 5.9

Correlations Among Attitudes Toward Abortion, Human Life, Sex, Gender Roles, Political Orientation, and Church Attendance by Religious Affiliation:Greenfield 1987

	Hum.Life	Sex	Gender Roles	Polit.Orient.	Church Attend.
Non-Catholics (N=166)					
Abortion	.62***	.50***	.37***	.38 ***	-.31***
Human Life		.43***	.30***	.21 **	-.33***
Sex			.48***	.39 ***	-.45***
Gender Roles				.37***	-.17 *
Polit. Orient.					-.32 ***
Church Attendance					
Catholics (N=125)					
Abortion	.55***	.42***	-.04	.19 *	-.47***
Human Life		.36***	.11	.19 *	-.34***
Sex			.25 **	.22 **	-.40***
Gender Roles				.18 *	-.07
Polit. Orient.					-.13 +
Church Attendance					

*** p<.001 ** p<.01 * p<.05 + p<.10

Here we show that Catholics and non-Catholics have responded to the changes in the abortion issue in different ways such that the belief structure surrounding abortion attitudes is markedly different for the two groups.

The first set of results are presented in Table 5.9 which show that both similarities and differences characterize the values orientation Catholics and non-Catholics bring to bear upon the abortion issue. Both groups show strong links between permissive attitudes toward abortion, sexual and reproductive matters, and human life issues. Furthermore, church attendance as a proxy for religiosity shows a strong negative relationship to all three belief domains within both religious groupings. The difference between the two groups emerges only with respect to the relationships among gender role attitudes, political orientation and abortion attitudes. Among non-Catholics, gender role attitudes and a liberal political orientation show strong significant correlations to beliefs and attitudes toward abortion and sex/reproduction. By contrast, Catholics show no significant relationship between gender role attitudes and abortion attitudes, and a liberal political orientation is only moderately related to beliefs and attitudes in all four domains.

The lack of a significant relationship between gender role ideology and abortion attitudes among Catholics indicates that they exempt this domain from a larger value orientation that shapes their responses to abortion, sexuality, and human life issues. The Catholic Church's opposition to abortions has been primarily cast within the framework of sexual morality and human life values. Hence the polarization of abortion attitudes among Catholics reflect different value orientations toward sexual morality and human life values, rather than a liberal-conservative gender role ideology. This point is further illustrated by the finding that among both Catholics and non-Catholics, abortion attitudes, sexual and reproductive norms, and human life values are negatively correlated with a higher frequency of church attendance: A liberal view toward gender roles shows weak to no significant relationship to church attendance. Both progressive and conservative Catholics may hold egalitarian views toward gender role arrangements in work and family life, and simultaneously hold a conservative position on abortion, sex, and contraception.

We replicated this analysis with the GSS indices that were constructed to check change in belief structures across different age groups of respondents. Table 5.10 shows the results from the analysis

Table 5.10
Correlations Among Attitudes Toward Abortion, Human Life, Sex, Gender Roles, Political Orientation, and Church Attendance by Religious Affiliation: General Social Surveys:1985

Non-Catholics (N = 1063)

	Hum.Life	Sex	Gend. Roles	Polit. Orient.	Church Attend
Abortion	.54***	.49***	.29***	.21***	-.39***
Human Life		.50***	.27***	.20***	-.40***
Sex			.43***	.29***	-.45***
Gender Roles				.23***	-.23***
Polit. Orient.					-.20***
Church Attendance					

Catholics (N = 395)

	Hum.Life	Sex	Gend. Roles	Polit. Orient.	Church Attend
Abortion	.49***	.51***	.22***	.16**	-.38***
Human Life		.40***	.16**	.00	-.35***
Sex			.39***	.19***	-.39***
Gender Roles				.26***	-.23***
Polit. Orient.					-.03
Church Attendance					

*** p<.001 ** p<.01 * p<.05 + p<.10

of the GSS data set. Given a larger sample base the GSS data set shows highly significant correlations across several indices. But the key pattern of relationships found in our data set are replicated in the GSS data set. Weaker links are found among Catholics than non-Catholics: between gender role attitudes and abortion attitudes (.22 vs. .29); between gender role attitudes and attitudes toward sex/reproduction (.16 vs. .29); and between gender role attitudes and human life attitudes (.39 vs. .43). In addition to this, the personal political orientation of Catholics shows weaker correlations than among non-Catholics to attitudes in the areas of abortion (.16 vs. .21), sex/reproduction (.19 vs. .29), and human life (.00 vs. .20).

We now turn to a closer inspection of these differences between Catholics and non-Catholics within the context of age differences. Panels A through C in Table 5.11 show correlations among the four belief domains within three age groups of Catholics. Panels D through F show the results of the same analysis for non-Catholics. We regrouped our respondents into three age categories rather than four in order to have enough cases in each of the six cells.

A comparison of age differences within the two religious affiliation groups shows interesting results. Among Catholics, significant high intercorrelations among attitudes toward abortion, sex/reproduction, and human life values are found only among the oldest age groups of respondents (56 and over). Each younger age group shows a less cohesive structure, such that the very young Catholics show a highly particular attitudinal structure within the narrow domain of abortion and human life values. By contrast, young non-Catholics show a highly integrated belief structure with significant intercorrelations among all four belief domains. The earlier finding that Catholics' views on gender roles has no significant relevance to their stance on abortion is replicated within each of the age groups.

These trends across the age groups suggest important shift in the moral orientation of contemporary young Catholics. Over time, Catholics have moved closer to the rest of the population in terms of attitudes and personal behavior in the areas of sex, contraception, and abortion. Differences in attitudes toward sex and contraception may have disappeared at a much earlier period, and significant differences in abortion attitudes are sustained largely within the framework of human life values. Many young Catholics may have departed from the church's teachings on pre-marital sex and contraception, but human life values may continue to distinguish the liberal and conservative

Table 5.11

Correlations among Abortion, Human Life, Sex and Reproduction, and Gender Role Attitudes among Catholics and Non-Catholics in Three Age Groups: Greenfield 1987.

Catholics

Under 30 (N=33)

	Hum.life.	Sex.Rep	Gen.Role
Abortion	.53 ***	.18	-.02
Human Life		.21	.22
Sex.Reprod.			.16

31-55 (N=53)

	Hum.life.	Sex.Rep	Gen.Role
Abortion	.43 ***	.29 *	-.18 +
Human Life		.05	.08
Sex.Reprod.			-.05

56 and Over (N=39)

	Hum.life.	Sex.Rep	Gen.Role
Abortion	.61 ***	.57 ***	-.25 +
Human Life		.52 ***	-.39 **
Sex.Reprod.			-.11

Non-Catholics

Under 30 (N=46)

	Hum.Life.	Sex.Rep.	Gen.Role
Abortion	.62 ***	.65 ***	.34 **
Human Life		.52 ***	.33 **
Sex.Reprod.			.42 **

31-55 (N=77)

	Hum.Life.	Sex.Rep.	Gen.Role
Abortion	.60 ***	.47 ***	.40 ***
Human Life		.30 ***	.18 +
Sex.Reprod.			.47 ***

56 and Over (N=39)

	Hum.Life.	Sex.Rep.	Gen.Role
Abortion	.62 ***	.37 **	.26 +
Human Life		.48 ***	.34 *
Sex.Reprod.			.28 *

*** $p<.001$ ** $p<.01$ * $p<.05$ + $p<.10$

positions held by young Catholics on the abortion issue.

In sum, our findings point to a highly particular and segregated attitudinal structure among Catholics to non-Catholics. Beyond the narrow domain of abortion and human life values, there is little certainty to predicting the views young Catholics bring to sex/reproduction and gender role issues. By contrast, young non-Catholics have moved to a more internally cohesive system of beliefs in the domains of abortion, human life issues, sex/reproduction, and gender roles.

Gender and the Ideational Context of Abortion

We turn to one final dimension on which to examine the belief structure underlying attitudes toward abortion. Gender is an important axis on which political and legal debate over abortion has evolved over the past three decades. Few empirical studies show a consistent significant difference in the extent to which men and women approve of abortions. Those that report gender differences in abortion attitudes indicate that women are more conservative on the abortion issue than men (Blake 1983). Various threads of analysis in earlier chapters showed significant differences between men and women in their attitudes toward pre-marital sex, beliefs about fetal personhood, and expectations regarding gender roles and responsibilities.

Women are more likely to view human life as beginning at earlier stages of a pregnancy than men; they are also more disapproving of casual pre-marital sex than men; but women tend to show more liberal views toward women's public and family roles than men do. Here we test whether men and women bring a different cluster of beliefs and values to the abortion issue. Table 5.12 presents the correlations among the four belief domains, political orientation and church attendance separately for men and women.

Among men and women similarities emerge in the links between a high approval of abortion, a permissive stance on issues related to human life and sex/reproduction. Critical differences characterize the moral stance men and women take on the abortion issue. Among men, a liberal-conservative stance on gender role issues has no significant relationship to their attitudes toward abortion. Their position on abortion is strongly rooted in human life values and

Table 5.12
Correlations Among Attitudes Toward Abortion, Human Life, Sex, Gender Roles, Political Orientation, and Church Attendance by Sex: Greenfield 1987

	Hum.Life	Sex	Gend. Roles	Polit. Orient.	Church Attend
A. Men (N = 139)					
Abortion	.63***	.42***	.10	.30 ***	-.45***
Human Life		.41***	.09	.15 *	-.45***
Sex			.27 ***	.25 **	-.53***
Gender Roles				.22 **	-.05
Polit. Orient.					-.26**
Church Attendance					

	Hum.Life	Sex	Gend. Roles	Polit. Orient.	Church Attend
B. Women (N = 152)					
Abortion	.59***	.55***	.36***	.32***	-.41***
Human Life		.43***	.42***	.28***	-.30***
Sex			.55***	.41***	-.39***
Gender Roles				.38***	-.31***
Polit. Orient.					-.26***
Church Attendance					

C. Absolute Means

MEN	.30
WOMEN	.40

*** p<.001 ** p<.01 * p<.05 + p<.10

normative orientation toward sex/reproduction. Among women, all belief domains are significantly intercorrelated and point to a more cohesive profile of values they bring to the abortion issue, as shown by the absolute means of all the correlations for men and women in Panel C (.30 for men vs. .40 for women). It is also interesting to note that men exempt their views on gender roles from their overall belief system. By contrast, women draw highly significant links between their position on gender roles and their views toward abortion, sexuality, and human life values.

This point is further illustrated by the finding that women show a more integrated profile of views on different dimensions of gender roles compared to men. Table 5.13 shows the correlations between the three dimensions that comprise the index of gender roles. Among women, a liberal view of gender role integration is significantly correlated with a support for domestic role sharing and a low emphasis on parental primacy in child care. In turn all three indices of gender role attitudes are significantly correlated with abortion attitudes. By contrast, men show more dimensionality in their views toward gender roles, and exempt their stance on various aspects of gender roles from their views toward abortion. In sum, these patterns suggest that men respond to the "moral" aspects of the abortion issue in placing their views toward abortion within the framework of human life values and sex/reproduction. On the other hand, women respond to the "rights" aspect of the abortion issue by including their views on gender role issues and their overall political orientation into their overall belief structure.

In light of the finding that men and women do not differ in their level of approval of abortions, the above mentioned differences have the following implication. Abortion politics and abortion morality are not directly polarized along the lines of gender. On the other hand, expectations regarding gender role arrangements, and their implications for sexual and reproductive life styles are more likely to explain the polarization of the abortion issue among women. Hence women who support abortions will show a liberal-permissive stance on issues related to sexuality and gender roles, while women who oppose abortions are more likely to hold a traditional view of both sexuality and gender roles. The fact that a liberal political orientation shows a strong positive relationship to all belief domains among women also implies that women who are polarized on the abortion

Table 5.13
Correlations between Gender Roles Attitude Indices and Abortion
Attitudes by Sex: Greenfield, 1987.

	Women		
	Gender Role Integration	Domestic Role Sharing	Abortion
Parental Primacy	.24**	.18**	.21**
Gender Role Integration		.03	.29***
Domestic Role Sharing			.18**

	Men		
	Gender Role Integration	Domestic Role Sharing	Abortion
Parental Primacy	.21**	.05	.07
Gender Role Integration		.28***	.12+
Domestic Role Sharing			-.03

*** p<.001 ** p<.01 * p<.05 + p<.10

issue will bring a broader set of value concerns to their political actions.

Summary

The major theme of the analyses presented in this chapter is the impact of social change on the structure of beliefs and attitudes our respondents bring to the abortion issue. New dimensions have been added to the experience of abortions in recent years and these concern the relative rights of family members in an abortion decisions. That these issues are directly relevant to the lived experiences of recent reproductive cohorts was shown in the ways in which our young respondents incorporated the issue of the relative rights of minors, parents, and spouses into their abortion belief structure. Our data also suggested that young respondents who attained sexual maturity in the aftermath of the legalization of abortions present a more integrated profile of views toward abortion, human life values, gender roles,and sexuality. Older respondents couch their views toward abortion within the domain of human life values and sex/reproduction, and exempt their views on gender roles from their response to issues within these domains. These differences are linked to the fact that our young respondents face decisions concerning sex, contraception, and pregnancy that are significantly different from those experienced by older respondents.

Beyond these broad differences, we found less support for a linear trend toward a more integrated structure of beliefs among younger respondents. Respondents in the 26 to 40 age range were markedly different from other age groups in showing a less coherent structure of beliefs. A comparison with data from the GSS data set showed support for some of our findings, but indicated trends across age groups that were also quite different from those found in our study. The findings concerning cohort trends in belief structures have not provided definitive answer to the question concerning age differences in attitudes toward abortion. An important next step would be to check trends in a national data set such as the GSS for different birth cohorts with a series of repeat measures. Such data would facilitate a more detailed specification of age categories, so that we can determine critical points in the reproductive life span of individuals that have the most impact on attitude formation and change. This would also allow us to distinguish between differences due cohort membership and those that are due to life course position.

Our analyses of differences along the lines of gender and religion revealed interesting results. Younger cohorts of Catholics show a highly focused structure of beliefs only on abortion and human life values. Our data suggest that there is greater dimensionality to the beliefs Catholics bring to the abortion issue compared to non-Catholics. By contrast, young non-Catholics have developed a tightly integrated system of beliefs with indicate consistent positions on abortion, human life issues, gender roles, and sexuality.

In a similar way, women compared to men show a highly cohesive system of beliefs that surround attitudes toward abortion. Gender role attitudes have a high salience for the position women take on matters related to abortion, sexuality, and human life. In addition to this women incorporate their attitudes in all four belief domains into their overall political orientation. In this respect, the young and women represent important political constituencies in the political debate over abortion. Perhaps the view that the "personal is political" has broader ramifications today when life style and personal morality issues are an integral part of the political outlook of women and youth.

6

Conclusion

Thus, "not with a bang, but a whimper," the plurality discards a landmark case of the last generation...The plurality does so oblivious or insensitive to the fact that millions of women and their families have ordered their lives around the right to reproductive choice, and that this right has become vital to the full participation of women in the economic and political walks of American life."

Justice Blackmun
Excerpt from Dissenting Opinion on Webster vs. Reproductive Health Services, July 3rd 1989.

Update on Abortion Politics

In the Fall of 1987, when this study was launched into the field, we did not expect any dramatic change in the U.S. abortion law. For almost 15 years the Roe decision which legalized abortion on the basis of the constitutional right to privacy had withstood repeated challenges from attempts to pass a Human Life Amendment that could subsequently outlaw abortions. In 16 cases dealing with the use of public funds for abortion or the requirement of spousal/parental notification, or waiting periods before abortions, the Court has reaffirmed a woman's private right to abortion. On July 3rd 1989, the Supreme Court ruled on Webster vs. Reproductive Health Services upholding a Missouri Law that imposed two new restrictions on legal abortions. First, women who seek abortions beyond 20 weeks of gestation will be required to undergo medical tests to assess fetal viability. Second, public facilities and employees are prohibited from performing or assisting with abortions that are not necessary to save the life of the mother. While the Court abstained from overturning its earlier ruling in Roe v. Wade, it relegated greater powers to individual states to decide their own abortion laws in the future. This also became evident in the Pennsylvania case in 1992 when the court upheld parts of the state's Abortion Control Act that required a 24-hour waiting period, counselling on alternatives to abortion, and parental or judicial consent for minors seeking abortions.

The major thrust of the Webster and Pennsylvania decisions has been to move the abortion issue from the courts to the state legislatures, thus paving the way for an arduous battle over detailed aspects of legal abortion in the years to come. The definition of fetal viability, the abortion rights of minors, and the use of public funds and facilities will be the focal points of this new phase of the abortion debate. As of 1990, 35 states in the country required some form of parental consent or notification for minors seeking abortions; 30 states restricted the use of Medicaid funding for abortions; 8 states had public funding restrictions; 2 states prohibited the involvement of public employees in abortion services; 4 states prohibited the use of public facilities for abortion services; and 9 states included a preamble in their laws on the protection of fetal life (in Karina 1989). In short, some states had modified their abortion laws in those areas that were left ambiguous by the Court ruling in 1973 even before the Webster decision.

The immediate effect of the Webster decision was felt in many states across the nation in which abortion became a divisive issue in elections for mayors, legislators, and governors. It is still unclear to what extent political victories in these states could be attributed to a candidate's stance on abortion, but the recent turn of events suggests that public opinion on abortion will become an important factor in shaping the future of abortion legislation. Until now, the fate of legal abortion was battled in the courts, and politicians could oppose or support abortions without having to effect changes in abortion policy. By transferring greater powers to state legislatures, the Court's stance in recent years has increased the salience of the abortion issue in the political domain.

As in many other areas of public policy, there is no clear correspondence among the views of political activists, the views of the general public, and abortion behavior. The extreme polarization of abortion perspectives among activists finds little support among the general public and our respondents. The public's views on abortion continue to remain ambivalent despite the increased exposure to abortions in recent years. This scenario raises the issue of the fit between reproductive values and reproductive behavior, and is relevant to the formulation of public policy. We return to this issue later in this chapter when we discuss the broader implications of public attitudes for the future of abortion politics. First we turn to a review of major findings from this study and suggest directions for further research.

The Abortion Belief Structure

The purpose of this study was to understand the structure of public attitudes toward abortion from a variety of perspectives. Toward this goal we utilized data from a factorial survey design and from a conventional survey that contained measures of attitudes and beliefs in the areas of sex/reproduction, human life, and gender roles. We have shown that abortion attitudes are shaped by both the characteristics of abortion decisions, as well as the social and ideological attributes of respondents. Abortion attitudes are also embedded in a larger ideational context and draw upon values and beliefs in the domains of sex/reproduction, human life, and gender roles. Furthermore, both the structure of abortion attitudes and the broader ideational context have changed historically, and show variation across sub-groups of individuals defined by age, religion, and gender. In sum, abortion attitudes are shaped by past experiences, current life circumstances, and the overall value orientation individuals bring to many aspects of social and personal life.

Abortion Situations and Abortion Morality

Abortion situations have changed historically, reflecting the change in social circumstances that prompt an abortion decision. Until the early part of the 20th century, abortions represented the desperate solution opted for by married women who became pregnant late in their reproductive phase of life. Over the course of this century this pattern has changed such that family size limitation is a reason for only a small proportion of all abortions. The majority of women who seek abortions today are unmarried, young, and childless. Prevention of unmarried motherhood and postponement of first births are key motivations behind the experience of abortions, whereas sterilization is resorted to more often by women who wish to prevent additional births in their later years of childbearing. The reasons women cite for their abortion decisions indicate competing life choices and decisions in a social context in which the pursuit of family life, and the pursuit of educational or employment goals are often in conflict. Abortion represents a necessary, yet morally problematic solution to a mistimed/unwanted pregnancy.

The factorial survey design facilitated a complex analysis of the structure of abortion attitudes in terms of the characteristics of contemporary abortion situations. Conventional surveys have largely relied upon responses to a uni-dimensional portrayal of the reasons for an abortion. The vignette design allowed the specification of reasons put forth for an abortion decision within the context of several background characteristics of pregnant women and their pregnancy circumstances. Nine situational dimensions in addition to the reasons given for abortion decisions were included in the design of the abortion vignettes: age, marital status, parity, financial status, health condition, gestation phase, the quality of couple's relationship at the time of the abortion decision, and various combinations of parental/partner approval of the abortion decision.

Four issues were explored with the vignette data. First, we examined responses to abortion vignettes to determine the situational factors that have the most impact on variation in public attitudes toward abortion. Second, we explored the interactive effects of different situational characteristics in modifying levels of approval. A third set of analyses focused on the reciprocal influences of life course characteristics shared by respondents and vignette women in shaping moral judgments of abortion decisions. At various points in these analyses we also compared the findings from the vignette analysis with findings from the analysis of conventional survey items. Together these analyses pointed to the relative salience of situational characteristics, the context effects of abortion vignettes, the impact of respondent characteristics, and strong similarities in the abortion belief structure across different approaches to measurement.

Relative Salience of Vignette Dimensions

The vignette analysis for the most part confirmed findings from previous studies of public attitudes toward abortion. Among the various dimensions that characterized specific abortion decisions evaluated by respondents, the overt reasons given by women for their abortion decisions, the phase of gestation, and the woman's health condition are central factors that shape public approval of abortions. Sharp distinctions emerged between the approval of health related reasons and the approval of social-personal reasons for an abortion; poor maternal health heightened approval of all reasons for an abortion; and an abortion contemplated beyond the fourth month of a pregnancy depressed the level of approval of all reasons for an abortion. The most important vignette dimension that accounted for more than two-thirds of the variance in abortion attitudes was the overt reasons women cite for their decision to terminate a pregnancy. Respondents gave the highest approval for abortions that would prevent physical/psychological harm to the mother and the lowest approval for many of social reasons that in fact are the major reasons for the abortion decisions made by most women. The health related reasons include rape by stranger, incestual rape, poor health, and fetal deformity - conditions that have elicited high levels of approval in national surveys. The social personal reasons that elicit only moderate approval include perceived financial constraints at the time of the pregnancy, a desire to limit family size or remain childless, preference to avoid unmarried motherhood, or the father's refusal to marry the woman. Age and household income of the pregnant woman, and the views of her parents and spouse/partner had a relatively low, but significant impact on the approval of abortion decisions.

Abortion Factor Structure

The rationale provided by individual women for their abortion decisions is central to understanding public responses to abortion situations. This is the dimension that has been the major focus in conventional survey items on abortion attitudes. Hence the vignette analyses underscore the overwhelming importance of this substantive dimension and provides empirical justification for the measurement approach taken by conventional surveys. The importance of this situational dimension was further illustrated in a variety of comparative analyses of responses to vignettes and conventional survey items used in this study. Our respondents were highly consistent in the level of approval given for the health and social personal reasons that appeared in survey items and abortion vignettes which varied along many other attributes of abortion situations.

Second, the similarities in the abortion belief structure across the two different methods (vignette and conventional survey) also emerged in the factor analyses of conventional survey items. Four distinct dimensions characterized the abortion belief structure in responses to survey items that focused on reasons for an abortion, or the presence or absence of parental/partner approval, or the duration of the pregnancy - Health, Social-Personal, Rights of Others and Couple Dissensus. The Rights dimension measures a unique aspect of abortion attitudes that has emerged in recent years and taps concerns related to the relative rights of parents, minor women, partners, spouses and fetuses (in the case of late abortions). These concerns were further distinguished from situations in which pregnant women did not share their partners' preference to terminate a pregnancy (Couple Dissensus). In other words, whether or not a woman voluntarily decides to terminate a pregnancy is as central to the acceptance of abortion decisions as the pregnancy circumstances that lead to an abortion decision. When parents disapprove of a minor's decision to abort, or when a husband disapproves of his wife's decision to abort, respondents vary widely in their level of acceptance of the woman's personal decision to abort the pregnancy.

Comparable attitude indices that measured approval of health and social-personal reasons for an abortion showed very high correlations across the vignette and survey data sets, pointing to a consistency in the judgment of various reasons provided for an abortion decision. The critical difference between questionnaire items and abortion vignettes is that the former measure abortion attitudes along a single dimension, whereas the vignette method measures these same attitudes in a more complex social context. The context specified the characteristics of the pregnant woman and the pregnancy circumstances. Thus a high correlation between similar measures of abortion attitudes across these two methods further underscores the fact that respondents largely focus attention on the rationale provided by pregnant women for their abortion decisions.

The distinctions that emerged between the Health, Social-Personal, and Rights dimensions of abortion attitudes also suggested a continuum of support for abortions that ranges from a restrictive approval of abortions to avoid physical harm to the mother or fetus to an unconditional support for abortions as a woman's right. Individuals who approve of abortion for a variety of discretionary reasons are also likely to view abortion as a private matter in which parents and spouses have limited rights. On the other hand, those who restrict their approval of abortion to health justifications alone are least apt to consider abortion as the uncontested right of individual women, if the decision reflects dissensus among many different parties involved. This finding suggests that public attitudes toward abortion center around a balance among a respect for fetal life, an understanding of the pregnant woman's dilemma, and a high emphasis on marital and family harmony in resolving reproductive decisions.

Context Effects of Vignette Dimensions

While the vignette analyses confirmed findings from conventional surveys, they pinpointed the impact of additional dimensions that have received minimal attention in previous research. A major result of the vignette analysis concerned the interactive effects of selected situational dimensions in shaping subtle departures from approval or disapproval of abortions. The tension between respect for the preservation of life and compassion for women's situations is also found in the complex ways in which knowledge of fetal age, woman's health condition, and reasons for an abortion interact in their influence on levels of approval.

The analysis yielded a more complex ranking, in which the highest approval was for health reasons and a decision to abort early in the pregnancy, followed by health concerns associated with a late abortion, followed by early termination of a pregnancy for social-personal reasons, and the least approval for an abortion late in the pregnancy premised upon a desire to limit family size, or to remain childless or unmarried.

In a similar fashion, the knowledge of the woman's general health status also modified approval of abortion decisions. Poor health resulted in a heightening of abortion approval for both health related and social-personal justifications. The health and gestation dimension of abortion attitudes tap deeply held and competing sets of concerns that pit the value of maternal life against the value of fetal life. In this instance, maternal life takes precedence when individuals accept an abortion that will save a mother's life and prevent prolonged physical and psychological harm. On the other hand, fetal life takes precedence when respondents judge as insufficient, the social-personal reasons women gave for their abortion decisions, and when the abortion would be performed during the later stages of a pregnancy. The value of fetal life thus attains greater salience as a pregnancy progresses.

By contrast, the life course characteristics of vignette women, such as age, marital status, and parity had no impact on respondents' judgments of abortions to prevent additional births or unmarried motherhood. For instance, our respondents did not significantly shift their level of approval for a decision to abort and remain unmarried as a function of the age of the pregnant woman (teens vs. twenties vs. thirties vs. forties). The vignette women's current parity also had no impact on whether respondent's judged an abortion to prevent additional births as more or less justifiable.

The fact that respondents do not differentiate their views toward abortion in terms of personal and life course characteristics of individual women suggests the following interpretation. Respondents are likely to significantly increase their approval of social-personal reasons women give for their abortion, only if in addition to these conditions the women are also in very poor health, or if the pregnancy will be aborted early in the pregnancy. A combined concern for maternal health and fetal life is thus central to the acceptance of social-personal reasons for an abortion. Barring any threat to the health of the pregnant woman, there is greater variation among respondents in the degree to which they find social-personal justifications such as family size limitation, preference to remain childless, or unmarried, as acceptable reasons for an abortion. This variation among respondents is more likely to be linked to their own life circumstances, personal characteristics, and value orientation. In other words, respondents' marital status, age, and parity --- three of the life course characteristics considered in our analyses --- are more apt to influence their approval of abortion decisions made by pregnant women who also vary along these characteristics. Hence the null finding on pregnant women's age, marital status, and parity masked an interesting interaction between respondents' and vignette women's life course characteristics.

Respondent and Situational Characteristics

We matched respondents and vignette women on three life course characteristics --- age, marital status, parity --- the analysis of which provided additional insight into the abortion belief structure. For example, we examined how respondents in different age groups (under 25, 26 to 40, 41 to 60, and over 60) judged the abortion decisions made by vignette women in their teens, twenties, thirties, and forties. The interaction of respondents' age and vignette age pointed to cohort effects in the judgement of abortion situations. Our oldest respondents, now in their sixties, gave highest approval for an abortion decision made by women in their forties, whereas the youngest respondents, in their early twenties, gave the highest approval for women in their teens. Respondents between 25 and 40 years, who vary widely in their own position on the reproductive life span, show greater variation in their approval of abortion decisions made by women of various ages.

In similar ways, the analyses of marital status and parity showed that respondents are more likely to sympathize with women who share their marital status or family size. The interaction of respondent's gender and marital status was of special interest: Solo women (never married and divorced) were most likely to sympathize with the abortion decisions made by unmarried vignette women, whereas married and widowed women were most disapproving of abortion decisions made by married vignette women. Marriage may stimulate conservative reproductive values, while the life circumstances of never married and divorced women stimulates sympathy for the decisions made by other single women.

Respondents who are currently childless show the highest approval for the abortion decisions made by childless women. By contrast, respondents who have had more than three children are least likely to approve of abortions to prevent additional births. Preferred family size is also a significant predictor of how respondents judge abortion decisions made by vignette women who differ by parity. Respondents who prefer to remain childless show the highest approval of abortion decisions made by childless women, and respondents who say they would like to have more than three children show the lowest approval of abortion decisions, regardless of vignette women's parity. Family size preferences may be proxy indicators of qualitatively different norms among respondents. Those who wish to remain childless would be most threatened by an unwanted pregnancy, and may therefore emphasize greater choice and discretion in personal reproductive decisions. By contrast those with large family preferences may be more willing to accommodate to poorly timed pregnancies or an additional child, and therefore reject most of the reasons for terminating a pregnancy. Individuals who currently have one or two children are probably very close if not at their desired family size, and hence they approve of abortions for pregnant women whose parity exceeds their own.

In sum, abortion morality largely revolves around a distinction between readily justifiable circumstances and those that are subject to closer scrutiny as a function of respondents' own life course characteristics (age, marital status, parity). The context effects and interactions among vignette dimensions indicate that individuals are sensitive to the complex set of factors involved in any given abortion situation. Concern for fetal life increases in salience as the pregnancy progresses, and imposes limits on approval of abortions. Concern for maternal health and well-being increases acceptance of abortion decisions that are premised on a variety of personal and health related justifications.

Suggestions for Alternate Vignette Designs

The use of both vignettes and a questionnaire raises methodological issues concerning the relative importance of these two sources of data. Questionnaire techniques have a long standing tradition in social science research, while the vignette method (as used in this study) is of recent origin. Vignette studies are complex, time-consuming, and expensive to design, and hence require careful planning and a solid rationale to justify their utility. The use of vignettes in this study was guided by its methodological benefits, as well as the conceptual questions raised by a focus on a multi-dimensional portrayal of abortion situations. By analyzing respondents' judgments of highly specific abortion situations, we are able to infer general patterns of the abortion attitude structure.

The finding that reasons for an abortion represent the central axis around which respondents shape their approval of abortions suggests additional directions for further research. In 1987, the Alan Guttmacher Institute initiated the first systematic survey of women who have had abortions to determine the reasons for their decisions. Results from this study suggest that both conventional surveys of public attitudes toward abortion and the vignettes designed in this study present only a partial picture of the complexity and variety of real life abortion decisions. First, the AGI study results indicate that women have more than one reason for their decision to terminate a pregnancy: young age, financial problems, self-judgment of not being mature enough to carry maternal responsibility, and incompatibility of work-family plans (Torres and Forrest 1988). Second, few women give physical harm from pregnancy or rape as a reason for aborting the pregnancy. Both conventional surveys and the vignettes designed for this study limit the characterization of each abortion decision to only a single reason, and present circumstances that do not approximate the range of reasons given by women at different points along the life course. Third, the reasons women give for their abortions also mirror concerns related to their position in the life course. Hence a fear that carrying a pregnancy to term will interrupt school work, or that parents will be less likely to provide emotional and financial support for the resulting child are some of the concerns that are more likely to emerge among pregnant teenagers. By comparison, an older married woman might fear the interruption of her professional career, the loss of a job, financial burdens, or troubles in the marriage relationship as a consequence of carrying the pregnancy to term. The implications of the results from such studies of real life abortion decisions for the design of future public opinion surveys are as follows.

Future research designs would benefit from elaborating the social-personal circumstances for an abortion, as the public shows the greatest dissensus in responding to these circumstances. In fact, very recent polls of public attitudes toward abortion have added new items that represent reasons given by young, unmarried women, who constitute a major proportion of pregnant women who choose to abort. Opinion surveys conducted by the New York Times and CBS, before and after the Webster decision in April, July, and September 1989, included two new items asking the public for their approval of abortions: legal abortion if the pregnancy would force the teenager to drop out of school, and if the pregnancy would interfere with a professional woman's career (Witwer 1989). A higher percentage (48) favor an abortion if it would prevent a teenager from dropping out of school, than if it would allow a woman to pursue her professional career (37).

Hence it would also be worthwhile to tailor vignette designs to the life course position of pregnant women, because the circumstances faced by teenage women are quite different from those faced by mature married women. For example, studies that wish to understand attitudes toward teenage pregnancy and public preferences for resolving a problematic pregnancy can design vignettes to depict pregnancy circumstances that are unique to teenage women. In this case relevant dimensions might include: family structure, current living situation, extent of financial dependence on parents, past sexual experiences, problems with use and access to contraceptives, importance of schooling in future plans, teenager's emotional stance toward the pregnancy, presence or absence of kin support for the pregnancy, the stability of the couple's relationship, social characteristics of the male partner, and perceived consequences of carrying the pregnancy to term. These dimensions cover the many reasons teenage women give for their abortion decision. These dimensions together can result in a rich description of the diversity of pregnancy circumstances faced by teenage women. These same dimensions take on a different set of implications in the lives of mature married women who face an unwanted pregnancy. Studies that attempt to portray such complexity of circumstances will be better able to model the structure of attitudes individuals bring to bear upon contemporary abortion decisions.

A more direct design implication of the results from the AGI study of abortion decisions concern the number of reasons presented for an abortion decision. Descriptions of hypothetical abortion decisions would have to shift from a focus on a single major reason for the abortion decision to the presentation of a mix of three or four different reasons for an abortion. From a technical point of view, the vignette method is uniquely suited for this purpose, since it allows the design and analysis of many different situational dimensions. The vignette design used in this study could be easily modified to include both greater variation in the specific reasons for an abortion and complex combinations of these reasons. In order to understand how the public evaluates multiple reasons women give for their abortion decision, the reasons that currently appear as levels within one dimension could be presented as separate dimensions. Since the vignette technique combines a single level from each dimension to present the description of a situation, each reason that would appear in combination with other relevant reasons for an abortion can be set up as a separate situational dimension. From an analytical point of view, we could then evaluate the relative importance of each reason on the overall approval of abortion decisions, as well as the interactive effects of combinations of reasons for an abortion.

In the present study, each vignette rated by the respondent also contained contextual information about the woman's life course characteristics, financial and health status, gestation phase, quality of the couple's relationship, the views of partners and parents. Our analyses of interactive effects among selected dimensions suggest that individuals respond to contextual information in evaluating abortion decisions. For example, respondents were more likely to increase their approval of financial problems as a reasons for an abortion only for very poor women. In a similar way, women who were in very poor health were more likely to receive greater approval for their abortion decision even if it was based upon a variety of social-personal circumstances. On the other hand, we found that respondents did not view a desire to remain single as a more valid reason for the abortion decisions made by very young women compared to older women: Neither did they vary their approval of abortions to prevent additional children if they knew the number of children the woman already had. In sum, the research on real life abortion experiences suggests new directions for the study of public opinion on abortion, and the factorial survey method is ideally suited to explore this issue.

The Ideational Context of Abortion

A second major issue in this study concerns the larger structure of beliefs and values that provide a context for abortion attitudes. The view that abortion attitudes are an integral part of an individual's overall worldview is a dominant theme in recent studies of abortion activists, but has received limited attention in studies of public attitudes toward abortion. Until now, most analyses of public attitudes toward abortion have focused on trends in support for legal abortions and linked support or opposition to abortion to social group characteristics such as religion, educational attainment, income, and the like. The data for such analyses have come from large scale national surveys that include repeat items on abortion and other social issues. Analyses of the relationship between abortion attitudes and attitudes in other belief domains have been limited to the inspection of a few available items on euthanasia, suicide, pre-marital sex, capital punishment, and some dimensions of gender roles.

In this study, three major domains were identified to explore the belief structure underlying abortion attitudes: human life values, gender role attitudes, and sex/reproduction. The analysis of these belief domains was structured along two levels of conceptualization. Preliminary analyses focused on the dimensionality of attitude domains, and related this dimensionality to the variation in social-group characteristics of respondents. Based upon the internal coherence of attitudes within each domain, we examined the relationship among all four belief domains. The results suggest that abortion attitudes are strongly rooted in human life values and norms concerning sex/reproduction, but they are weakly related to gender role attitudes.

Human Life Values and Abortion

Within the domain of human life issues we found that attitudes toward euthanasia and suicide show a structure that is very similar to abortion attitudes: Approval of euthanasia and suicide are distinguished in terms of health concerns and social-personal concerns. The factor analyses of items that measured approval of euthanasia for terminally ill patients, and approval of suicide under conditions of an incurable illness, bankruptcy, and if the person is tired of living resulted in two distinct factors that we labelled Terminal-Illness Suicide/Euthanasia and Personal-Social Suicide. This factor structure suggested that respondents distinguish between health factors that justify the termination of life in the case of both suicide and euthanasia, and social-personal situations in which suicide is generally considered unacceptable.

Furthermore, social group characteristics that differentiate approval of euthanasia and suicide parallel those that differentiate approval of health reasons for abortion. A strong commitment to traditional religious beliefs that is reinforced by frequent church attendance results in an absolutist view of human life, such that the taking of human life through euthanasia, suicide, or abortion is highly unacceptable even under conditions of extremely poor health. By contrast, a secular view of life results in tolerance of suicide, euthanasia, and abortion to avoid painful, prolonged suffering. Hence traditional religious beliefs provide the overarching framework within which individuals cast their opposition to euthanasia, suicide, and abortion.

The issue that has been central to the abortion debate is the definition of fetal life and personhood. That this issue is at the heart of abortion values is demonstrated first by the lack of consensus among our respondents in defining human life, and second, by the very high correlation between views regarding the beginning of life and attitudes toward abortion. The majority of our respondents believe that human life begins before birth, and close to a third believe that human life begins at conception or when the fetus is viable. Beliefs about fetal life and personhood draw upon both religious commitment and reproductive values and experiences. The importance of family size in predicting views toward fetal life suggests that opposition to abortion among those who have many children is in part rooted in the centrality of children in personal life, and these people link the personhood of the fetus and the sanctity of human life to conception and very early pregnancy as the beginning of 'human life'. This linkage has also been found in studies of pro-life activists who interpret their reproductive lives within the context of religious values (Luker 1984).

Sex/Reproduction and Abortion

In our attempt to tap values in the domain of Sex/Reproduction we asked our respondents for their views on a variety of issues ranging from pre-marital sex, homosexuality, contraceptive access to teenagers, extra-marital sex, teenage parenthood, and various forms of artificial reproduction. A factor analysis of responses to various questions on sexuality and contraception resulted in five distinct dimensions of attitudes in this domain: Attitudes toward pre-marital sex in the context of a committed relationship, attitudes toward casual pre-marital sex, homosexuality, extra-marital sex, and teenage contraceptive access. This dimensionality suggested non-overlapping moral concerns across different aspects of sexuality and reproduction as well as variation in attitudes among respondents as a function of their age, gender, church attendance, and educational attainment. Permissive views toward pre-marital sex, homosexuality, extra-marital sex, teenage access to contraception, and various forms of artificial reproduction were positively related to higher educational attainment. By contrast, a higher frequency of church attendance was negatively related to permissive views toward these issues. The positive effect of educational attainment on permissive views toward sexual and reproductive issues points to the secular influences of higher education in stimulating tolerance of individual discretion in sexual and reproductive matters. And the negative relationship between age and permissive attitudes toward sexuality underscores the historical context in which different reproductive cohorts became exposed to issues related to sex, contraception, and pregnancy. Among our young respondents, who attained sexual maturity during the 1960s 1970s, and 1980s, pre-marital sex, contraception, homosexuality, and legal abortions were topics that were openly discussed in public as issues of individual choice and discretion. Older respondents may have retained conservative views toward matters of sexuality that were prevalent when they themselves were young. On the other hand, the possibility that attitudes in the domain of sex/reproduction may change over the life course of individuals can also mean that older respondents may have shifted to more conservatives views on pre-marital sex or contraception as a result of the duties and responsibilities of parenthood.

It is also important to note that attitudes toward various aspects of sex and reproduction do not differ significantly by religious affiliation, as they do by religiosity. Differences between Catholics and non-Catholics are found only in the abortion domain, not on other attitude measures concerning sexual and contraceptive behavior. Unfortunately, we were not able to examine differences by religious affiliation in greater detail by distinguishing Protestants by denominations or Catholics by ethnic origins. The category of non-Catholics used in our analyses contains a mix of Protestants, those reporting 'no affiliation', and a very small minority of Jews. However, our findings on Catholic/non-Catholic differences in attitude toward sexuality, contraception, and abortion underscore an important point. Since the 1960s Catholics have become similar to Protestants in their attitudes and behavior in the area of pre-marital sex, contraceptive use, and fertility. Furthermore, as many Catholics resort to abortion as adults from other religious groups. From a social change perspective, the lingering difference between Catholics and non-Catholics in their attitudes toward abortion is a reflection of significant differences among older cohorts of Catholics and Protestants, but not the younger cohorts of Catholics and Protestants who differ little in the extent to which they engage in pre-marital sex, use birth control pills, or resort to abortions to prevent an unwanted pregnancy. This issue was explored in an attempt to relate attitudinal differences by religious affiliation with age of our respondents.

While the factor structure showed a multi-dimensional profile of attitudes in the domain of sex/reproduction, attitudinal indicators were strongly intercorrelated, suggesting an underlying liberal-conservative dimension. The only exception to this pattern was found for attitudes toward teenage parenthood. Much to our surprise, our sample showed very high approval of a teenager's decision to carry a pregnancy to term. This finding implies that within the context of an abortion survey, respondents support unmarried motherhood when the alternative is abortion. Their tolerance for teenage parenthood also arises from a respect for the views of parents and partners, in situations where they support the minor woman's decision to carry the pregnancy to term.

Gender Roles and Abortion

Studies of abortion activists have emphasized the centrality of gender role ideology to views on abortion, but studies of public attitudes toward abortion have found no consistent relationship between gender role attitudes and abortion attitudes. Empirical studies of the relationship between abortion attitudes and gender role attitudes have relied upon indicators of sex role attitudes found in national surveys, and the choice of items varies from one analysis to another. From one point of view, the domain of gender roles encompasses a microcosm of many aspects of social life, and hence attitudes and beliefs regarding the roles of men and women will necessarily reflect a great degree of dimensionality.

The measures used in this study tapped attitudes toward empowerment of women in national politics, salience of work over family life, women's work roles and family responsibilities, the importance of children in marriage, parental involvement in child care, and equal sharing of childcare and domestic chores by husbands and wives. Factor analysis of these items showed three underlying constructs, which we labelled Parental Primacy, Gender Role Integration, and Domestic Role Sharing. The relationships among these three dimensions of gender role attitudes and with abortion attitudes ranged from moderate to weak. This finding suggests the following interpretation.

The factor structure shows that the three aspects of gender role ideology do not represent a single underlying construct that captures a liberal-traditional continuum of attitudes and beliefs. Many of our respondents simultaneously hold liberal views toward some aspects of gender roles and more traditional views toward other aspects of gender roles. For example, approval of equal sharing of domestic chores and child care between husbands and wives is distinct from attitudes toward women's empowerment in politics and work. The fact that the majority of our respondents approve of equal involvement of husbands and wives in domestic chores and childcare, but vary widely on issues related to women's employment and parental responsibilities for childcare suggests that the ideology of equality is more readily accepted within the domestic domain. This finding is clearly at odds with recent literature that points to an increased involvement of mothers in paid employment, and little change in domestic role sharing among women and men (McLaughlin et al 1989). Mothers who work full-time in the labor force continue to carry major responsibility for home maintenance and child care, and egalitarian division of responsibilities in the domestic domain has be slow to merge in response to women's increased and continued participation in the labor force (Hochschild 1989).

The lack of consistent results across different studies in establishing a relationship between gender role attitudes and abortion attitudes also point to problems in measurement, and the need for more carefully constructed items in future studies. The research challenge lies in identifying good measures of gender role attitudes that tap the variation in support and opposition to abortion. That no simple liberal-conservative continuum underlies attitudes and beliefs in the domain of gender roles is also illustrated by the fact that even among pro-life activists the opposition to abortions does not arise from an opposition to the advancement of women's political and economic rights (Luker 1984), but rather from traditional views toward sexuality and reproduction.

Abortion attitudes are strongly linked to attitudes in the domains of Human life and Sex and Reproduction, but weakly linked to gender role ideology. The three domains of abortion, sex/reproduction, and human life show significant intercorrelations, which point to an underlying unity of values individuals bring to issues within these domains. In addition, the finding that gender role attitudes show the strongest relationship to attitudes in the domain of sex/reproduction suggests an indirect link between abortion attitudes and gender role ideology. As more women opt for higher education and become entrenched in the labor force for longer periods of their reproductive life time, the necessity for closely spaced and planned births will result in a reevaluation of work and family priorities. The need to prevent unwanted births as the acceptance of additional children becomes problematic may result in a change in views toward abortion, sterilization, and gender roles.

The political-ideological links among the four belief domains have emerged over the course of the history of abortion politics. Human life values have been a central part of abortion morality for a much longer period of time, just as sexual and reproductive norms have shaped fertility patterns. The connection between gender role issues and abortion attitudes, as it is articulated in the contemporary abortion debate, has emerged with structural changes in the experiences of work and family life. However, abortion attitudes also draw upon deeply held beliefs and values about obligations toward family members, respect for human life, and the meaning and purpose of sexuality and procreation. These values produce conflicts for individuals faced with a decision to terminate an unwanted pregnancy, and detract from an unconditional acceptance of abortion. The differences in the value orientation our respondents bring to the abortion issue are also rooted in the social-historical context of their reproductive lives. Three social group indicators - age, religion, and gender - provide an opportunity to examine variations in abortion attitudes within the social-historical context of individual lives.

Age, Gender, and Religion

A third major topic in this study was the impact of social change on the values individuals bring to bear on the abortion issue. We examined age differences in attitudes toward abortion in order to place abortion attitudes within the historical context in which our respondents reached sexual maturity, and personally confronted decisions concerning sex, contraception, and pregnancy. Over the past few decades the experience of abortions, the political salience of abortion, and the moral issues central to abortion politics have changed such that the abortion issue carries a different meaning for young women and men today than it did for older generations in their youth. New dimensions of the abortion debate now concern the relative rights of pregnant women, fetuses, and family members in an abortion decision. That these issues are directly relevant to the lived experiences of recent reproductive cohorts was illustrated in a variety of ways. First, very young respondents now in their early twenties showed a highly integrated structure of attitudes within the abortion domain, as well as across all four belief domains investigated in this study. Older respondents in their sixties, seventies, and eighties who completed their childbearing before the legalization of abortions were less apt to consider abortion as a woman's rights issue. Furthermore, older respondents exempt their views on gender roles from the stance they take on abortion, human life issues, and sex/reproduction. These age differences suggest cohort differences in the values the young and the old bring to the abortion issue.

We found little support for a linear trend toward a more integrated structure of beliefs within each younger age-group of respondents. Respondents in their twenties showed significant positive correlations between their views on gender roles, abortion, sexuality/reproduction, and human life issues. Respondents in their forties and fifties similarly showed a highly integrated structure of attitudes across all four belief domains. The oldest respondents in their sixties, seventies and eighties showed significant positive correlations among abortion attitudes, human life attitudes, and attitudes toward sexuality/reproduction, but not gender role attitudes. But respondents currently 26 to 40 years of age differed from both younger and older respondents, in that they showed the least coherent structure of attitudes across the four belief domains.

A comparative analysis of age differences in belief structure using data from the 1985 General Social Surveys showed partial support for our findings. The differences between very young and very old respondents that suggested a high coherence of attitudes across all belief domains among the very young, and a relatively loose structure of attitudes among older respondents were sustained. On the other hand the GSS data indicated other differences that were in contrast to findings from our Greenfield data set: Respondents who are 25 to 40 years of age showed closely related views in all four domains in the GSS data set, but they showed the least coherent structure in our own data set. Hence both the GSS data set and the Greenfield data set do not provide strong evidence for a linear pattern of increasing ideological coherence among each younger cohort of respondents.

There are at least two limitations to drawing firm conclusions regarding cohort differences in the abortion belief structure from our data. First, a clear demonstration of cohort effects requires repeated measures of attitudes over time for different birth cohorts. In the absence of such longitudinal data, age differences in attitudes mask multiple effects due to maturation, life course position, and cohort membership. A next step in exploring these issues would require a detailed specification of age categories and the use of national trend data to secure repeated measures for different birth cohorts. A detailed specification of age categories would allow us to pinpoint the critical point in the reproductive life span of individuals when their attitudes toward sexual and reproductive issues are shaped. But the tremendous variation in timing and patterning of reproductive life events among families today suggests that we will not find a single inflection point along the life course when values in many life domains converge into a coherent belief structure.

A second limitation in drawing strong inferences about cohort shifts in value orientation is related to the local peculiarities of our sample. The Greenfield sample contains a greater proportion of Catholics than representative national samples. Hence an interaction of effects due to age and religious affiliation that emerge strongly within this sample could result in a different aggregate profile of attitudes across age groups.

The evidence for interactive effects of age and religion was found in the different cohort profiles shown by Catholics and Non-Catholics, although results must be interpreted with caution because of the small cases bases when our sample is divided by both age and religious affiliation. Our analyses indicate that Catholics differ from non-Catholics in the extent to which they approve of abortions, and bring a different cluster of beliefs and values to bear upon the abortion issue. Non-Catholics show a highly integrated structure of attitudes that shape their views toward abortion, human life issues, sex/reproduction and gender roles. By contrast, Catholics show less coherence to their beliefs and values across these domains: their views toward abortion are placed within the context of human life values. These differences are most pronounced between very young

Catholics and non-Catholics. In light of the historical trend toward diminishing Catholic-Protestant differences in attitudes and behavior in the areas of pre-marital sex, contraception, and abortion these findings point to different responses to social change among Catholics and non-Catholics. Catholics have gradually exempted their beliefs regarding gender roles, sexuality, and reproduction from their moral views toward abortion, at the same time that non-Catholics developed an internally cohesive system of beliefs in these different domains. Over time many lay Catholics have departed in their behavior and values from the Church's position on contraception, sterilization, divorce, and pre-marital sex. For older Catholics, many aspects of family life were influenced by a higher degree of participation in church and parish activities, and conservative views toward sexuality, gender roles, abortion, and contraception drew upon religious values.

In a similar vein, women compared to men show a more tightly knit system of beliefs surrounding their attitudes toward abortion. A liberal position on abortion among women is consistently linked to permissive views toward sexuality/reproduction, human life issues, and a liberal political orientation. Gender role attitudes are much more important to the position women take on issues related to abortion, sexuality, and human life, than is the case for men. While men and women show no significant differences in the extent to which they approve of abortions for a variety of reasons, the different position they hold on gender role issues and sexual and reproductive matters results in a different moral calculus that underlies their respective attitudes toward abortion. Among women, both opposition to abortions and support for abortions are closely related to opposing views on human life issues, gender roles, and sexuality. Among men, support or opposition to abortion is not strongly linked to their position on gender roles, or to their overall liberal-conservative political orientation.

Behavior, Attitudes and Abortion Politics

In this concluding section we discuss the relationship between public attitudes toward abortion and behavior in this domain, and suggest implications for the future of abortion policy in the United States. A question that has intrigued both scholars and activists alike concerns the lack of fit between public attitudes toward abortion and their behavior in this domain. Statistics gathered since the legalization of abortion underscore the importance of abortion in the reproductive lives of young Americans. More than 20 million women have had legal abortions since abortion became legalized in 1973. Currently, more than a million women resort to abortions every year. Paradoxically, trend data on public opinion gathered since 1965 and findings from our own study indicate that the public shows only moderate support for the actual circumstances abortion clients faced in reaching their decisions. We have few measures in our study to directly address this broader question. But it is useful to begin with two findings that highlight the complex relationship between abortion values and personal reproductive experiences.

The findings on two simple measures of personal reproductive experiences indicate that respondents' family size and exposure to abortions have significant and opposite effects on abortion attitudes. Approval of abortion declines significantly with an increase in respondents' family size, and a personal exposure to abortion or the knowledge of the abortion experiences of friends or relatives results in a significant increase in the acceptance of abortion. Since our measures are based upon reports at one point in time, we cannot draw causal inferences regarding the influence of abortion experiences on abortion attitudes, and vice versa. An assumption of reciprocal influences of attitudes and behavior leads us to conclude that individuals who have personally experienced an abortion, and those who know of abortion experiences of friends and relatives may have developed more favorable views toward abortions as a result of such exposures. On the other hand, a liberal position on abortion may predispose individuals to consider abortion a viable solution to an unwanted pregnancy.

In a similar way, the impact of family size points to the mutual influence of values and personal experiences. Individuals who have many children are, by actual behavior, demonstrating the salience of children in their personal family life; and those who solved an unwanted pregnancy by having the child may find it difficult to view the child as unwanted after its birth. To our knowledge, there are no detailed studies that have traced the decision making processes that lead to abortion decisions, and the subsequent impact of such decisions on the attitudes individuals hold toward abortion. Most longitudinal studies of reproductive decisions focus on macro data on timing, sequencing, and number of completed births, and infer the impact of social and cultural factors on these decisions. Most studies of women who have experienced abortions usually suffer from sampling problems, and have generally focused on the immediate psychological sequelae of abortion experiences. Obtaining adequate data on the abortion experiences of individuals is difficult because of the highly sensitive nature of abortion, which continues to be a personally complex and conflictual choice for many women.

The ideal study to address the issue of the links between abortion attitudes and abortion behavior would have to include a broader conception of reproductive values and reproductive behavior. Such a study would trace individuals through the reproductive life span in terms of formation and change in values on pertinent life domains, and the decisions made regarding sex, contraception, marriage, and childbearing. Until future research on reproductive behavior takes into account the importance of reproductive values, we cannot address the complex relationship between abortion attitudes and abortion behavior.

However, two explanations are relevant to understanding the lack of fit between social values on abortion and the experience and incidence of abortions in contemporary society (Rossi and Sitaraman 1988). The first suggests that those who experience an abortion exempt their experiences as personal departures from the social norm. For example women who decide to have an abortion for a variety of reasons view their decision as a personal necessity and may continue to uphold moral opposition to abortions in general. Second, from a historical point of view, high infant and maternal mortality due to a high susceptibility to disease and natural disasters, required families to have many children to assure the survival of a few. In this long evolutionary context, deep rooted pro-natalism has been the cultural background against which deliberate control of fertility was exercised by family and individuals. Individuals and families in high fertility societies may have simultaneously held to these norms, and departed in their personal experiences at those times when fertility control optimized family survival. Both in the past and at present there are many discrepancies between individual-family strategies and larger societal concerns related to population control.

From the point of view of social change in values and behavior, ambivalent attitudes toward abortion represent variation in the views found among different social groups as they move through a transitional phase in the transformation of values, including those relevant to abortion. This point was illustrated by our analysis of the impact of social change on the abortion belief structure. Among elderly respondents who faced pregnancy decisions when abortions were both unsafe and illegal, the very fact of illegality restricted access to abortions, and perhaps reinforced normative sanctions against abortions. In this context, many women had abortion while retaining traditional values that disapproved of their own actions. Even in contemporary societies, legalization has eased the access to abortions, but it has failed to resolve the moral conflict faced by individuals who decide to terminate a pregnancy.

One Czechoslovakian study traced the psycho-social development of children born to women who were twice denied an abortion for the same pregnancy. David et al (1988) note that a third of these women denied that they had ever applied for an abortion. The records available from the Prague Abortion Appellate Commission indicate that these women provided more than one reason for their desire to terminate a pregnancy, the most common reasons being housing shortage, financial constraints, unmarried status, and an unstable relationship -- social and economic reasons that parallel those found among women in the United States. Interestingly, 65 percent of these abortion appeals were rejected on the basis of "insufficient" reasons. While the women who were twice denied an abortion constituted only a minority of all women who applied for an abortion, their denial of access to an abortion suggests the incompatibility of societal values regarding parenthood and personal circumstances that lead to an abortion decision. An even more important point made by David and his colleagues concerns the changing conception of particular pregnancies as wanted or unwanted, such that individuals who resolve an unwanted pregnancy in childbirth may subsequently develop positive views toward that pregnancy following the birth of the child. The micro context of reproductive decision making thus sheds light on the processes by which individuals negotiate moral views toward abortion with personal experiences.

Viewed on a continuum of reproductive strategies to curtail parental investment in children (Hausfater and Hrdy 1984) the incidence of abortion varies through historical time and cultures. Societies that have a lower incidence of abortions, also show evidence of a higher incidence of infanticide, abandonment, and differential investment in the care of children by birth order and sex, along with high fertility. In a provocative thesis on child abandonment, Boswell (1989) maintains that the practice of abandonment was a safe and widespread means of fertility control from antiquity to the 18th century in Western Europe. Strong sanctions against infanticide, and the greater risks to maternal health associated with abortion relative to pregnancy and childbirth led to the development of abandonment as a social mechanism to alleviate the burden of unwanted pregnancies. Unlike infanticide, abandonment involved placing unwanted children in public places so that their survival might be assured by the "kindness of strangers" who took custody of the children. Throughout this long history, laws and social customs regulating abandonment shifted from a informal system of social welfare to a highly institutionalized system of foundling homes that emerged in the 18th century. With the rise of Christianity, abandonment was regulated through the ritual of "oblation" : children left by parents at church doors as a "gift of a child to God" came to be raised as monks or nuns. It is interesting to note that laws regulating abandonment at various points in their early history focused less on the punishment of parents, and more on the legal rights of abandoned children. While Boswell ends his history of abandonment in 18th century Europe, we might add that abandonment is an unfortunate fate experienced by children in many poor countries today, where lack of easy access to contraceptives, and unsafe abortion practices leave women to make wrenching life choices.

A much less visible form of curtailment of parental investment in children is found in the differential provision of health care and nutrition to different offspring. The high incidence of infanticide, abandonment, and differential care of offspring does not necessarily imply a callous attitude toward human life in those societies. The adoption of such extreme measures is also likely to be patterned along culturally acceptable deviations from the norm, where a high premium placed upon maternal health and survival of existing children results in the adoption of drastic measures to control family size, especially late births.

From this perspective, the high incidence of abortions in developed countries results in part from the lack of fool-proof contraceptives, access to safe legal abortions, and strong sanctions against abandonment and infanticide. As compared to the past, abortions involve fewer health risks to pregnant women than pregnancy and childbirth. Societal concerns over fertility rates below replacement level are in sharp contrast to the needs and desires of families and individual women who wish to postpone births, limit family size, or remain childless. While many opponents of abortion cite adoption as a viable solution to an unwanted pregnancy, the particular circumstances that shape current patterns of fertility control render this option less desirable. Among teenagers and young unmarried women the task of carrying the pregnancy to term disrupts continued involvement in schooling and jobs. Furthermore, the legal complications involved in adoption arrangements, and the preference for children of particular racial backgrounds eliminates adoption as an option for many women.

The fact that the public shows only moderate support for the many reasons that lead to real life abortion decisions also raises an important question concerning the implications of the relationship between public values and behavior for the future of abortion policy. There are several reasons for believing that access to legal abortions will continue to be needed: The lack of any fool-proof contraceptive in the near future, recent concerns related to sexually transmitted diseases, and the fact that pre-marital sexual abstinence is not a viable goal to reduce unwanted pregnancies. Developments in in-utero fetal research have also led to the diagnoses of a variety of fetal defects early in pregnancy suggesting a greater need for abortion in these cases as many women opt to have only one or two children. But such diagnoses of fetal defects can only be concluded around 16 to 18 weeks of pregnancy. Currently the majority of the public support abortion in the case of fetal deformity. It is unclear to what extent the movement in support of the rights of the handicapped could alter the current public support for abortions under conditions of fetal deformity. However, unless efforts are made to directly address the reasons why women have abortions, no amount of moral debate and education will reduce the need for legal abortions. The complex structure of public attitudes toward abortion provides a useful corrective to the simplified polarity of perspectives found among abortion activists. There may also be more compassionate ways to resolve the highly polarized debate over abortion.

Public Attitudes and Abortion Politics

Our analyses of the links between public attitudes toward abortion and support for the pro-choice and pro-life position on abortion showed that respondents base their support for abortion groups on the extent to which they approve of abortions. Furthermore, our respondents consider a simultaneous support for the views expressed by pro-choice and pro-life groups as highly incompatible. Abortion attitudes were only moderately correlated with a liberal political orientation, with very young respondents and women most apt to incorporate their views on abortion, human life, gender roles, and sex/reproduction into a liberal political orientation. This finding points to the political salience of the abortion issue for youth and women, such that a liberal political orientation embraces permissive views toward abortion, together with a host of other life style and personal morality issues. Older respondents who reached adulthood in an earlier era exempt their views on abortion, sexuality, gender roles and human life from their overall political orientation.

Another interesting finding from these analyses concerned the changing relationship between religiosity (church attendance) and a liberal political orientation. Among each younger age group of respondents, we found a progressively stronger negative correlation between high frequency of church attendance and a liberal political orientation. We interpret this finding to suggest broader historical changes in the definition of political liberalism and conservatism, and a greater polarization of values along religious and political lines. The continued salience of religiosity in shaping abortion attitudes of both young and old respondents and the additional salience of political orientation for the views young respondents and women bring to the abortion issue implies a long term trend that links secularism and a liberal political ideology.

In light of these findings, it is not surprising to read that recent polls target women and youth as important constituencies in shaping the future of abortion politics. Until now studies of the impact of public opinion on abortion on political outcomes in elections do not suggest the public votes on the basis of their support for the candidate's stance on abortion. That this situation may shift in light of the recent Supreme Court decision on abortion has resulted in attempts by both pro-life and pro-choice groups to identify voters on the basis of the salience of the abortion issue for their political behavior. Within the Republican party the concern over candidates' stance on abortion has been heightened by defeats in two gubernatorial races in New Jersey and Virginia where the two democratic candidates took strong pro-choice positions. Some Republican party members, such as Olympia Snowe of Maine, the co-chair of the Congressional Caucus for Women's Issues would prefer that the party abandon its opposition to abortion rights (Shirbman 1989).

It is unclear as to how different state restrictions such as fetal viability tests may affect access to abortions. First, the two requirements upheld by the Supreme Court in the Webster decision may have little impact on access to legal abortion for many women. Most abortions are performed at between 12 and 14 weeks of gestation, and hence few women would have to undergo tests to ascertain fetal viability at 20 weeks of gestation. Second, the requirement that public employees and hospitals not involve themselves in abortion services may have little impact, as the majority of abortions are performed in private clinics and hospitals. On the other hand, many fear that attempts to grant greater state control of abortion may intensify the political struggle over abortion, as each state legislates on many different aspects of legal abortion. Furthermore, the response of different states to the Court's decision is likely to vary by the historical legislation of abortion in these states, with conservative states imposing greater restrictions on access to abortions compared to states with a liberal history of abortion legislation. The determination of pro-choice groups to lobby for the importation of the abortion pill, RU486, has led many to predict a quick end to the abortion issue.

One important area in which the politics of abortion has had the most serious impact is in the area of fetal research. Since the legalization of abortion in 1973, anti-abortion lobbyists have attempted to curtail federal funding of various forms of fetal research. Fetal research varies from in-utero research to the use of fetal tissue transplantation (Gold and Lehrman 1989). The transplantation of fetal tissue obtained from induced abortions into severely ill patients is particularly important in the treatment of diabetes and Parkinson's disease. The opposition to fetal research has come from anti-abortion activists who have claimed that such research could potentially encourage abortions among women, and in general leads to a "dehumanized" view of fetal life. Vigorous lobbying on the part of pro-life activists under the auspices of a sympathetic, conservative administration has resulted in continued threats to federal funding of important bio-medical research.

Another possible outcome of the shift in the locus of the abortion debate from courts to state legislatures is that it can open up a new set of possibilities in the area of abortion policy. These possibilities concern the linking of abortion with legislation on maternal health, childcare, social welfare, and contraceptive education. Thus far the polarized dialogue of abortion activists has detracted public attention from the common concerns they share on a variety of issues.

The United States differs markedly from other developed countries in this regard. In a comparative analysis of approaches to abortion and divorce laws in many developed countries, Glendon (1987) points to sharp differences in the legal approach to the abortion issue in the United States and Western European countries. Glendon argues that abortion law based on the view of constitutional rights to privacy represents a highly individualistic conception that is unique to the United States. American law shows little concern for the fetus, or maternal health, or childcare. In other words, the law guarantees the right to abortion while sidestepping the social circumstances that lead to an abortion decision. By comparison, Glendon argues that the approach of countries like France and Germany has been to reaffirm the importance of human life, while in practice allowing for abortions under circumstances of acute 'distress'. These laws, in turn, have been backed up by a wide variety of public support programs to reduce the need for abortions and avert the burdens of an unwanted pregnancy. The 1979 French Law, for example, reads as follows:

> The law guarantees respect for every human being from the commencement of life. There shall be no derogation from this principle except in cases of necessity and under the conditions laid down by this law. . .The teaching of this principle and its consequences, the provision of information on the problems of life and of national and international demography, education toward responsibility, the acceptance of the child in society, and family-oriented policy are national obligations." (in Glendon 1987: 16)

The French law requires that abortion be performed early (10 weeks), and that the pregnant women receive counselling and information regarding alternative ways to resolve the pregnancy, contraceptive education, and a brief waiting period before the performance of the abortion. The government also facilitates access to birth control, and provides generous support for unwed mothers and married mothers. Among staunch supporters and opponents of abortion in the United States this approach to abortion regulation may be viewed with suspicion and uneasiness. From another perspective, the French approach to abortion legislation represents a "humane, democratic compromise " (Glendon 1987:20).

There are two positive implications of compromise legislation on abortion. First, a simultaneous respect for fetal life and for the woman in situations of distress would find support among the majority of Americans whose views mirror these dual concerns. Second, Glendon argues that a compromise legislation, in conjunction with active public support for a variety of family policies can alleviate the problems of unwanted pregnancies, and simultaneously convey a responsible message to the public. The politics of abortion in countries where such a compromise position pervades law and policy is less intense and polarized. There is a growing concern in feminist circles that the extreme views represented by abortion activists in the United States detracts from a focus on the actual experiences of women who have abortions (Elshtain 1986, Ooms 1986). By focusing heavily on a individualistic conception of rights, that is highly isolating to many people, extreme supporters of abortion have failed to take into consideration the dependency that permeates relationships between women and children, and between women and their families. Glendon draws attention to an important ideological difference in the legal approach taken to abortion in the United States and Western European countries like France and Germany. In the United States, a right to privacy in matters of sex and contraception has meant "the right to be left alone;" in the European legal system with its more communalistic focus on social welfare, individual rights are of less importance, and reproductive choice has meant genuine access to alternatives including abortion. Similarly, extreme opponents of abortion ignore the real life circumstances that lead women to terminate a pregnancy.

From another point of view the exclusive focus on extreme views on the morality of abortion has blurred the common ground shared by women who are pro-choice and those who are pro-life. The central thesis of anthropologist Faye Ginsberg's (1989) recent study of the emergence, articulation, and resolution of abortion politics in a small mid-western community illuminates the common ground shared by abortion activists on both sides of the issue, and provides hope for the resolution of the abortion debate in the larger society. Ginsberg traces the activism of pro-choice and pro-life women in Fargo, North Dakota to their personal biographies, and to the longer history of women's movements in the United States that have centered around the relationship among women's identity, work, and family life. Pro-life feminists fear the challenge of modern society to qualities of nurturance and domesticity that are rooted in women's reproductive lives and shape their moral responses to life choices. In this context abortion represents an erosion of values such as obligations toward the community and others, and the care of the weak and dependent. Furthermore, Ginsberg argues that pro-life opposition to abortion arises not simply from an essentialist view of gender differences, but from a concern for the types of stances women take toward their reproductive capacities. A decision to abort implies denial of the unique qualities of nurturance and a host of other values that women bring to their reproductive experiences. For pro-life activists, abortion encourages male irresponsibility and reduces obligations toward women and children. According to the leader of the Lutherans for Life:

> It is realistic, accurate and humane to recognize that pregnancies exist which are distressful to the woman and her family. Unfortunately, because abortion on demand erodes a sense of collective responsibility for the woman in actual crisis, she is abandoned to heartless individualism. In a society where programs, services and funding are geared toward abortion rather than toward addressing the causes which make a particular pregnancy a problem, the woman in stress is forsaken. Adjustment of health care plans could eliminate one form of coercion to abort... Insurance policies to cover newborns from birth would relieve the economic pressures confronting those who discover that they are to be parents of a handicapped child (in Ginsberg 1989:215)

Ginsberg's account of the abortion debate in this midwestern community has a different ending from other stories of abortion activists. At the end of a long period of confrontation, the activist participants in this study took an active step toward resolving their differences. Responding to an article by the author, the activists gathered to explore a new group called "Pro-Dialogue". The emergence of 'Pro-Dialogue' is rather unusual in the history of contemporary politics of abortion, yet its emergence in this North Dakota community is consistent with its long cherished tradition of tolerance. The group was formed based upon a realization that activists on both sides of the issue share much common ground beyond their differences in the area of abortion. "Pro-Dialogue" may represent an anomaly and a rare event in the eyes of abortion activists elsewhere in the country, but it gives a glimmer of hope that tolerance and compromise are real options. The group's activities have emphasized greater dialogue than concerted action, as Ginsberg points out, but this dialogue is worth recounting as it shows directions for a more compassionate, yet radical resolution of the abortion debate.

We began by having each person tell their reasons for coming to the meeting. The most frequent reasons given was "I just want to get to know the people on the other side of the issue. I've never really talked about abortion with someone who's on the other side."

. . .Another said "We should be allies on most of women's issues --- but our disagreement on one issue (abortion) has kept us from cooperating on all of the other issues that would insure a better life for all people"

As we talked and listened that night, we discovered some very important common ground. We wished that women would not be faced with pregnancies:

---that they couldn't afford,
---that at times they weren't ready for
---by people they didn't love
---or for any of the many reasons women have abortions.

That common ground gave us something concrete...a goal
we could work toward together."To direct our energies
toward reducing as much as possible the need for
abortion". . .We were

Picketers of Abortion Clinics
and
Patient Advocates who walked with women through the picket lines
to the clinics

(Minutes from the meeting of Pro-Dialogue, Ginsberg 1989:224)

Bibliography

Arney, W.R. and W.H. Trescher. Trends in Attitudes Toward Abortion:1972-1975. *Family Planning Perspectives,* 1976,8:117.

Barnatt, S.N. and R.J. Harris. Recent Changes in Predictors of Abortion Attitudes. *Sociology and Social Research,* 1982,66,3:321.

Benin, M.H. Determinants of Opposition to Abortion: An analysis of hard and soft scales. *Sociological Perspectives,* 1985:28,2,:199.

Blake, J. The Supreme Court's Abortion Decisions and Public Opinion in the United States. *Population and Development Review,* 1977,3,:45.

Blake,J. Abortion and Public Opinion in 1960-70 Decade. *Science,* 1971,171:540.

Blake, J. and J.H. del Pinal. Negativism, Equivocation and Wobbly Assent: Public 'Support' for the Pro-choice Platform on Abortion. *Demography,* 1981,18,3:309.

Blake, J. Catholicism and Fertility: On Attitudes of young Americans. *Population and Development Review,* 1984,10,2:329.

Blumstein, P. and P. Schwartz. *American Couples: Money, Work, Sex.* Morrow Press, New York, 1983.

Boswell, John. *The Kindness of Strangers: The Abandonment of Children in Western Europe from Late Antiquity to the Renaissance.* Pantheon Books, New York, 1988.

Butler, J.D. and D.F. Walbert (eds.) *Abortion, Medicine and the Law.* Facts On File Publications, New York, 1986.

Callahan, S. and D. Callahan. *Abortion: Understanding Differences.* Plenum Press, New York, 1984.

Center for Disease Control. *Abortion Surveillance Reports.* Atlanta, Georgia, 1983.

Chafe, William H. *The American Woman.* Oxford University Press, London, 1972.

D'Antonio, W.V. The American Catholic Family: Signs of Cohesion and Polarization. *Journal of Marriage and Family,* 1985,47:395.

David, Henry P. et al. *Born Unwanted: Developmental Effects of Denied Abortion*. Springer Publications, 1988.

Davis, James A. and Tom W. Smith. *General Social Surveys: Cumulative Codebooks*. National Opinion Research Center (producer),Chicago, 1988.

Deitch, C. Ideology and Opposition to Abortion: Trends in Public Opinion, 1972-1980. *Alternative Lifestyles*, 1983,6,1:6.

Donovan, P. The Holy War. *Family Planning Perspectives,* 1985,17:5.

Donovan, P. When the Conventional Wisdom Is Wrong: A Reexamination of the Role of Abortion as an Issue in Federal Elections, 1974-1986. *The Alan Guttmacher Institute,* New York, 1988:16.

Ebaugh, H.R.F. and C.A. Haney. Church Attendance and Attitudes toward Abortion: Differentials in Liberal and Conservative Churches. *Journal for the Scientific Study of Religion,* 1978,17:407.

Ebaugh, H.R.F. and C.A. Haney. Shifts in Abortion Attitudes: 1972-78. *Journal of Marriage and Family,* 1980,42,3:491.

Ebaugh, H.R.F. and C.A. Haney. Abortion Attitudes in the United States: Continuities and Discontinuities. in P. Sachdev (ed.) 1985:163.

Elshtain, J. B. Reflections on Abortion, Values, and the Family. in S. Callahan and D. Callahan (eds.) *Abortion: Understanding Differences,* Plenum Press, New York, 1984.

Elshtain, J.B. *The Family in Political Thought.* University of Massachusetts Press, Amherst, 1982.

Finlay, B. Sex Differences in Correlates of Abortion Attitudes Among College Students. *Journal of Marriage and Family* (August), 1981:571.

Francoeur, R.T. Reproductive Technologies: New Alternatives and New Ethics. *Siecus Report,* 1985,xiv,1:1.

Ginsberg, F. *Contested Lives:* The Abortion Debate in an American Community. University of California Press, Los Angeles, 1989.

Glendon, Mary Ann. *Abortion and Divorce in Western Law.* Harvard University Press, Cambridge, Massachusetts, 1987.

Gold, R. B. and D. Lehrman. Fetal Research Under Fire: The Influence of Abortion Politics. *Family Planning Perspectives,* 1989,21(January/February):6.

Granberg, D. Pro-life or Reflection of Conservative Ideology? An Analysis of Opposition to Legalized Abortion. *Sociology and Social Research,* 1984,62:414.

Granberg, D. and B.W. Granberg. Pro-life versus Pro-choice: Another look at the abortion controversy in the United States. *Sociology and Social Research,* 1978,65,4:424.

Granberg, D. and B.W. Granberg. Abortion Attitudes, 1965-1980: Trends and Determinants. *Family Planning Perspectives,* 1980,12,5:250.

Granberg, D. and B.W. Granberg. Social Bases of Support and Opposition to Legalized Abortion. in P.Sachdev (ed.) *Perspectives on Abortion.* Scarecrow Press, Metuchen, N.J., 1985.

Granberg, D. The Abortion Activists. *Family Planning Perspectives,* 1981,13:157.

Granberg, D. The Abortion Issue in the 1984 Elections, *Family Planning Perspectives,* 1987, 19:59.

Guth, J.L. The New Right in R.C. Liebman and R. Wuthnow (ed.) *The New Christian Right.* Aldine Publishing Co. N.Y., 1983.

Hall, E.J. and M.M. Ferree. Race Differences in Abortion Attitudes. *Public Opinion Quarterly,* 1986,50:193.

Hausfater, G. and S.B. Hrdy. Introduction. in G. Hausfater and S.B. Hrdy (eds.) *Infanticide: Comparative and Evolutionary Perspectives.*Aldine, New York, 1984.

Himmelstein, J. The New Christian Right. in R.C. Liebman and R. Wuthnow (eds.) *The New Christian Right,* Aldine Publishing Co. New York, 1983.

Hochschild, A.R. *The Second Shift:* Working Parents and the Revolution at Home Viking Press, New York, 1989.

Joffee, C. *Regulating Sexuality.* University of Pennsylvania Press, Philadelphia, 1987.

Karina, W. From Roe to Webster: Court Hands Abortion to the States. *State Government News,* November, 1989:12.

Kater, J.L.Jr. *Christians On The Right:* The Moral Majority in Perspective.Seabury Press, N.Y., 1982.

Kingsley, Davis. *Human Soceity.* MacMillan Press, 1949.

Kinsey, Alfred et al. *Sexual Behavior in the Human Female.* W.B. Saunders, Philadelphia, 1953.

LaRossa, R. and M.M. LaRossa. *Transition to Parenthood.* Sage, Beverly Hills, California, 1981.

Lesthaeghe, R. and J. Surkyn. Cultural Dynamics and Economic Theories of Fertility Change. *Population and Development Review,* 1988,14:1.

Luker, Kristin. *Abortion and the Politics of Motherhood.* University of California Press, Berkley, 1984.

Markson, S.L. The Roots of Contemporary Anti-Abortion Activism. in P. Sachdev, ed., *Perspectives on Abortion,* Scarecrow Press, Metuchen, N.J., 1985:33.

Mason, Karen O. and L. Bumpass. U.S. Women's Sex Role Ideology, 1970. *American Journal of Sociology,* 1975,80:1212.

McCready, and A. Greeley. *General Social Surveys,* July 1972 and July 1973. National Opinion Research Center, Williams College, Massachusetts, 1973.

McLaughlin, Steven D. et al. *The Changing Lives of American Women.* University of North Carolina Press, Chapel Hill, 1988.

Means, C.C. A Historian's View. in Robert E. Hall (ed.) *Abortion in a Changing World.* Columbia University Press, N.Y.1970:16.

Messer,E. and K.E. May. *Back Rooms: Voices from the Illegal Abortion Era.* St.Martin's Press, New York, 1988.

Mohr, J.C. *Abortion in America.* Oxford University Press,London, 1978.

Mohr, J.C. The Historical Character of Abortion in the United States Through World War II. in Paul Sachdev (ed.) *Perspectives on Abortion.* Scarecrow Press, New Jersey, 1985:3.

New York Times, Supreme Court to Hear Argument on Law Limiting Abortion Access, 1989, January 10.

New York Times. June 30, 1992.

Ooms, T. A Family Perspective on Abortion. in S. Callahan and D. Callahan (eds.), *Abortion: Understanding Differences,* Plenum Press, New York, 1984.

Petchesky, R. *Abortion and Woman's Choice:* The State, Sexuality and Conditions of Reproductive Freedom. Longman, N.Y., 1984.

Popenoe, David. *Disturbing the Family Nest:* Family Change and Decline in Modern Societies. Aldine de Gruyter, New York, 1988.

Potts, M. The Intellectual History of Abortion. in P. Sachdev
   (ed.) *Perspectives on Abortion,* 1985:15.
Rich, A. C. *Of Woman Born:* Motherhood as Experience and
   Institution.Norton, New York, 1976.
Riley, Matilda. Overview and Highlights of a Sociological Perspective,
   in A.B. Sorenson; F. Winert and L.E. Sherrod (eds.) *Human
   Development and the Life Course:* Multi-disciplinary
   Perspectives. Lawrence Erlbaum Associates, New Jersey, 1976.
Rindfuss, Ronald. R.P.S. Morgan, and G. Swicegood, *First Births in
   America,* University of California Press,Berkley, 1988.
Rosoff, Jeannie I. The Politics of Birth Control. *Family Planning
   Perspectives,* 1988,20,(November/December):312.
Rossi, A.S. Abortion Laws and their Victims. *Transaction,* 1966,3,6:7.
Rossi, A.S. Public Views on Abortion. in Alan F. Guttmacher M.D.
   (ed.) *The Case for Legalized Abortion Now.* Diablo Press,
   California, 1967:26.
Rossi, A.S. *The Feminist Papers.* Columbia University Press. New
   York, 1973.
Rossi, A.S. *Gender and Parenthood.* American Sociological
Review, 1984,49:1.
Rossi, A.S. and B. Sitaraman. Abortion in Context: Historic Trends
   and Future Changes. *Family Planning Perspectives,* 1988
   (November/December) 20:273.
Rossi, A.S. and P.H. Rossi. *Of Human Bonding: Parent-Child
   Relations Across the Life Course.* Aldine de Gruyter, New
   York, 1990.
Rossi P.H. and S.L. Nock (eds.) *Measuring Social Judgements: The
   Factorial Survey Approach.* Sage Publications, Beverly Hills,
   1982.
Rossi P.H. and A. Anderson. The Factorial Survey Approach: An
   Introduction.in P.H. Rossi and S.L. Nock (eds.) *Measuring Social
   Judgements.* Sage Publications, Beverly Hills, 1982:1.
Rothman, Barbara Katz. *The Tentative Pregnancy: Prenatal Diagnosis
   and the Future of Motherhood.* Viking, New York, 1986.
Ryan, M. *Womanhood in America: From Colonial Times to the
   Present.* Watts, New York, 1983.
Sachdev, P. *International Handbook on Abortion.* Greenwood Press,
   New York, 1988.

Scott, J. and H. Schuman. Attitude Strength and Social Action in the Abortion Dispute. *American Sociological Review,* 1988,53:785.

Scott, J. and H. Schuman. Generations and Collective Memories. *American Sociological Review,* 1989,54:359.

Shirbman, D. GOP, Facing Choice Between Party's Principles and Political Realities, Agonizes over Abortion. Wall Street Journal, 1989,December 5.

Singh, B. and P. Leahy. Contextual and Ideological Dimensions of Attitudes Toward Discretionary Abortion. *Demography,* 1978,15:381.

Snowden, R., G.D.Mitchell. and E.M. Snowden, *Artificial Reproduction: A Social Investigation.* G. Allen and Unwin, London, 1983.

Thornton, A and D. Camburn. Fertility, Sex Role Attitudes, and Labor Force Participation. *Psychology of Women Quarterly,* 1979,4:61.

Thornton, A., D.F. Alwin and D. Camburn. Causes and Consequences of Sex-Role Attitudes and Attitude Change, *American Sociological Review,* 1973,48:211.

Tietze, C. *Induced Abortion: A World Review.* Population Council, New York, 1983.

Tietze, C. Demographic and Public Health Experience with Legal Abortion:1973-1980. in Butler and Walbert (eds.)1986:289.

Torres, A. and J.D. Forrest. Why Do Women Have Abortions? *Family Planning Perspectives,* 1988,20:169.

Town of Greenfield. *Street Census of Greenfield.* Greenfield, Massachusetts, 1987.

U.S. Bureau of the Census. *Historical Statistics of the United States: From Colonial Times to 1970.* U.S. Government Printing Office, Washington,D.C., 1975.

Vinovskis, M.A. Abortion and the Presidential Election of 1976: A multivariate analysis of voting behavior. in C.E. Schneider and M.A. Vinovskis (eds.) *The Law and Politics of Abortion.* Lexington Books, Boston, 1980:184.

Welter, B. The Cult of True Womanhood, 1820-1860. *American Quarterly,* 1966,18:151.

Westoff, C.F., E.Moore and N. Ryder. The Structure of Attitudes toward Abortion. *Milbank Memorial Fund Quarterly,* 1969,47:11.

Westoff, C.F. and E.F. Jones. The End of 'Catholic' Fertility. *Demography,* 1979,16:209.

Westoff, C.F. Unintended Pregnancy in America and Abroad. *Family Planning Perspectives,* 1988,20:254.

Woolsey, S.H. Pied Piper Politics and the Child Care Debate, *Deadelus,* 1977,Spring:127.

INDEX